The horse established the physical pace of society during some four thousand years, and the beginning of its decline as transport in the thirties of the last century left a world to all intents and purposes pretty much as it had been at the end of the third millennium B.C. – agricultural in its economy, parochial in its thinking, and still generally subject to the whims of nature.

The railway system, now desperately fighting the competition of road and air transport, has set society's pace for less than one hundred and fifty years. But during its short reign it has played a crucial part in the world's transformation. This is the significance of Harold Perkin's lucid, carefully documented study. It is not merely one more book for the steam locomotive enthusiast – although *The Age of the Railway* answers many of his questions. It is above all an absorbing account of the way in which the Industrial Revolution and its fundamental weapon, the steam engine, have revolutionised man at – it is not too much to claim – every level of his existence. *The Age of the Railway*, Professor Perkin says in his preface, is an essay in the *connectedness of things*, and especially things social.

Harold Perkin is Professor of Social History at the University of Lancaster. He is the author of *The Origins of Modern English Society, 1780–1880; Key Profession: the History of the Association of University Teachers;* a Report on *Innovation in Higher Education* for the Organisation for Economic Co-operation and Development, *New Universities in the United Kingdom;* and editor and part-author of *History: an Introduction for the Intending Student* (Routledge and Kegan Paul, Autumn 1970). He is also editor of the well-known series of books, Studies in Social History, published by Routledge and Kegan Paul and the Toronto University Press. He has appeared on television many times, including his own series of educational programmes for Granada on 'The Railway Age' and 'The Automobile Age'.

Harold Perkin

The Age of the Railway

Panther

Granada Publishing Limited
First published in 1970 by Panther Books Ltd
3 Upper James Street, London W1R 4BP
Reprinted 1971

Copyright © Harold Perkin 1970
Made and printed in Great Britain by
C. Nicholls & Company Ltd
The Philips Park Press, Manchester
Set in Monotype Times

for Deborah
who likes railways

Preface

This is not just another book about the history of railways, interesting and enjoyable as that might be for the small boy – or girl (see the dedication) – in all of us. It is an attempt to introduce to the general reader, young and old, the new kind of history, social history, which is now beginning to be widely studied in schools, colleges and universities. It does this by approaching the history of our own country in the last century and the early years of this one through the medium of transport and communications in general, and in particular through the impact on the lives of our grandfathers and great-grandfathers of the revolution wrought by the steam locomotive, the first mechanized, power-driven prime mover of land carriage known to man. In the process it touches on many aspects of life in the past: the standard of living and the structure of society before and after the transport revolution, the transition from life in the village and countryside to life in great towns and cities, the development of large-scale industry and big business, the beginnings of leisure and holidays for the mass of the population, class conflict and the development of democracy, trade unions and the Labour Party, as well as the building of the railways themselves, their progress in speed, efficiency and comfort, and the beginnings of the ultimate decline of steam. Through this approach to social and general history it is hoped that the ordinary reader will see at one view the importance of transport and communications in everyone's life, and the railway enthusiast the wider context and implications of his special interest. For both, the 'great connecter' is a symbol of the connectedness of things, especially things in the history of our own society.

The book grew out of the first of two series of programmes, on 'The Railway Age' and 'The Automobile Age', which I wrote and presented some time ago for Granada Television. They were watched and, from their many letters I believe, enjoyed both by schools and by late-night viewers throughout the country. I should like to record my gratitude for his original suggestion to that irrepressible railway enthusiast, Jack Smith, the producer of the programmes, and for their unstinted and vastly enjoyable teamwork and co-operation to both him and the director, Eric Harrison. For once it is no exaggeration to say that without them this book would not have been written.

Borwicks,
Caton,
Lancaster.   Harold Perkin

April, 1970

Contents

Illustrations

Acknowledgements

Permission to reproduce paintings, prints and photographs in their possession is gratefully acknowledged to the following: the British Waterways Board for Plate 5 (the Regent's Canal), the *Illustrated London News* for Plate 4 (train at Grimsby, 1848, and labour yard at Bethnal Green, 1868), the Trustees of the Lady Lever Collection, Port Sunlight, for Plate 1 (2) (George Stubbs' "Hay carting"), Manchester City Corporation for Plates 6 (cellar dwellings) and 7 (Ford Madox Brown's "Work"), the Trustees of the National Gallery for Plate 1 (1) (George Stubbs' "The Phaeton"), Royal Holloway College, Englefield Green, for Plate 5 (W. P. Frith's "The Railway Station"), and Mr. W. Eglon Shaw of the Sutcliffe Gallery, Whitby, for Plates 8–16 (photographs by Frank M. Sutcliffe, 1853–1941).

Introduction

ALL civilization depends on communication – between
man and man, town and town, country and country,
perhaps in the future between planet and planet. Civilization itself began with the concentration of population in
the great river valleys of Sumeria, Egypt, the Indus and
the Yellow River, where the rivers themselves provided
the means of transport as well as water for irrigation.
Having learned to domesticate draught animals, notably
the ox and the ass (or its close relative the onager), these
'hydraulic' civilizations were conquered by waves of barbarians with the superior means of transport and mobile
warfare afforded by the horse. First, between about 1700
and 1400 B.C., the Indo-European charioteers from the
hills between Mesopotamia and the Caspian Sea came as
the Kassites to conquer Sumeria, as the Aryans to conquer the Indus cities of Harappa and Mohenjo-daro, as
the Hyksos to conquer Egypt, as the Mycenaeans to
conquer Greece, and as unnamed charioteers to conquer
Hsia China and found the Shang Dynasty; secondly,
between about 800 and 500 B.C. the true horsemen of the
Euro-Asian steppelands, the Celts, Cimmerians, Scy-
thians, Persians and men of the Altai Mountains came to
conquer and were in their turn absorbed and assimilated
by the existing civilizations.

The speed, endurance, intelligence and manageability
of the horse enabled these rude barbarians and their

successors not only to conquer their wealthier and more
sedentary neighbours, but also to defend and govern the
great empires which rose and fell in the Old World for
more than twenty centuries. For nearly two and a half
millennia civilization beat to the rhythm of the horse's
hooves. The ox might draw the plough and tread out the
corn, the camel measure out the sandy wastes of the
desert to join civilizations together by a tenuous link of
trade, the elephant cross the Alps and try the power of
Rome, but it was the horse with its swiftness and
manoeuvrability which was the key to economic,
political and military power. The man on horseback was
the symbol of power from the days of Alexander to those
of Napoleon.

But if civilization beat to the rhythm of the horse's
hooves, it could beat no faster. It took as long to ride
from London to Manchester in King George III's day as
it did from Londinium to Mancunium in the Emperor
Hadrian's. The world was waiting for a new and more
efficient horse. When it came, the 'iron horse' began a
new epoch in the history of the world. That epoch began
in Britain, in the north of England, in the Railway Age.
The invention of the railway, next to that of the power-
driven factory, is Britain's greatest contribution to the
progress of civilization, for it was here that the real
conquest of space began. Whatever new frontiers of
space men may conquer in the last third of the twentieth
century, the first conquest of physical distance by
mechanical power was *the* revolution in communications
from which all the rest have stemmed.

Indeed, it was here that the modern world began. For
the building of the railways was only the most spectacular
aspect of that dramatic increase in man's control over

nature, that enormous growth in the productivity of human labour, that remarkable rise in the scale and complexity of human co-operation and social organization, which we inadequately call the Industrial Revolution. The latter was even more a social than an economic revolution, since it transformed human life itself. Its function was to raise by a multiple – in Britain in the nineteenth century alone, roughly fourfold – *both* the number of people who could live on a given area of land *and* their average standard of living. In the process it created new communities on a vastly larger scale than the small towns and villages of the old, pre-industrial society. In these new, huge towns and cities, the whole pattern of life changed: the old paternal relationships of squire and tenant, farmer and labourer, master and servant died hard, and new, less personal relationships of employer and employed, producer and consumer, and upper, middle and working classes took their place, in a new society at once freer and harsher than the old. The denser population and greater complexity of life demanded new forms of social control as well as both a moral revolution in people's behaviour towards each other and a revolution in government at central and local levels. In short, it was a much more than industrial revolution which, from the way people worked and where they lived, to the way they thought about themselves and their place in the universe, affected every aspect of life.

In this enormous social and political as well as economic upheaval the railways were only one aspect, and as much an effect as a cause. But they were an important aspect, and still more a magnificent symbol, of the more-than-industrial revolution. That revolution is still in process of transforming the world, as one country after another demands the higher living standards and the greater economic and military power that go with modern industry. If we wish to understand what is happening to the world today, both in our own and in other countries, it is with Britain just before and during the Railway Age that we must begin.

This book, therefore, is not the history of the rise and decline of a particular mode of transport – not just another book about railways – but an attempt to tell in words and pictures the story of the transformation of British society during the last century through the impact upon it of the Industrial Revolution's most spectacular achievement: the development of the steam railway.

Chapter One

The Man on Horseback

WHEN George III came to the throne in 1760, communications in Britain were little better than in the days of the Romans. If there was a more complete network of routes, and every market town and almost every village was 'on the map' and linked by post with London, the roads themselves were certainly worse. Those the Romans built had deteriorated with the storms and floods of fourteen centuries, and the rest were mostly tracks worn down to the subsoil by the passing traffic. Since the Romans left there had been little road *building* as distinct from *repairing* – which chiefly meant throwing gravel, broken stone, rubble or whatever materials came to hand into the worst ruts and potholes. They were, quite literally and legally, beaten tracks. The king's highway in law was merely a right of passage for the king and his subjects, and where for any reason it was blocked by mud, floods or dangerous nuisances such as manure heaps or the encroachments of farmers, travellers had the right to break through hedges, and make a detour through the fields on either side. Before the agricultural enclosures, which came chiefly after 1760, the fields were open over large parts of eastern and southern England, and elsewhere there were large commons and moors, so that it was easy, especially in the winter when the roads were at their worst, for the traffic to fan out over a wide area, picking the firmest route it could. Across the sandy heaths of Norfolk Arthur Young could remember that the coaches approaching Norwich 'would sometimes be a mile abreast of each other in pursuit of the best track'.*[1] By contrast, along the rocky precipices of the Lake District or Pennine roads there would scarcely be room for two horsemen to pass. A writer in the *Gentleman's Magazine* in 1752, praising England for having raised herself to 'so high a pre-eminence over other nations that all foreigners both envy her and admire her', went on to say that 'the only solid objection I can make to this amiable recess, secreted, as it were by the hand of nature, from the gross of the European continent, is the wretched state of the public roads'.[2]

Many of the roads certainly were wretched. Five years earlier another writer in the same magazine had said:

In my journey to London, I travelled from Harborough to Northampton, and well was it that I was in a light Berlin, and six good horses, or I might have been overlaid in that turnpike road. But for fear of life and limb, I walked several miles on foot, met twenty waggons tearing their goods to pieces, and the drivers cursing and swearing for being robbed on the highway by a turnpike, screened under an act of parliament.[3]

The roads were at their best in and around London, and yet Lord Hervey in November 1736 found George II's

* See notes at the end of each chapter.

Court at Kensington Palace cut off from the City by 'a great impassable gulf of mud'.[4] Even de Saussure, a French visitor of the same period, who thought the highways around London 'magnificent, being wide, smooth, and well kept', was 'most cruelly shaken' in a hackney coach by the unevenness of the London pavement.[5] Over the rest of the country the state of the roads varied with the soil and the season. The roads on the Wealden clays of Kent, Surrey and Sussex were notoriously deep and heavy going even in summer, and intolerable in the winter, when wheeled transport came practically to a standstill. A petition to Parliament from the citizens of Norwich in 1725 described the road from there to London as 'in a very ruinous and dangerous condition'.[6] In the west country, Lady Irwin at Bath in October 1729 found that, 'The road between Altrop and this place is so extremely bad that the coachman won't undertake it in under four days, though it is but 64 miles.'[7] According to Arthur Young, in about 1760 'the roads of Oxfordshire were in a condition formidable to the bones of all who travelled on wheels'.[8] In the midlands the roads were so bad that most of the trade of the Potteries in the 1750s went by packhorse.[9] In the north-west there was, until 1760, no road for wheeled transport out of Liverpool, and such of the cotton and other imports for Manchester and East Lancashire as did not go by the Mersey and Irwell River Navigation went by packhorse.[10] A House of Commons Committee on a Highways Bill in 1740 confirmed that the roads between Leeds, Selby, Wakefield, Halifax and Bradford were ruinous and impassable in winter. In Northumberland, according to a traveller in 1749, all the roads around Whitfield were mere trackways for ponies: 'There was not a cart in the country.'[11] In

Scotland wheeled traffic was so unfamiliar that when a cartload of coal was brought in 1723 from East Kilbride to Cambuslang near Glasgow, 'crowds of people went out to see the wonderful machine; they looked with surprise and returned with astonishment'.[12] In fact, apart from the Highland military roads being built after the 1745 Rebellion by General Wade, the roads north and west of a line from Flamborough Head in Yorkshire to Lyme Regis in Dorset were mostly soft, unmade roads suitable only for driving cattle, with a raised causeway on one side for packhorses and mounted travellers. In 1739 two travellers from Glasgow to London rode all the way to Grantham on such causeways, standing aside from time to time to let pass strings of thirty to forty packhorses.[13] The soft roads by the side were chiefly droveroads, bringing the cattle and sheep of Scotland, Wales and the north, whose cloven hooves would not stick in the mud like those of horses, to the midlands and the south for fattening, especially for the London market.

The roads were in this state because, except for a few turnpike trusts, it was nobody's business to make or repair them properly, from the foundations. Since the first real Highways Act of 1555, it is true, the constables and churchwardens of every parish had to call together the parishioners in Easter Week to 'elect and choose two honest persons of the parish to be surveyors and orderers for one year of the works for amendment of the highways in their parish', and these surveyors had the right to call on every occupier of enough arable land for one plough to provide a cart and oxen or horses and two able men, and on every other householder to come himself or send a substitute with necessary tools, to repair the roads on four appointed days in the year, raised in 1562 to six.

From 1662 this 'Statute labour', as it was called, could be supplemented or replaced by hired labour, paid for by a levy or rate of up to 6d. in the pound on the annual value of land or on £20 capital value of personal property in money or goods. But, in spite of the fact that both the surveyors and the householders could be heavily fined for failing in their duty, the work was usually done in a perfunctory manner, merely filling up the ruts and potholes of the previous year with the scrapings of the old road, to be churned up again by the next coaches and waggons to roll by.

The trouble was that the major highways of the kingdom were often little used by the local inhabitants of the parishes through which they passed, whose main aims were simply to avoid being fined for non-performance and to give as little excuse as possible to through-travellers for trespassing on the fields by the roadside, and who thought that the people who used the road should pay the cost of its upkeep. In 1663 this was recognized in the case of that part of the Great North Road from London to Scotland which ran through Hertfordshire, Cambridgeshire and Huntingdonshire, when the first Turnpike Act was passed, giving the Justices of the Peace in those counties the right to appoint professional surveyors to repair the road and set up turnpikes or toll-gates with collectors to receive the tolls and turn the money over to the county surveyors for their labour and materials. The Act was short-lived and ineffective outside Hertfordshire, and the second Turnpike Act, for part of the London to Colchester road, was passed only in 1695–6. More Acts were passed in the first half of the eighteenth century, and from 1706 private enterprise was called in to supplement or replace the

1. *Main roads and navigable rivers, early 18th century*

parish and county authorities, in the shape of named
trustees who were to appoint the surveyor and collectors,
receive the moneys, and to raise the capital for improving
or repairing their stretch of road either by mortgaging
the tolls or farming out for an annual rent the right to
collect them.[14] Up to 1750, however, these turnpike trust
Acts were comparatively few, and covered only a few
hundred miles of road, mostly on the main highways in
and out of London (see Map 1).[15] More important, their
effect on the quality of the roads was bound to be
limited as long as road engineering was almost non-
existent and confined to the mere repair of the existing
roads. The turnpike roads, as we have seen, were often as
bad as the rest, and travellers could often see no difference but the tollgate. Per Kalm, the Swedish pastor
who walked through England in the 1740s, wrote:

These high roads had not the character, as with us in Sweden,
that the road lay higher than the land around, but here exactly
the opposite is the case, viz., so that the road goes in most
places deep down in the earth, to a depth of two, four, or six
feet, so that many would believe the road was only some dry
stream-course. There is commonly on one side of the road, if
not on both sides, on the walls or the high sides, a foot-path
for foot passengers [strictly, the causeway for horse traffic].

That the roads are so deep seems to come from this, that in
this country very large waggons are used with many horses in
front, on which waggons a very heavy load is laid. Through
many years' driving, these waggons seem to have eaten down
into the ground, and made the road so deep.[16]

In so far as the government interfered at all, beyond
passing the few, and mainly private, Turnpike Acts, it
was mainly to fit the traffic to the roads rather than the

roads to the traffic. James I in 1621 had forbidden by proclamation the use of four-wheeled waggons or the carriage of more than one ton weight on any vehicle, and this was repeated by Charles I in 1629, but it was clearly ineffective, as the 1662 Highways Act complained: '[because of] the extraordinary burdens carried upon waggons and other carriages, divers of the said highways are become very dangerous and almost unpassable'. In addition to supplementing statute labour with a highway rate, the 1662 Act therefore began the practice of regulating the width of wheels and the number of horses per vehicle as well as their weight: no waggon or cart carrying for hire on the public roads should have wheels less than four inches wide, be drawn by more than seven horses, or carry more than twenty hundredweight in the winter (1 October – 1 May) or more than thirty hundredweight in summer. The purpose of the wider wheels was to distribute the burden over a larger area of contact with the road and to provide a larger rolling surface which would help to flatten and consolidate it instead of cutting it into ruts. The clause was repealed in 1670, when it was laid down that waggons with more than five horses should have them harnessed in pairs, so as to widen the track, and the maximum number of horses was increased in 1696 to eight (in pairs). In 1718 carriers' waggons were restricted to six horses and their carts (two-wheeled) to three, and waggons which had tyres (usually of iron) less than two and a half inches wide and fitted with rose-headed nails (raised nail heads which gave a better grip but which cut up the road) also to three horses, under penalty of forfeiting the supernumerary horses. In 1741 the maximum number of horses per waggon was reduced to four, and turnpike trustees were allowed to set up 'weighing engines' at their tollgates and charge the prohibitive toll of 20s. for every hundredweight over sixty. An Act of 1751 allowed six horses, but *required* trustees to demand the 20s. toll on excess hundred-weights.

Broad wheels triumphed in 1753, when vehicles using the turnpike roads were to have wheels no less than nine inches broad, but this was found impossible to implement and two years later waggons with nine-inch wheels were exempted from toll for three years, and waggons and carts with six-inch wheels paid reduced tolls, while those with narrower wheels might be charged 25 per cent more than the normal rate. Broad-wheeled waggons could also have eight horses, six-inch wheeled could have six, whilst narrow-wheeled vehicles were limited to four. The final sophistication came in 1773, when waggons with six-inch wheels set on axles of different lengths so as to roll a nine-inch track on each side could have seven horses instead of the normal maximum of six. Legislation on the width of wheels, on the maximum weight to be carried for different widths, and on differential tolls for different widths, continued to be passed down to 1823, and was not finally repealed until 1835, by which time road engineering had rendered it unnecessary.[17] But in the mid-eighteenth century it was one of the few known ways of saving the road system from utter collapse.

In these conditions travel was slow and expensive. Most people who could afford to travelled on horseback. The man on horseback, from the Cabinet Minister riding to Whitehall, the aristocratic gentleman riding to Bath or the pluralist country parson riding to take service in one of his several churches, to the post-boy blowing his horn to clear a way for the royal mails, was the symbol of travel in eighteenth-century England, and far more typical than the stage coach or the private carriage. But the horse was an expensive beast – from £20 to £50 for an ordinary riding mount, or from over one to three years' wages for a labourer – and it cost from 5s. to 10s. a week to feed – a week's wages for one or two labourers. Most people, the poor who had to travel to get work or the not-so-poor who wanted to travel cheaply, like Pastor Kalm or Fielding's Joseph Andrews and Parson Adams, therefore walked. It was not necessarily slower than riding, at least on an un-changed horse. Experienced foot guides and messengers would 'undertake to run down the best horse you can buy in seven or eight days', and a woman named Mally Messenger, who died at Keswick in 1856 at the age of ninety-three and who had often walked to London and back in her youth, had been known to beat a horseman over the distance of 283 miles.[18] Footposts had been introduced in Tudor times, and were monopolized by the royal patentee Thomas Witherins in 1635, as being considerably faster than the common carrier. In the eight-eenth century a 'running footman', usually a shock-headed Irish 'kerne' whose 'glibbe' or bushy fringe of hair over his eyebrows was the mark of his trade, was a social necessity for a nobleman, to carry messages and to run before his master's carriage to proclaim his impending arrival.[19]

A horse, nevertheless, was the normal means of trans-port for the moderately well-to-do, as it was for Celia Fiennes who travelled *Through England on a Side-Saddle* in the 1690s, or for John Wesley who, between 1739 and 1791, rode a quarter of a million miles to found his 356 chapels and preach 40,000 sermons. A horse could go twenty-five to fifty miles a day, according to the weather and the difficulty of the road, though it might not keep it up for more than a few days together. If you wanted to travel faster you could 'ride post', changing your horse every ten to fifteen miles at the official postmaster's stable, for the hire of post-horses was a government monopoly. The system had grown out of the ancient royal prerogative of purveyance by which the king could command the use of his subjects' goods at a fixed rate, and so could send a messenger with an 'open placart' or letter of command to public officers to supply horses for his journey at a penny a mile. In 1511 Henry VIII had appointed Brian Tuke Master of the Posts to organize a system of 'standing posts in pay' on the main roads from London to Scotland and the major cities and seaports.[20] By degrees it had come to be made available, both for letters and for travel, to the ordinary citizen who could afford to pay the high charges. The post-boys, who were really men, distinguished by their 'packet' or postbag and horn, used the same horses and travelled at four to six miles an hour, but the ordinary citizen in a hurry could manage ten or twelve. But it was not cheap: about $2\frac{1}{2}$d. or 3d. a mile, summer or winter, plus a charge of 6d. or 8d. for the guide whose services were compulsory, to safeguard and return the horses.[21] A journey from London to Manchester would thus cost £2 10s. – £3, plus tips and one or two nights' stay on the road – up to £4, or four months' wages for a labourer.

If you were really rich, you could go in your own coach, with your own horses if you were content to travel slowly, or hiring post-horses at the same rate of $2\frac{1}{2}$d. or 3d. a mile per horse if you wished to travel faster. Or you could go by post-chaise, a fast, light carriage for

two or three persons, drawn by two horses, at 1s. to
1s. 6d. a mile, including postillion – £10–£15 from
London to Manchester, or about a year's wages for a
labourer.[22] James Boswell, the future biographer of Dr
Johnson, shared a chaise from Edinburgh to London in
November 1762 with a Mr Stewart, first mate on an East
Indiaman and son of a Jacobite who had forfeited his
estate for his part in the 1745 Rebellion. It took them
just over four days, stopping the nights at Berwick,
Durham, Doncaster and Biggleswade, and because
between Stamford and Stilton a young unruly horse ran
away with the driver, the chaise overturned and 'Stewart's
head and my arm were somewhat hurt'.[23]

The stage coach at that time would have taken ten or
twelve days. Stage coaches had only begun in the reign of
Charles I, and were not very numerous until the eighteenth century. Down to the 1780s, when John Palmer
took advantage of the improving roads to introduce his
fast mail coaches, they were mostly slow and cumbersome. It took a whole day in summer, two in winter,
from London to Brighton or Oxford, two to Bristol or
Birmingham, three to Manchester or Sheffield, four to
Liverpool or Leeds, a week to Plymouth or Newcastle,
ten days or more to Glasgow.[24] The fare was much the
same as riding post, but without the charge for the guide
(though it was usual to tip the coachman for each stage):
2½d. or 3d. a mile, summer or winter, plus the cost of
meals and beds at the inns on the way[25] – say, £3 from
London to Manchester, or about three months' wages
for a labourer. This was the fare for inside passengers,
and outside passengers would pay about half, but until
the roads were improved in the late eighteenth century it
was rare to carry passengers on the roof or in the boot,

since they were likely to be thrown off on the rougher parts of the journey. At this price, coaching was confined to the well-to-do, and especially to those who for some reason – age, sex or infirmity – did not wish to ride post.

Those who could not afford either could travel by the still slower and more lumbering stage waggon at its steady two to four miles an hour. These were regular covered waggons, the faster ones called 'fly vans', intended mainly for goods, especially parcels and perishables, which could not wait for the big bulk-carrier waggons, but carried a few passengers among the boxes and barrels for $\frac{1}{2}$d. or 1d. a mile.[26] They were much used by maid-servants and other retainers travelling between their masters' country houses and London residences.

Besides the hazards of the weather and the mire, ruts, potholes, floods and precipices of the roads, there was the constant danger to all, coaches and waggons, horsemen and foot passengers, from highway robbers. The 'knights of the road' were of course mounted, for swiftness of encounter and getaway, but there were also footpads who would attack anyone who looked weak enough and worth robbing. Fielding's Joseph Andrews and Parson Adams when travelling on foot were set upon and robbed and stripped. Over large parts of the country, however, it was comparatively difficult in the small communities of the day to pursue a life of crime for long without being discovered, and so the bulk of the highway robberies took place around the few great towns where the thieves could hide among the crowds and most easily dispose of their plunder. The most favoured haunts were the heaths around London, and there the traffic was so thick and continuous that it was becoming difficult to carry out raids except at night without raising a hue and cry all along the road. There were daring robbers, of course, like Macheath in John Gay's *The Beggar's Opera*, often in league with innkeepers who tipped them off about wealthy victims or with corrupt officials like Jonathan Wild who protected them from the law, but by and large the highwaymen were more important in fiction than in real life. More property was probably purloined by dishonest coachmen, carriers and porters than by outlaws, or lost by damage through rough handling or storm and flood.

Goods, as we have seen, could go by the fast stage waggon or fly van, but most of those which went by land went by the big carriers' waggons where the roads permitted and by packhorse or mule where they did not. The waggons were the galleons of land carriage, huge and lumbering and painfully slow, the carrier and his lad usually walking by the side of their team rather than riding. They were limited in weight, as we have seen (latterly under the 1741 Act to three tons gross), and they were restricted at various times to from four to eight horses, though there was much evasion of the law on both counts. In spite of these restrictions, no one doubted that it was the great waggons which did most to cut up the roads and reduce them to rocky deserts or bottomless quagmires. In the north, the midlands and the west, and in winter almost everywhere, most goods were carried by packhorse. Gangs of thirty or forty tethered in line, the leading horse carrying a bell to warn approaching travellers to stand aside, would be led along the causeways at the side of the soft roads. Seventy of them used to leave a single inn in Liverpool daily for Manchester. Around the Potteries in Josiah Wedgwood's day, pack-

horses and asses would be seen 'heavily laden with coal –
tubs full of ground flint from the mills, crates of ware or
panniers of clay', and 'floundering knee-deep through the
muddy holes and ruts'.[27] Sheffield tools and cutlery were
carried by packhorse to London. Wool and malt went by
the same means from Derbyshire and Nottinghamshire
to Manchester and the West Riding. Coal from the Forest
of Dean went on horseback to Bath and Bristol. In
Devon 'the common traffic and business of this county is
mostly done by horses with panniers and crooks' – the
latter a wooden frame for carrying prodigious loads of
hay, straw, wood or vegetables – and the country people
even rode in wood and leather panniers called 'gam-
bades'.[28] The packhorse usually carried a double pack of
240 lb. (over two hundredweight), so that it took twenty
or thirty to carry as much as one waggon pulled by six or
eight, admittedly bigger and stronger, animals. The cost
of transport was the same for both, and by Acts of 1691
and 1748 fixed at the Easter Quarter Sessions by the
Justices of the Peace of each county, usually for journeys
between certain well-known market towns. The charges
usually worked out at about $\frac{1}{2}$d. a hundredweight per
mile in summer and $\frac{3}{4}$d. in winter, sometimes rather less
for bulk loads and over longer distances. The Derbyshire
Justices in 1717 fixed the rate from Derby to London, a
distance of 126 miles, at 6s. per hundredweight in summer
and 7s. 6d. in winter, or just over $\frac{1}{2}$d. and just under $\frac{3}{4}$d.
a mile respectively.[29]

At such rates it was impossible to carry cheap and
bulky commodities like grain and coal very far and still
sell them at a profit. If land carriage had been the only
means available, trade in many industrial materials
would almost have been strangled and Britain could not

have been as prosperous as she undoubtedly was by the middle of the eighteenth century, when she was the leading trading county in Europe. The answer was that most heavy goods went by water. As Andrew Yarranton put it in 1677,

Of necessity we must always be Sailing round about the Island, carrying and recarrying such heavy Commodities from Port to Port, to be taken into the more Inward parts of the Kingdom, otherwise the charge of carrying such goods by Land, would rise to a very vast charge, the High-ways of our Island being very uneven, and the ways therein in Winter time very bad.[30]

By the bounty of nature, Britain was blessed with an excellent network of navigable rivers, leading down to the universal highroad, the sea itself, and since the 1660s these had been improved and supplemented by a series of 'Navigation' Acts. As a result, few areas in England were more than fifteen miles, a day's haul-and-return for a horse and cart, from navigable water – chiefly the moors and mountains of the Pennines, the Lake District, Dartmoor, Salisbury Plain, and part of the Downs, together with a still large and industrially important island around Birmingham (see Map 1). Some of these navigations, like the Mersey and Irwell, the Aire and Calder, the Kennet, and the Exe were large and technically advanced undertakings, including 'cuts' and locks on the scale of the later canals, which indeed they anticipated in everything but the 'deadwater' principle (an artificial supply of water from springs, streams and reservoirs instead of utilizing an existing flow).[31]

Water transport, whether on natural or artificial navigations, was enormously cheaper than land. As Adam Smith pointed out, 'Six or eight men . . . by the help of water-carriage, can carry and bring back in the same time the same quantity of goods between London and Edinburgh, as fifty broad-wheeled waggons, attended by a hundred men, and drawn by four hundred horses.'[32] It paid the Horsehay Iron Company in Shropshire as late as 1775 to send pig iron down the Severn, round the Welsh coast and up the Dee to Chester, instead of the fifty miles by road, and Cambridge undergraduates to send their trunks from London by sea to King's Lynn and up the Ouse and Cam rather than the fifty-one miles by road. For wind power was free, or at least cost no more than the capital investment in boat and sails and the labour of a relatively small number of sailors to work them, while the horse that carried 240 lb. on its back or pulled half a ton on wheels could, on a good towpath, pull twenty-five tons or more on water. Not that horses could be used everywhere: many of the navigations lacked suitable tow paths, and boats had either to be sailed or laboriously poled along, or manhandled by gangs of 'halers' hauling on the ropes and working sometimes up to their waists in the river.[33] Nevertheless, even on the worst and most difficult of waterways the cost of transport was still cheaper than by road. How much cheaper it is difficult to say, since the watermen, unlike the land carriers, were not controlled by the Justices of the Peace, and could charge what the traffic would bear; but eighteenth-century estimates varied from one third to one twelfth of the land freight. In the 1750s it cost 12s. a ton to send goods from Manchester and Liverpool by the Mersey and Irwell Navigation, compared with 40s. a ton by road.[34]

Consider what this abundance of cheap water-transport meant to industry, which had been growing at an accelerating pace since Tudor times. British industry even before the Industrial Revolution used coal for all kinds of processes from salt boiling and firing pottery to glass making and even, since Abraham Darby's introduction of coke-smelting in 1709–14, to iron-founding – not to mention the enormous use of coal for house-fires in London and many other towns. According to Adam Smith, the coal trade between Newcastle and London alone employed more shipping than the whole foreign trade of the country, which was also booming. It was uneconomical to carry coal more than about fifteen miles by road, and so without water transport a large part of British industry would have collapsed.

In spite of the bad roads, then, Britain was well-served in the eighteenth century with heavy transport and, since human beings are much more mobile than goods and so could move around on foot or on horseback when they could not go on wheels, with a system of passenger transport which was not inadequate to the needs of the time.

What sort of society did these communications, slow and cumbersome by our standards but as good or better than most other countries in that age, support? In 1760 Joseph Massie, a remarkable pamphleteer, published a broadsheet entitled *A Computation of the Money that hath been exorbitantly Raised upon the People of Great Britain by the Sugar Planters, in One Year from January 1759 to January 1760; shewing how much Money a Family of each Rank, Degree or Class hath lost by that rapacious monopoly.* . . . Although intended for a polemic purpose, his figures are reasonably objective, are compatible with the better-known calculations of Gregory King for 1688 and of Patrick Colquhoun for 1803, and give a useful bird's-eye view of English society in 1760.[35] What do they tell us about the old society which still depended on the horse and wind-power for the bulk of its transport? First of all, it was a small society, since the existing levels of food production and the manufacture of other necessities of life such as clothes and housing could not support a large population. If we multiply Massie's 1,471,600 families by four and a half, which is thought to be the size of the average family at that time, we get a figure for the population of England and Wales in 1760 of 6.6 million, and this is confirmed by modern estimates, which all range between 6.5 and 6.7 million. Secondly, and for the same reason, it was a poor society, as one would expect when almost everything had to be made by hand and manhandled to its destination with only the help of wind and horse. The national income he estimated at £60.9 million, which was only £47 6s. per family, or about £9 10s. per head a year; in terms of bread prices, say, about £150 per family a year or £3 a week today. Yet by the standards of that time England, if not Scotland, Wales or Ireland, was a rich country, and the average income was somewhat higher than those of Holland and France, the next richest, and far higher than the countries of southern or eastern Europe. If the national wealth had been shared out equally no one would have been affluent, but unlike many, perhaps most, countries in the world, no one would have starved.

But the national wealth was *not* shared out equally. As in all contemporary societies with the least claim to civilization and an organized system of government, there was an enormous difference in wealth between the ruling few and the many poor. At the top there were the aristocracy and gentry, a tiny class of landlords, 18,070 families, scarcely more than one in a hundred (1.2 per

cent), who shared according to Massie one seventh of the
national income (14.3 per cent). At the bottom the mass
of the 'lower orders' or 'labouring poor', nearly three
fifths of the population (866,000 families, 58.9 per cent),
shared little more than a quarter of the income (25.7 per
cent). But in other European countries this bottom layer,
though constituted rather differently, of subsistence
peasant farmers rather than mainly landless labourers,
would have been much larger – three quarters of the
population in France, four fifths in most of eastern
Europe, nine tenths or more in Russia – and even poorer.
The great difference in England was the size and prosperity of the 'middle ranks', the two fifths of Massie's
families (587,500, 39.9 per cent) who received no less
than three fifths of the national income (60 per cent). To
the enormous significance of this large and wealthy
section of English society we shall return.

Meanwhile, the most powerful and important section
by far was the landed class. A handful of great lords, the
Dukes of Newcastle, Bedford, Devonshire and some
others, received £30,000 a year or more in rent, besides
what they might get in government salaries and pensions,
but the bulk of the landed gentry, the real country
squires, received rentals of a few hundred pounds a year,
but still many times the average family income. It had to
be so, since they were the principal servant-keeping class,
and they usually employed in their households and home
farms from about five to forty servants. The aristocracy
and gentry were not only the richest class, individually at
least, but they were in the strictest sense the ruling class.
As the only group with both the leisure and the wealth for
politics in a system of government run mainly by amateurs, they were the rulers of England at every level from

the Cabinet to the parish. The King's Ministers were, with a few exceptions in the law offices of state, great landowners or their relations. The civil service, as we should now call it, consisted of their appointees from among their friends and relations. The House of Lords was to all intents and purposes a House of landlords. Four fifths of the House of Commons comprised land-owners and their relations, and the rest were chiefly their friends and dependants. In the counties the lords lieutenant and high sheriffs were drawn from the greatest landlords, while the effective county government for almost all purposes was in the Bench of Justices of the Peace, drawn from the landed gentry. In the villages the squire's word, whether or not he was a J.P., was law, backed up by the threat of eviction or the withdrawal of his custom from the village traders. Three quarters of the population lived in the countryside, but even in the smaller towns the local landowners were often almost as influential as in the villages, and it was only in the com-paratively few great cities – and no town outside London had more than 50,000 inhabitants, and most had less than 20,000 – that the men of the middle ranks, the greater merchants and lawyers, could control their own affairs and elect their own M.P.s.

The landed aristocracy and gentry were the men on horseback *par excellence*. The horse had been the symbol of their domination of English society since the Norman Conquest, from which they significantly, but in most cases mistakenly, traced their descent. King Harold's thanes who rode to Hastings in 1066 and then, to their undoing, dismounted to fight, were beaten and dispossessed by Norman invaders who fought on horseback, towering over the Anglo-Saxons and crushing them. The man on

horseback dominated English society for the next seven
or eight centuries. Even when feudal knights and chain
mail had long since disappeared, and many if not most
Norman families themselves had been replaced by new
ones from below, the horse and the coat of arms remained as the exclusive symbols of the aristocracy and
gentry. The reason is obvious: just as the rich must be
few if they are to buy the labour of other men, so only the
few could buy the still more expensive labour of the
horse which, as we have seen, cost as much to feed and
house as two labourers. For centuries the pleasures of
riding, in the medieval tournament (strictly, a mock-
battle) and the hunt, the mobility of the horse for the
business of governing and the pastimes of social inter-
course, and the power of the horse in war and political
dominion, were almost confined to the landed few and
their dependants and servants. The man on horseback
towered above the rest of society in power, wealth and the
enjoyment of life.

Yet since the later Middle Ages, the English man on
horseback had come to differ in increasingly important
ways from his European counterpart. By a long process
beginning with the breakdown of feudalism and the commutation of the serf's labour services into money rents
after the Black Death, going on through the enclosures
and engrossing (throwing many small farms into a few
large ones) in Tudor times by which most English
peasants disappeared and were replaced by large tenant
farmers employing landless labourers, and ending with
the Civil War in the mid-seventeenth century, as a result
of which feudal tenures were abolished and replaced by
modern freehold, the English landed class turned lordship
into ownership and instead of feudal lords became real

owners of the land.[36] This was the most important change in the whole of English history. Instead of drawing labour services or fixed feudal dues in money or kind from their estates, like the Russian or French landlords who could not increase their incomes without cheating or oppressing their peasants, the English landlords could do what they liked with their land. The could farm it, let it to the most efficient farmer for the highest rent, mine the minerals under it, build on it or let it on long leases to developers, or of course sell it for any of these purposes. This freedom to do as they pleased with their land, as we shall see in the next chapter, was to have a great effect on the coming of the Industrial Revolution and the building of the railways. Even by 1760 their keen interest in agriculture, trade and industry and the increased rents arising from any kind of economic development had helped to make Britain the wealthiest country for its size in Europe.

This helps to account, too, for the exceptional size and prosperity of the 'middle ranks'. The rising incomes of the landed class were spent on consumer goods and improvements to their estates which put money into the pockets of the manufacturers and traders and, as it were, 'primed the pump' of the whole economy so that almost everyone had money to spend and almost everyone benefited from the resultant prosperity. Income and small amounts of capital were thus widely diffused, and thousands of small but ambitious businessmen actively sought opportunities for increasing their profits and expanding their turnover. As Patrick Colquhoun was to put it in 1814,

It is not . . . an excess of property to the few but the extension of it among the mass of the people which appears most likely to prove beneficial with respect to national wealth and national happiness. Perhaps no country in the world possesses greater advantages in this respect than Great Britain, and hence that spirit of enterprise and that profitable employment of diffused capitals which has created so many resources for productive labour beyond any other country in Europe.[37]

These were the men who, along with the landlords who encouraged agriculture, mining and transport improvements and the farmers who were to learn how to feed three times the population of 1760, were to play so large a part in the Industrial Revolution. Sharing many of the ideals, pleasures and ambitions of the landed class, the middle ranks came also to share their means of transport. Every prosperous merchant, lawyer and farmer came to possess at least one good riding horse, and many of them contrived to hunt with their landed friends, patrons or relations, while their wives set their hearts on a carriage and pair. 'Keeping up with the aristocratic Joneses' was one of the most important motivations in English eighteenth-century society, and if it applied to periwigs, waistcoats, knee-breeches and panniered dresses, it applied even more to horses and carriages. Just as fashions in dress went further down the scale in eighteenth-century England than anywhere else, so did the fashion for horse-riding and driving. And even in agriculture, where Continental peasants still relied on the ox, the English farmer almost everywhere was harnessing his plough and harvest cart to the superior strength and speed of the horse.

Even the labouring poor were not unaffected by the change in the nature of English landlordship. At first, at least after their gain in freedom and indeed in prosperity by the abolition of serfdom, they had lost heavily by it.

Tudor enclosing and engrossing had meant that large numbers of peasants were evicted, and they and their descendants turned into landless labourers.[38] Along with the rising population and the great inflation of the sixteenth century, in which wages had lagged far behind food prices, this had created the great poverty crisis of the Tudor period, and the need for the unique English Poor Law to mitigate it. It had also led to two other developments, both very rare elsewhere. One was the segregation of most agricultural workers from the occupation of the soil, so that the bulk of the country population were not subsistence peasants, as over most of the civilized world, but wage-earners working for comparatively large commercial farmers. The other, since this more efficient system of farming could not employ them all, was the widespread development of an industrial system much larger and more highly organized than elsewhere. The surplus labourers came to be employed, mostly in their own homes in the country villages and the suburbs of the corporate towns, by large capitalists who supplied the raw materials – the wool, iron, wood, etc. – and sometimes even the tools and equipment – the loom, anvil, lathe, etc. – and paid them a piece-wage for the work.

This domestic outwork system, as it is called, grew up alongside and finally almost replaced the older domestic craft system, in which the master craftsman with his journeyman and apprentice, usually belonging to a guild and living in a corporate town, worked on his own materials and sold direct to the customer or merchant.[39] Some of the merchant-employers were on a very large scale, employing 500, 1,000 or even 2,000 outworkers, sometimes through agents or middlemen, called 'puttersout' in Lancashire or 'bag-hosiers' in the east midlands knitting industry. Thus, even before the Industrial Revolution, some of the industrialists were as rich and highly organized as the later millowners and ironmasters, and their workers just as dependent for their daily bread on money-wages as the later factory workers.

There had also grown up, over the same period and using the same landless labour, a number of larger works, somewhat akin to modern factories: paper mills, potteries, sugar refineries, soapworks, saltworks, blast furnaces, copper and tin smelting works, and so on. But with very few exceptions these were on a small scale, employing at most a score or so of workers, and, more important, they were not modern factories, with lines of machines driven by a central source of power, but mainly groups of handworkers – paper-makers, potters, ironmoulders, brassfounders, and the like – gathered for convenience around the grinding mill, boiler or furnace which supplied their raw or semi-fabricated material. Perhaps the only real factory in early eighteenth-century England was the Lombe brothers' silk mill on the Derwent near Derby in 1719, with its 300 throwing machines driven by a giant water wheel. Such modern-seeming industrial workers were not only in a minority but scattered in small and mainly rural establishments near the water power, the clay, the saltings, the metal ore, the woodland charcoal, and so on, across the countryside. The majority of industrial workers were individual outworkers and their families working in their own homes for a capitalist merchant, to whose warehouse they tramped weekly with the finished goods on their own backs or on those of donkeys or packhorses.

In addition to all these, the landless labour force supplied thousands of transport workers on the roads and the waterways – post-boys and packhorsemen, coachmen and guards, waggoners and their boys, bargees and 'halers', dockers and sailors, and many more, none of whom, save the last, appears separately in Massie's figures. Without them, all the vast trade of this richest of trading countries, and all its industry and agriculture, its towns and its government, would have ground to a halt. Even leaving them on one side, no less than 19 per cent, nearly one in five, of the population were engaged in trade and distribution as merchants, tradesmen, inn-keepers and alesellers, and accounted for 25 per cent of the national income.

Perhaps the most striking result of the growth of landless labour, however, and the most striking thing about Massie's estimate, is the large proportion of the population not primarily employed in agriculture. Even though most people in that old society were never far from the land, and most industrial workers still turned out to help bring in the harvest, it is a remarkable fact that, when we have allocated half the general labourers to agriculture, according to Massie more than half the population (52 per cent) earned their living primarily from industry, trade and the professions. If his guess is anywhere near the truth, it must have been the first time in any country that non-agricultural surpassed agricultural pursuits. That a well-informed observer should believe such a thing is a measure of how far England had progressed in industry and commerce before the onset of the Industrial Revolution.

Agriculture, nevertheless, was still by far the biggest single occupation, and most of the industries were closely based on it, notably the textile industries, brewing, flour-milling, leather goods, and many more. Prosperity and

poverty ebbed and flowed with the seasons and the
changing harvest, so that in winter and spring everyone
lived harder and most went hungrier than in summer and
autumn, and a bad harvest meant not only high bread
prices but less to spend on manufactured goods and so
less work for the industrialists and their workers. In
other words, a bad harvest meant a slump in trade and
industry, and a good harvest meant a boom. Thus, in
spite of considerable industrial progress, England in 1760
was still very much in the old pre-industrial world where
men were the passive dependants on the whims of the
climate and the niggardliness of nature.

In one other way, too, men were entrapped by nature
and unable to break free from its trammels. The bad
roads and the slow and cumbersome communications
meant that in one sense England, still less Britain or the
United Kingdom, scarcely existed as a real entity or focus
of loyalty. For most men their 'country' still meant their
own locality, their district or their county. Many people
had never left their parishes, and most people had never
been further than the nearest market or, at most, county
town – though waggoners and coachmen, post-boys and
packhorsemen, boatmen and, curiously enough, the
domestic servants of the well-to-do, were the great
exception to this. And this geographical immobility had a
profound effect on the shape and structure of society. In
the villages and tiny towns in which the majority of the
people lived everybody knew everybody else, and the
squire, the parson, the larger farmers, traders and craftsmen were known too and dominated the lives of all the
rest. There was little elbow-room for modern class
institutions, such as trade unions or political societies,
and where they appeared they were usually suppressed by

the ruling oligarchy as examples of 'insubordination'.

The important links in the old society, therefore, were not the horizontal connections of class, between workers or others on the same social level, but the vertical connections of what was called 'patronage' or 'dependency', between landlord, tenants and farm labourers, between squire, parson and villagers, between master and servants, between merchant-employer and outworkers, and so on. It was the duty of superiors, landlords, masters, to take care of their inferiors, tenants, servants, labourers, and also to discipline them when they misbehaved; it was the duty of inferiors to obey. Anything else was insubordination, and to be punished, as a father chastised his children. Paternalism was thus two-faced: with its benevolent face it smiled on and rewarded the loyal and obedient; with its disciplinary face it frowned on and punished the disloyal and insubordinate. A few of the more independent spirits in the middle ranks, yeomen (owner-occupying) farmers, large traders and master craftsmen, were sufficiently emancipated from economic dependence on the ruling aristocracy and gentry to express their independence in the way most open to them, by leaving the Church and joining their own Dissenting chapels. But the great majority of tenants and workers had no such freedom, and it did not occur to them to ask for it. With these few exceptions the dependency system stretched from top to bottom of society, for the smaller squires looked to the larger and the larger to the county aristocracy for a lead in all matters of politics and government, and even the village poor were drawn into the system, for whatever the law said, only those poor people who belonged to the system, who were recognized as dependent, loyal and subordinate, were given charity or parish relief, and outsiders, strangers, vagrants and others who did not belong were turned empty away, and sent back to their home parish under the Settlement Act of 1662.

Of course, the nobility and bigger gentry did travel much more than the rest – to the county town for the Quarter Sessions of J.P.s which governed the county, and the Assizes, which were big occasions not merely for trying criminals but also for the social life of the county families, who wined, dined and danced at the assembly rooms; and also to London in 'the Season' between Christmas and May, for the Court, Parliament and London 'Society'. For all the strings of patronage and dependency met at the top, in London, in the Court and the Cabinet, which dispensed patronage – jobs in the government, pensions and sinecures, contracts and favours, honours and peerages – in return for loyal political service in Parliament and in local government. And so in a sense there was *one* nation-wide class in eighteenth-century society: the landed class, the men on horseback, who could afford to travel and meet each other in the county towns and in London, to enjoy themselves, arrange marriages and other alliances, and to govern the rest of society. And because the English landed class were real owners of the land and stood to gain in increased rent from anything which improved its value, they had a stake in every kind of economic growth. Above all, they had an interest in improved methods of transport. It was the English landlords, therefore, who played the most important part in pioneering the new roads and canals of the Industrial Revolution, which in turn paved the way for the Railway Age.

Further Readings

W. T. Jackman, *The Development of Transportation in Modern England* (2nd edition, Cass & Co. Ltd., 1962), Chapters 1–3.

H. J. Dyos and D. H. Aldcroft, *British Transport: an Economic Survey from the Seventeenth Century to the Twentieth* (Leicester U.P., 1969).

Sidney and Beatrice Webb, *The Story of the King's Highway* (Longmans, 1920).

J. Crofts, *Packhorse, Waggon and Post: Land Carriage and Communications under the Tudors and Stuarts* (Routledge & Kegan Paul, 1967).

T. S. Willan, *River Navigation in England, 1600–1750* (Cass & Co. Ltd., 1936).

Peter Mathias, 'The Social Structure in the 18th Century: a Calculation by Joseph Massie', *Economic History Review*, August 1957.

Sidney Pollard and D. W. Crossley, *The Wealth of Britain, 1085–1966* (Batsford, 1968), Chapter 5.

Charles Wilson, *England's Apprenticeship, 1603–1763* (Longmans, 1965).

Peter Laslett, *The World We Have Lost* (Methuen, 1965).

Dorothy Marshall, *English People in the 18th Century* (Longmans, 1956).

J. H. Plumb, *England in the 18th Century* (Penguin Books, 1950).

Harold Perkin, *The Origins of Modern English Society, 1780–1880* (Routledge & Kegan Paul, 1969), Chapter 2.

Notes

1. Quoted by J. Crofts, *Packhorse, Waggon and Post: Land Carriage and Communications under the Tudors and Stuarts* (Routledge & Kegan Paul, 1967), p. 16.

2. *Gentleman's Magazine*, 1752, XXII.517.
3. *Ibid.*, 1747, XVII. 232.
4. John, Lord Hervey, *Memoirs of the Court of George II* (ed. J. W. Croker, 1848), p. 362.
5. César de Saussure, *A Foreign View of England in the reign of George II* (English trans. 1902), pp. 146–7, 165–6.
6. Francis Blomefield, *Topographical History of Norfolk* (1805–10), III. 441.
7. Letter to Lord Carlisle, 27 Oct. 1729, *Historical MSS Commission*, XV, Appendix 6, p. 61.
8. Arthur Young, *View of the Agriculture of Oxfordshire* (1809), p. 324.
9. Eliza Meteyard, *Life of Josiah Wedgwood* (1865–6), I. 266–8.
10. J. A. Picton, *Memorials of Liverpool, Historical and Topographical* (1875), II. 106; Thomas Baines, *History of the Commerce and Town of Liverpool* (1852), p. 418.
11. M. A. Richardson, *The Borderer's Table Book* (Newcastle-upon-Tyne, 1846), II. 20.
12. H. Graham, *The Social Life of Scotland in the 18th Century* (1906), p. 167.
13. James Cleland, *Enumeration of the Inhabitants of the City of Glasgow and County of Lanark* (Glasgow, 1832), p. 156.
14. W. T. Jackman, *The Development of Transportation in Modern England* (Cass & Co. Ltd., 1962 edition), chap. ii
15. *Ibid.*, Appendix 13, pp. 742–4.
16. Per Kalm, *An Account of his Visit to England . . . in 1748* (trans. J. Lucas, 1892), p. 381.
17. Jackman, *op. cit.*, chap. iv.
18. Crofts, *op. cit,*, pp. 52, 56.
19. *Ibid.*, pp. 51, 52.
20. *Ibid.*, p. 61.
21. Jackman, *op. cit.*, pp. 110, 138.
22. *Ibid.*, pp. 138, 321–3.
23. J. Boswell, *London Journal, 1762–63* (Bannerlea, 1952 edition), pp. 51–3.

24. Jackman, *op. cit.*, pp. 90–8, 335–9.

25. *Ibid.*, pp. 138, 344–5.

26. *Ibid.*, pp. 346–7.

27. Meteyard, *Wedgwood*, pp. 267, 275.

28. Rev. S. Shaw, *A Tour to the West of England in 1788* (1789), p. 263.

29. Jackman, *op. cit.*, pp. 139–40, 346–8.

30. Andrew Yarranton, *England's Improvement by Sea and Land* (1698), II. 92.

31. Cf. T. S. Willan, *River Navigation in England, 1600–1750* (Cass & Co. Ltd., 1964 edition), *passim*.

32. A. Smith, *Wealth of Nations* (1905 edition), I. 19.

33. T. S. Ashton, *An Economic History of England: the 18th Century* (Methuen, 1955), p. 71; Willan, *op. cit.*, pp. 105–8.

34. Jackman, *op. cit.*, pp. 206–9.

35. All three sets of figures are given by Peter Mathias, 'The Social Structure in the 18th Century: a Calculation by Joseph Massie', *Economic History Review*, August, 1957, pp. 42–5. Massie's 50 categories have in the following paragraph been grouped under the three contemporary concepts of 'aristocracy and gentry', 'middle ranks' and 'lower orders' or 'labouring poor'.

36. Cf. Harold Perkin, *The Origins of Modern English Society, 1780–1880* (Routledge & Kegan Paul, 1969), pp. 52–5.

37. P. Colquhoun, *A Treatise on the Wealth, Power and Resources of the British Empire* (1814), p. 6.

38. Cf. R. H. Tawney, *The Agrarian Problem of the 16th Century* (Longmans, 1912).

39. Cf. George Unwin, *Industrial Organization in the 16th and 17th Centuries* (Oxford, 1904).

Chapter Two

Why the Railways Came

THE iron horse – the steam locomotive – was to begin a new epoch in the history of the world. But *why* did the railways come? And why here in Britain, in the early nineteenth century? It is not enough to say 'because a set of clever men invented them', for inventors need the challenge and the opportunity, a problem to be solved, a demand to be met, and businessmen and money to back them and apply their inventions far and wide.

The short answer, of course, is: because of the Industrial Revolution. The new factories, the new towns, the larger population, the increased volume of raw materials and finished goods which had to be carried – and the much greater numbers of businessmen, salesmen and agents and so on who wanted to travel – created the need for a new, faster and more efficient mode of transport, and the new technology, the mass-produced iron and mechanical engineering skills, produced the means of supplying it. But that merely takes us back to the Industrial Revolution itself, and the questions of why it came at all, and why in Britain first. And the answers, strangely enough, lie to a large extent with the man on horseback, the landed gentleman who dominated British society. The English landowner, almost literally, paved the way for what was to be the first Industrial Revolution in any country.

He did this in two ways, directly and indirectly. Indirectly, he created – for his own ends and unintentionally – the right kind of society for an Industrial Revolution. Directly, he played the key part in providing what modern economists have called the preconditions of industrialism: the new agriculture to supply the food for the industrial workers and the much larger population; the planning and much of the building of the new towns; the mining of coal and metal ores for the heavy industries; above all, the new roads and canals which preceded and led on to the railways themselves.[1]

First, the landed class created the right kind of society for an Industrial Revolution. We all know that Britain was lucky in her geography. She had the water-power, coal, iron ore and other minerals, and easy access to the sea near what was becoming the crossroads of world trade. But so had many other countries in Western Europe, which did not have an Industrial Revolution until half a century or more after Britain had shown the way. In Britain industrialism came before and caused the railways. Elsewhere the railways, already invented by Britain, came before and helped to cause industrialism. What gave Britain the lead was the men to grasp the opportunity presented by this combination of economic resources and expanding world trade: not only the inventors but the enterprising capitalists to apply their inventions, the ready and able workers to make and work the machines, and a ruling class willing to provide the land for industrial development and to pass the legislation for agricultural improvement and transport undertakings. This was not just a lucky accident. It was because British society was already different in important ways from Continental, and because the landowners had made it so.

We have already seen that the landlords in Britain, by a long process lasting several centuries, had made themselves real owners of the land, with a stake in every kind of economic growth. This they had done by a continuous struggle carried out in the law courts, in Parliament, and finally on the battlefields of the Civil War. But real ownership of their estates was not without a price, though one which the landlords very willingly paid. First of all, in order to keep their estates together and prevent them from fragmenting among all their descendants, who would soon have become as numerous and as poor as some of the Continental minor aristocracies, they practised primogeniture, or inheritance by the eldest son. This meant that all the younger sons had to be sent out into the world, usually with an education and an annual allowance or a 'portion' (lump sum of capital), to earn their living in business or the professions. Elsewhere the sons of the aristocracy were prevented, on pain of *dérogeance* – degradation or loss of status – from going into any occupation save the service of the Crown or the Church. In Britain, younger sons took their capital and their ambitions into trade and the professions and not only helped to swell the numbers and prosperity of the middle ranks but also helped to tie them more firmly to the ideals and outlook of the aristocracy. Now if their own younger sons were in business, and if the ownership of an estate rather than the status of an aristocrat (or landed gentleman in Britain, where the gentry were the equivalent of the Continental *petite noblesse*) was what made you a country gentleman, then the British land-lords, unlike their Continental counterparts, had to allow men from the middle ranks to buy land, and to treat them as gentry when they did.

Thus in Britain there was a continuous downflow of younger sons of the landed class into the middle ranks, and a continuous upflow of 'new men' from business and the professions into the landed class. To this, since the aristocracy and gentry were anything but snobbish when it came to marrying money, one should add a continuous downflow of dowried daughters and a continuous upflow of heiresses. Thus there was a two-way flow of people and wealth between the landed class and the middle ranks which had much the same effect on society and the economy as the circulation of the blood, enriching and stimulating every part and helping it to grow. The younger sons, instead of idling away their time like their Con-tinental cousins, worked hard to make a fortune and get back to their proper station in life. Business men 'ploughed back the profits', not only to get rich but to buy a landed estate and set themselves up as country gentle-men. When they did so, they made room for others coming up behind them on the ladder of success, and so the game of getting rich and social climbing went on, with repercussions right down to the very bottom of society. As a Manchester cobbler put it in 1756,

See, as the Owners of old Family Estates in your Neighbour-hood are selling off their patrimonies, how your Townsmen are constantly purchasing; and thereby laying the Foundation of a new Race of Gentry! . . . who, knowing both how and when to be content, retire, decently to enjoy their well-got Wealth, leaving the Coast open, for new Adventurers, to follow their worthy Example.[2]

The effects of this two-way flow were manifold, some frivolous, others profound. One curious paradox was that Britain was a more snobbish society than any in Europe. English snobbery was and is proverbial. For snobbery is a way of putting people in their place – their proper place in society. It was not much needed on the Continent, where people knew their place and were less tempted to step out of it. Continental aristocracies were proud and aloof, and clung to their honour and privileges, but they had stronger means than snobbery of keeping inferiors in their places in an essentially closed society. Britain, by contrast, was an open society, in which everyone tried to 'keep up with the Joneses'. Among many others, Henry Fielding the novelist complained in 1750 that

while the Nobleman will emulate the Grandeur of a Prince; the Gentleman will aspire to the proper state of a Nobleman; the Tradesman steps from behind his Counter into the vacant place of the Gentleman. Nor doth the Confusion end here: It reaches the very Dregs of the People.[3]

Foreign visitors like the Swedish Per Kalm and the French P. J. Grosley were amazed to find English farm labourers wearing periwigs and knee-breeches and their wives wearing large hats and panniered dresses – just as in Stubbs's paintings.[4]

'Keeping up with the Joneses' simply meant that the British, from top to bottom of society, were ambitious and wanted to get on in the world, which an open society allowed and encouraged them to do. Yet this seemingly frivolous ambition became the engine which drove the

British economy on to the Industrial Revolution. The inventors and industrialists strove to amass a fortune, buy an estate and set up as country gentlemen, like generations of 'new men' before them. Sir Richard Arkwright, the pioneer of cotton spinning, built Willersley Castle and set up four sons as landed gentlemen; Sir Robert Peel, another cotton spinner, bought Drayton Manor and the pocket borough of Tamworth from which he launched his son's career to the premiership; Josiah Wedgwood, the great potter, bought Barlaston and built himself an elegant Georgian house; his friend Matthew Boulton, partner of James Watt in the making of steam engines, bought the estate of Great Tew; and almost every successful industrialist did much the same.

On a smaller scale the workers who built the factories, made the machines and operated them for the industrialists were trying to do much the same thing: to raise their wages and better themselves. And because in Britain, unlike the Continent, the bulk of the people were not penny-pinching, subsistence peasants but wage-earners used to earning money and spending it as soon as earned, they were more easily persuaded into the mills, mines and factories to earn the wherewithal to buy the whiter bread, the stronger beer, the cotton dresses and woollen coats, the pots and pans, clocks and watches, furniture and fire grates, which the new industrialism was producing in such abundance. As Henri Meister, a Swiss journalist from Paris, observed in the 1790s,

There is as great an inequality of ranks and fortune in England as in France; but in the former the consequence and importance of a man as a member of society is far more respectable. Individuals of the lower classes are better cloathed, better fed and better lodged than elsewhere; and often, as far as I could learn, with no better means than the same classes enjoy with us. Pride and a desire to preserve the public esteem seem to force upon them that attention to their conduct and outward appearance.[5]

Keeping up with the Joneses, or social emulation, was in fact the main driving force behind the Industrial Revolution in another, and perhaps the most important, way. Both industrialists and workers could only make the new mass-produced goods if somebody would buy them, and buy them in ever-increasing quantities. This could only happen if not merely the rich but the middle ranks and lower orders could be induced, not all at once but by degrees, to buy the same things. Take, for example, the new whole cotton cloth, especially the fine muslin, which the new factory-spun yarn enabled to be made in Britain for the first time. In the 1770s and 1780s, when it was absolutely new and still comparatively expensive, it was worn in great swathes in the panniered dresses and huge bonnets of the aristocracy and gentry. By the 1790s and 1800s it was worn by the middle ranks as well in the clinging, transparent shifts of the Directory and Empire lines. By the 1810s and 1820s it was being worn by everybody from the duchess to the mill girl in the swelling skirts and puffed sleeves of the Regency period.[6] In the course of a generation or so a fashion created by industrialism had spread from top to bottom of society, and in doing so had helped to expand many times over the volume of production and reduce the price from that of a luxury to that of a commonplace necessity.

Yet the Industrial Revolution could not have happened unless the landed class had wanted it to. It was not that they made the revolution themselves, although some of them did turn industrialist in their spare time: the

Earl of Derby had a cotton mill at Preston, the ninth Earl of Dundonald ruined himself in trying to develop new chemical processes at his works at Walker-on-Tyne, while among hundreds of coal-owning gentry the Sneyds of Keele, where the new university now stands, also ran ironworks and brickworks.[7] Their main task, however, was to prepare the way for industrialism, in agriculture, mining, town development and, above all, in transport.

All the landowners had a stake in agricultural improvement, so necessary if the new town dwellers and factory workers were to be fed, through the increased rents which could be charged after improvements, especially after enclosure. The new four-course rotation – clover, wheat, turnips, oats or barley – instead of the three-course – wheat, oats or barley, fallow – not only produced a crop every year instead of only two years in three, but produced heavier crops and, for the first time, arable fodder crops instead of the limited hay harvest of the meadows, thus enabling much larger numbers of animals to be kept. More animals meant more fresh meat and milk, especially in the winter, and more manure for the fields and so heavier crops. On the whole the landlords themselves were not agricultural innovators, although some of them were quick to seize on new ideas on their home farms. Sir Robert Walpole was growing field turnips as early as 1702, and if in 1730 he had been turned out of the government instead of his brother-in-law, we should not hear of 'Turnip' Townshend, perhaps, but of 'Wurzle' Walpole. The great agricultural inventors were large tenant or yeomen farmers like Jethro Tull of the seed-drill, Robert Bakewell of the Derbyshire ram and the Colling brothers of the Durham ox, but it was great landowners like the Duke of Bedford and Thomas

Coke of Holkham who popularized their ideas. And above all it was the landowners in the villages and in Parliament who took the initiative in bringing about the enclosures which were ultimately decisive in spreading the agricultural revolution.[8]

Good agriculture meant prosperity, but mining could mean a fortune. The British landowners were unique, west of the Urals, in owning the mineral rights (apart from gold and silver, which still belonged to the Crown). Elsewhere in Europe they all belonged to the Crown, and the main aim of the landlord was to keep his minerals secret and the king's surveyor off his estate. In Britain every landowner dreamed of finding coal, iron, copper, lead or some other valuable ore on his property. The Duke of Northumberland mined coal in Northumberland, the Duke of Buckingham alum in the North Riding, the Duke of Norfolk and the Marquess of Rockingham coal in the West Riding, the Earls of Derby and Crawford coal in Lancashire, the Dukes of Devonshire and Newcastle coal and lead in Derbyshire, Lords Gower and Grenville coal and iron in Staffordshire, Lord Ashburnham iron in Sussex and coal and lead in Wales, the Duke of Bedford copper in Devon, Lord Falmouth tin in Cornwall, and hundreds of other landowners coal wherever it could be found. Mining was the next best thing to a rich marriage for increasing the fortunes of a landed family.

Town planning and development was another opportunity for windfall gains for landowners with estates in the right places. London was the best place of all, and the Dukes of Bedford, Portland and Devonshire among others increased their rent-rolls enormously by laying out the fashionable streets and squares of the West End. The

Earls of Derby and Sefton gained from the development of Liverpool. The Dukes of Norfolk laid out the new streets of industrial Sheffield and built the new town of Glossop from scratch. Later, in the railway age, the Dukes of Devonshire laid out and built the new towns of Eastbourne and Barrow-in-Furness, and Sir Peter Hesketh-Fleetwood built the new town, holiday resort and port of Fleetwood, and named it after himself.[9] For someone had to plan the new streets and thoroughfares of all the new and expanding towns, and sell or lease off the building plots to the builders and contractors, and who could this be but the large local landowners?

Most of all, however, the new agriculture, mines, factories, towns and ports of the Industrial Revolution needed new and better transport and communications to connect them all up and make them work together. The food and raw materials had to be carried to the towns, the cotton from India and America had to be transported from the ports to the mills, the yarn had to be distributed to the handloom weavers or the powerloom weaving sheds, the iron from Wales or Shropshire and the West Riding or Lincolnshire had to be carried to London, Birmingham and Sheffield to be made into cutlery, tools and other hardware, and most of all the coal had to be carried from the mines of the north, the midlands and South Wales all over the country for the domestic fires of the towns and the thousands of furnaces and boilers in a vast and growing number of different industries. Landowners everywhere had a stake in better transport to encourage trade and enable their farmers and urban tenants to pay higher rents, but coal and mineral-owning landlords had the biggest stake of all, since the cost of transporting cheap, heavy and bulky goods was

the largest part of the price and the biggest hindrance to
increased sales and larger profits. Moreover, since the
mining and smelting industries, unlike agriculture or
domestic manufactures, generate heavy loads from a comparatively few concentrated points over a small number
of heavily used routes, they soon wear out the roads, and
offer a challenge and an opportunity to find ways of
improving the roads or finding alternatives to them. It
was no accident, therefore, that it was the owners of
mineral-bearing land who pioneered the revolution in
transport.

The waterway was the easiest answer, and we have
already seen that the navigable rivers were developed
and used as much as possible. Coal was shipped from the
Tyne, the Wear, the Severn and South Wales to all the
ports and rivers of Britain. But there was always the problem of getting it to the waterside. Within the mines
themselves an ancient device had long been used for
moving heavy loads: a little truck with wheels running on
wooden planks or rails to reduce the friction, with some
device – a spigot, pulley-shaped wheels, or wheels shaped
like a half-pulley or with a flange – to keep it on the track.
Such a truck, pushed by the miners, was used in the
Black Forest ironworks in the late Middle Ages, first
illustrated in a German treatise on mining law published
in 1519,[10] and beautifully detailed in Agricola's *De Re
Metallica* in 1556. It may have been introduced into
England by the German brass founders and copper
miners brought to Borrowdale in the Lake District by
Queen Elizabeth I's chief minister, Lord Burleigh;
though a 'tram' or special track for a truck existed at
Barnard Castle, County Durham, in Queen Mary's
reign.[11]

This primitive and remote ancestor of the railway the English mineowners took a stage further, by harnessing a horse to the truck and making it much bigger, chiefly for transporting the coal from the pithead to the water-side. Wooden tracks or waggonways, as they were called, enabled a horse to pull two or three tons instead of half a ton or less on an ordinary road. One of the earliest of them was built about 1605 by Sir Francis Willoughby to get his coal from Wollaton near Nottingham down to the Trent. A few years later, about 1630, the waggonway is said to have been introduced from the East Midlands to Newcastle by Huntingdon Beaumont, a landowner's son and colliery 'viewer' or engineer, who lost all his money but began the widespread network of waggon-ways or 'Newcastle roads' all around the Tyne.[12] Mostly they were simply wooden tracks laid over the surface of the ground, and large sums of money or annual rents in the form of a royalty on the tonnages carried were paid for 'wayleaves', or the right to take them across other owners' land. Some, however, were elaborate engineering works, like the Tanfield Tramway, built about 1671, with the oldest still existing railway bridge, the Causey Arch, with a span of 100 feet, built in 1726.[13]

From the north-east the system spread to other parts of the country, notably the north midlands, Shropshire and South Wales. In the early eighteenth century when, as a result of Abraham Darby's coke-smelting process, iron became cheaper, thin plates of iron were used to rein-force the track at bends and other wearing points. Cast iron also began to be used, at some time between 1734 and 1753, for the wheels, which might be flanged, like modern ones, to hold them on the track. A tramway with rails and flanged wheels was built by Ralph Allen, the

Master of the Cross Posts, a typical 'new man' who bought himself a country seat at Prior Park in Somerset, to bring building stone from his Combe Down quarries to Bath.[14] Charles Brandling obtained the first Railway Act in 1758 to enable him to acquire the land for a railway to take his coal from Middleton Colliery to Leeds.[15] Abraham Darby II, son of the inventor of coke smelting, laid the first cast-iron rails at his Coalbrookdale Ironworks in Shropshire in 1767.[16] John Curr, the Duke of Norfolk's agent, laid a similar cast-iron road from Nunnery Colliery to Sheffield in 1776, but transferring the flange from the wheel to the track so as to make what came to be called a plateway, for flat-tyred wheels, while the modern edge rail was introduced on the Loughborough Canal Dock railway in 1788–9.[17]

All such horse-drawn tramways or railroads, however, were very much second best to water transport, to which, as in the last case, they acted chiefly as short-distance feeders. A horse could pull four or five tons on a tramway, perhaps up to ten tons on a level one (which was rare), but it could pull up to fifty tons on a waterway, and with much less wear and tear of the equipment. Wherever possible water transport was preferred as being easier and cheaper, and waggonways and tramways reserved for steep and difficult country with downhill loads like that above the Tyne. As we have seen, the many River Navigation Acts between 1660 and 1760 more than doubled the mileage open to barge traffic, and some of them, like the Mersey and Irwell or the Aire and Calder Navigations, were practically new waterways, with new 'cuts', pound locks, towing paths, and all the appearance of canals. Two navigations in particular formed important connecting links with the canal age. The Newry

Navigation built in Northern Ireland between 1730 and 1742 and the Sankey Brook Navigation from St Helens to the Mersey in 1755–7 were to all intents and purposes man-made waterways, the latter planned as a river improvement but executed as a deadwater canal.[18]

The first deadwater canal planned and built as such and not along the line of an existing river was, of course, the famous Bridgewater Canal built in 1759–61. The Duke of Bridgewater wanted to get his coal from his mines at Worsley to Manchester more cheaply than by road to the Irwell and then at exorbitant tolls up the old navigation to Salford. The mines were deep in a hillside, and John Gilbert, the duke's agent at Worsley, had the brilliant idea of both draining them and carrying the coal away by means of a canal starting in a tunnel at the coal face and ending at the Irwell below Salford. The duke obtained an Act of Parliament, but the scheme depended on the co-operation of the Mersey and Irwell Navigation Company, and so he decided to carry the canal by an aqueduct over the Irwell and on into Manchester itself. To help carry out the scheme he engaged a semi-literate millwright, James Brindley, introduced to him by his brother-in-law, Earl Gower, who owned mines in Staffordshire and Shropshire, and had employed Brindley to survey a possible canal from the Potteries to the navigable part of the Trent. Brindley had made his name building ingenious machinery for the silk mills at Macclesfield, Congleton and Leek, including the mill-races which were in effect small canals with complicated sluices, and what he called in his notebooks 'fire injons' (steam engines on the Newcomen atmospheric model) for pumping water out of mines in the Potteries. Between them John Gilbert and Brindley engineered the canal brilliantly, and the duke was able to halve the price of coal in Manchester, and inaugurate a new era of cheap transport.[19]

The success of the first Bridgewater Canal inspired the duke and other landowners and businessmen to project many more. The first was an extension of the Bridgewater down to the Mersey at Runcorn, thus avoiding the difficult passage and also breaking the monopoly of the 'Old Navigation', the Mersey and Irwell, and reducing the freight charge between Liverpool and Manchester from 12s. to 6s. a ton. Lord Strange and the other proprietors of the Old Navigation fought him through Parliament, but judicious lobbying and a certain amount of outright bribery got the necessary Act in 1762, though even then the opposition of Sir Richard Brooke, whose Norton Priory estate lay across the final stretch near Runcorn, delayed completion of the canal until 1776.

Meanwhile, the duke, his brother-in-law Earl Gower and the great potter, Josiah Wedgwood, revived the scheme for a Grand Trunk Canal to join the Trent and Mersey by way of the Potteries, thus connecting Liverpool to Hull and cheapening supplies of china clay from the west and flint from the east, as well as providing outlets for the coal and earthenware of the north midlands. The Act was carried in 1766 against the opposition of the Mersey–Weaver and Trent Navigations, both of which were by-passed in whole or in part, and Brindley built the ninety-three-and-a-half-mile canal, which was opened throughout its length, after great difficulties with the one-and-a-half-mile tunnel at Harecastle, in 1777, reaching the Mersey by way of the Bridgewater Canal at Preston Brook.

Brindley's success with the Bridgewater and Grand Trunk Canals led to his appointment as consulting engineer for a whole network of waterways designed to link up the Trent and Mersey with the Thames and Severn, and so to connect all the major English ports, Liverpool, Hull, Bristol and London, via Birmingham and the Midlands. This was the famous 'Cross' of canals, the Grand Trunk forming the northern arms of the X, the Staffordshire and Worcestershire (opened 1771) the south-western from that canal at Great Haywood to Stourport on the Severn, and the Coventry Canal from Fradley Junction on the Grand Trunk via Marston Bridge on the Oxford Canal (both opened about 1790) to the Thames, forming the south-eastern arm. Brindley also built the Birmingham Canal (opened 1772) and the Droitwich Canal (opened 1771), which reinforced the route to the Severn, and the Chesterfield Canal to bring the North Derbyshire coal down to the Trent. All this work was too much for one man, as many of his landed and business clients complained, and much of it was done through his assistants, and completed after his death in 1772. But it ensured that by 1790 the whole heartland of England had been opened up to water transport.[20]

What this meant in terms of trade and prosperity can be seen from the reception given to canal Acts in the local press. As a Birmingham newspaper reported at the time, 'on receiving the agreeable news that His Majesty had been at the House of Peers and signed the Bill for making the Navigable Canal from this Town to Wolverhampton, the Bells were set to ringing, which continued the whole day'.[21] During the great surge of industrial growth of the 1790s there was a 'canal mania' when over fifty canal Acts were passed, thirty of them in 1793 and 1794 alone, and canal shares changed hands at enormous prices. As a result of this and a later boom in the 1820s,

just before the railways came, England from Kendal to
Portsmouth, from the Severn to the Thames, came to be
covered with a vast network of canals, and even Scotland
was trisected by the Forth and Clyde and the Caledonian
Canals. Many of them were major engineering works
built by Brindley's successors, Henshall, Dadford,
Rennie, Smeaton, Outram, and many more – a new race
of civil engineers who anticipated on a smaller scale the
great achievements of the railway age. Among the
greatest of them was Thomas Telford, who rose from
being a working mason to become the father of civil
engineering, not merely as founder of the Institute of
Civil Engineers in 1818 but as pioneer of the system of
large-scale contracting which later built the railways.[22]
The inscription on his greatest single work, the Pont-
cysyllte Aqueduct which carries the Ellesmere Canal in
an iron trough 1,000 feet long 121 feet above the River
Dee near Llangollen, sums up the partnership which
made the canals and the Industrial Revolution:

> The Nobility and Gentry of
> The adjacent Counties,
> Having united their efforts with
> The great commercial interests of this Country
> In creating an intercourse and union between
> ENGLAND AND NORTH WALES,
> By a navigable communication of the three Rivers
> SEVERN, DEE, AND MERSEY,
> For the mutual benefit of Agriculture and Trade,
> Caused the first stone of this Accqueduct of
> PONTCYSYLLTE,
> To be laid on the 25th day of July, 1795,
> When Richard Myddelton, of Chirk, Esq. M.P.
> One of the original patrons of the
> ELLESMERE CANAL,

Was Lord of this Manor
And in the Reign of our Sovereign,
GEORGE THE THIRD,
When the equity of the Laws, and
The security of Property,
Promoted the general welfare of the Nation;
While the Arts and Sciences flourished
By his Patronage, and
The conduct of civil life was improved
By his example.
The navigation over this Acqueduct
was opened 26th November 1805.[23]

The canals were both the effect of the Industrial Revolution and the extra boost needed to keep it going. They meant cheaper coal and iron, clay and bricks, cotton and grain for the factories and towns, but this was only the start. Adam Smith at the time said the division of labour, the application of ingenious machinery, and so the efficiency and productiveness of labour depended on the extent of the market. The canals linked almost every factory and industrial town to the national market, and through the rivers and ports to the world market. The great surge of industrial expansion in the last two decades of the eighteenth century has been called by W. W. Rostow the 'take-off into self-sustained economic growth'. Although not all modern economic historians would accept all the implications of that phrase, the upturn of the curve of economic growth around that time is very like the trajectory of an aeroplane taking off. In the twenty years between the Peace of Paris, which ended the American War of Independence in 1783, and the Peace of Amiens, which called a temporary halt to the Napoleonic Wars in 1802, industrial production

doubled, foreign trade trebled, iron production nearly
quadrupled, cotton production quintupled.[24] This was
the turning-point in industrial growth which was to lead
on to the dramatic increase in population and affluence
in the railway age itself.

Yet this very acceleration created its own problems.
The needs of industry for heavy transport soon outgrew
the old roads, waggonways and tramways, and even
began to demand something faster, more efficient and
more flexible than the canals. A tremendous effort was
made to quicken passenger transport even on the canals.
The Bridgewater Canal carried passengers from the
early years in special boats with first-, second- and third-
class cabins, charging 2s. 6d., 1s. and 10d. respectively
from Warrington to Manchester. The Forth and Clyde
Company, which began to carry passengers in two cabins,
one for ladies and one for gentlemen, in 1783, later
developed the 'swift boat', introduced in 1809, to record
speeds. They did the twenty-five miles from Glasgow to
Falkirk in three and a half hours, pulled by two horses,
one ridden by a postillion, which were changed every two
miles. In the 1830s under the threat of the new railways
they achieved speeds of ten miles an hour, their swan-
neck prows riding the bow wave like a motor-boat.
Similar 'fly-boats' were introduced in England, on the
Lancaster Canal between Kendal and Preston, and
elsewhere. There were even excursion trips, such as that
on the Chester Canal from Beeston to the Chester Races
in 1776, or the ten miles of pleasant scenery with opportunities for refreshment at one of the 'highly interesting
aqueducts' which the Edinburgh and Glasgow Union
Canal offered for 6d. in 1834.[25]

The Forth and Clyde also experimented with the

steam-boat, invented by William Symington in 1787, and
his second paddle-boat was tried out there two years
later: 'in the presence of hundreds of spectators, who
lined the banks of the canal, the boat glided along,
propelled at the rate of five miles an hour'. Lord Dundas,
the governor of the canal company, took up the idea, and
employed Symington to build a tug, the *Charlotte Dundas*,
which successfully pulled two seventy-ton barges in
1802. But the company feared the damage to the canal
banks from the wash, and the *Charlotte Dundas* was
beached and left to rot. The same fate met the *Buona-
parte*, designed by Robert Fulton of New York for the
Duke of Bridgewater, which successfully hauled eight
twenty-five-ton barges on his canal in 1797. The engine
was taken out and used for pumping water from the
foundations of Stretford aqueduct. Only when light
steam engines were developed as a result of the railways,
in the 1850s, did steam play much part, and then not a
major one, on the canals.[26]

Neither fly-boats nor steamers, however, could meet
the demand for rapid passenger transport. The very
expansion of economic activity meant that businessmen
needed to travel more often and more swiftly, and they
also needed a faster and more reliable postal service. To
meet both needs John Palmer persuaded the government
in 1784 to let him introduce his new mail coaches–fast,
light vehicles with only four inside and no outside passengers, which covered the journey from London to
Bristol in sixteen hours, about half the previous time.
The scheme soon spread to other parts of the country,
and similar speeds were achieved to most of the major
trading centres.[27] But faster coaches depended on better
roads, and better roads came surprisingly late. Over 4,000

turnpike and other road Acts were passed between 1750 and 1830, covering about 20,000 miles of road,[28] but it was only in the last few decades before the railways came that really good roads began to be made. 'Blind Jack' Metcalfe of Knaresborough, perhaps the first modern road engineer, built about 180 miles of good turnpike road in and around the Pennines between 1765 and 1792. He pioneered all the main principles of road building: a firm foundation preferably on the subsoil, or on a mat of heather or ling where the ground was soft or marshy, a filling of hard road metal (stone) built up to a convex surface above the level of the surrounding soil, and drainage ditches on either side to carry off the surface water.[29] But his work was very little imitated outside his own area until after his death in 1810.

Thomas Telford, the great canal engineer and bridge builder, turned his attention to roads in 1816, when the government appointed him to take charge of the building of the Glasgow to Carlisle road, at a cost of £50,000. He engineered the road with bridges and easy gradients, and on his own sixty-nine miles employed an expensive but very effective method of laying a broken rock foundation by hand and building up in layers to a convex gravel surface. As Telford proudly remarked of the result,

To persons who were in the habit of travelling in Lanarkshire previous to these improvements, the change was surprising as well as gratifying; instead of roads cut into deep ruts through dangerous ravines, jolting the traveller, and injuring his carriage, – or leading him, if on horseback, plunging and staggering, circuitously over steep hills, the traveller has now smooth surfaces, with easy ascents, rendered safe by protecting fences. Such advantages being equally beneficial to all ranks of society, are of the first importance to a civilized nation.

He went on to engineer new roads from Edinburgh to Morpeth on the way to London, from Shrewsbury to Holyhead including the famous Menai Suspension Bridge, a network of roads in the Scottish Highlands, and elsewhere.[30]

But the colossus of roads was John Loudon McAdam, a small Scottish laird (landowner) who observed the inadequacies of parochial road mending as a road commissioner and experimented with improved methods of construction on his own estate. His final method, which was not new but a development of that of his predecessors Lester and Paterson, was much cheaper than Telford's, since it ignored the expensive hand-laid foundation, and simply laid a ten-inch layer of small broken stones upon a well-drained soil, which was then compacted into a bonded, water-proof and only slightly convex surface – very like a modern road, except that the road metal was water-bound instead of tarred. McAdam sent a description of this to Sir John Sinclair, chairman of the Board of Agriculture (not a government department but a private, though influential, society), who brought it to the attention of a parliamentary committee on highways. McAdam soon became known as *the* expert on road construction, from 1816 was appointed surveyor to most of the turnpike trusts around Bristol, and in 1827 surveyor-general of the metropolitan turnpikes. Most of the major roads of the kingdom were remade on his system, and even the streets of London were dug up, the paving stones broken into 'macadam' by gangs of pauper women and children, and then relaid on his instructions. At the same time he and his son and successor, James McAdam, began and carried on the movement for consolidation of the turnpike trusts which reduced them to a much smaller number of larger and more efficient organizations.[31]

As a result of the new McAdam roads and the better management of the trusts, there was another burst of improvement in the speed of coaches in the 1820s and 1830s. Indeed, the really fast coaches, with record average speeds of nine or more miles an hour, did not come until the early years of the railways, when the coaching system was already under sentence of death. The London to Edinburgh mail coach was down to fifty-nine hours by 1818, and forty-five and a half hours by 1836, an average speed of nine and a half miles an hour (excluding stops for meals, etc.). That from London to Manchester took twenty hours in 1830, eighteen hours fifteen minutes in 1836, an average of about ten miles an hour. The London to Shrewsbury took eighteen hours in 1822, fifteen hours forty-five minutes in 1835, an average of nearly ten miles an hour. The London to Bristol took eleven hours forty-five minutes in 1836, an average of over ten miles an hour. Such speeds could only be attained by changing the horses at least every hour, and even then only by working them to death: the average working life of a coach horse was at most three or four years. And with the high cost of horses and feeding stuffs the cost of fast coaching was proportionately high, on average about $2\frac{1}{2}$d. a mile outside and 4d. a mile inside.[32] Attempts were made to make the horse more efficient and productive, by reducing the friction and increasing the load in public transport, as was already done on the private tramways and plateways. In 1801 the first horse-drawn public freight railway, the Surrey Iron Railway from Croydon to Wandsworth, was incorporated, and opened in 1803. In 1807 the first public passenger railway, the Oystermouth round Swansea Bay, later the Swansea and Mumbles Railway, was opened, and there were various imitators during the next twenty years.[33] But these were all makeshifts, which did not solve the problem of finding a new and more efficient horse.

The real solution appeared with Richard Trevithick's high-pressure steam engine of 1800. This was as big an improvement on Watt's stationary steam engine as Watt's was on Newcomen's atmospheric engine, for its high power to weight ratio allowed it to carry itself about. Trevithick at first tried to apply it to road transport, and built a successful steam carriage at Camborne, Cornwall, which on Christmas Eve, 1801, went faster than walking pace but broke down on a steep hill. A later model, demonstrated in London in 1803, managed speeds of four to nine miles an hour. But the roads of that era were too rough for steam traction, and road transport was not suited to an engine which was most effective when built on a large scale to pull loads of twenty-five tons and upwards. Trevithick married his engine to the smooth metal road of the plateway (with flat-tyred wheels) on Penydaren Tramroad at Merthyr Tydfil in South Wales in 1804, and to the railway itself (with flanged wheels) at Gateshead-on-Tyne in 1805. Though they successfully pulled from ten to twenty-five tons, both these first primitive locomotives were too heavy for the contemporary track, and were converted to stationary engines.[34]

It was left to a group of rival colliery engineers to solve the problem completely. With plenty of cheap coal at their disposal and heavy loads to move over short distances, they had the means and the incentive to experiment. The first successful solution was Blenkinsop and Murray's locomotive at Middleton Colliery near

Leeds in 1812, which hauled itself along by means of a cog operating along a toothed rack on the track. A better solution was Blackett and Hedley's *Puffing Billy*, which worked on the smooth rail of Wylam Waggonway on the Tyne in 1814. But it was George Stephenson, a self-educated engine man at Killingworth Colliery on the Tyne coalfield, who turned the crude colliery engines into a revolutionary means of public transport. His loco-motives, beginning with the *Blücher* (named after both the allied Prussian general and a local colliery) in 1814, impressed a group of coal-owners and merchants led by the Quaker Edward Pease, who, having found a canal too costly to build over the terrain, were planning a horse-drawn railway from Darlington on the Auckland coal-field to deep water at Stockton on Tees. Pease and Stephenson met on the day that the Stockton and Darlington Railway Act received the royal assent. Out of that meeting grew the first steam-hauled public railway, which opened, for freight only, on 27 September 1825, the first train hauled by the locomotive *Locomotion*, driven by George Stephenson.[35]

The Stockton and Darlington had powers, under its second Act of 1823, to haul passengers as well as freight, but it only did so on exceptional occasions such as the ceremonial opening, and not as a regular thing. Passen-ger coaches operated in competition, paying tolls to the company, like stage coaches on a turnpike road or barges on a canal, and the receipts were only 3 per cent of the total in 1826–8. Moreover, the traffic was curiously mixed, and shared by horse, locomotive and stationary steam engine.[36] The undoubted success of the twenty-seven-mile railway, the longest and most complex one so far devised, attracted the attention of engineers and businessmen from all over the country, and above all a group of Liverpool and Manchester men, led by Joseph Sandars, who in 1826 obtained an Act for a railway between their two cities. They engaged George Stephenson to build for them the first modern railway, and so began the Railway Age.[37]

Further Reading

W. T. Jackman, *The Development of Transportation in Modern England* (2nd edition, Cass & Co. Ltd., 1962), Chapters 4–7.

Charles Hadfield, *British Canals: an Illustrated History* (2nd edition, Phoenix House, 1959).

Hugh Malet, *The Canal Duke* (Eccles & District Hist. Soc., 1961).

L. T. C. Rolt, *Thomas Telford* (Longmans, 1958).

'Roy Devereux' (Mrs R. McAdam Pember-Devereux), *J. L. McAdam* (Oxford University Press, 1936).

Howard Robinson, *The British Post Office: a History* (Oxford University Press, 1948).

H. P. Spratt, *The Birth of the Steam Boat* (Griffin, 1958).

C. E. Lee, *The Evolution of Railways* (Railway Gazette, 2nd edition, 1943).

H. G. Lewin, *Early British Railways: a Short History of their Origin and Development, 1801–44* (Locomotive Publishing Co., 1925).

C. F. Dendy Marshall, *A History of British Railways Down to . . .1831* (Locomotive Publishing Co., 1938).

H. W. Dickinson and A. Titley, *Richard Trevithick* (Cambridge University Press, 1934).

Notes

1. Cf. Perkin, *op. cit.*, pp. 74–8.
2. J. Stot, *A Sequel to the Friendly Advice to the Poor* (Manchester, 1756), p. 19.
3. Henry Fielding, *An Enquiry into the Causes of the Late Increase of Robbers* (1750), p. 6.
4. Kalm, *op. cit.*, p. 52; P. J. Grosley, *A Tour to London* (trans. T. Nugent, 1772), I. 75.
5. J. H. Meister, *Letters written during a Residence in England* (English trans. 1799), p. 8.
6. Cf. James Laver, *Fashion and History from the French Revolution to the Present Day* (Harrap, 1945).
7. For sources on landlords' entrepreneurial activities see Perkin, *op. cit.*, pp. 74–8.
8. Cf. G. E. Mingay and J. D. Chambers, *The Agricultural Revolution, 1750–1880* (Batsford, 1966), chap. iii.
9. W. Ashworth, *The Genesis of Modern British Town Planning* (Routledge & Kegan Paul, 1954), chap. ii; J. D. Marshall, *Furness and the Industrial Revolution* (Barrow, 1958), H. J. Perkin, 'The Development of Modern Glossop', in A. H. Birch, *Small Town Politics* (Oxford, 1962), chap. ii; J. H. Sutton, 'Early Fleetwood, 1835–47' (unpublished M. Litt. dissertation, University of Lancaster, 1968).
10. *Der Ursprung Gemeyner* (The Origin of Mining Law) (1519).
11. For the origins and early development of horse-drawn railways see C. E. Lee, *The Evolution of Railways* (2nd ed., 1943), R. A. Peddie, *Railway Literature, 1556–1830: a handlist* (1931), and Jackman, *op. cit.*, pp. 461–73.
12. R. S. Smith, 'Huntingdon Beaumont, Adventurer in Coal Mines', and 'England's First Rails: a Reconsideration',

Renaissance and Modern Studies, 1957, I. 115–53, and 1960, IV. 119–34.

13. Jack Simmons, *The Railways of Britain: an Historical Introduction* (Routledge & Kegan Paul, 1961), p. 2.

14. A. M. Ogilvie, *Ralph Allen's Bye, Way and Cross Posts* (1897); the tramway is shown in an engraving of Prior Park by Anthony Walker, 1752, in the British Museum, reproduced in Benjamin Boyce, *The Benevolent Man* (Cambridge, Mass., 1967), plate 3.

15. W. G. Rimmer, 'Middleton Colliery near Leeds', *Yorkshire Bulletin of Economic and Social Research*, 1955, VII. 41–57.

16. C. E. Stretton, *A Few Notes on Railway History* (1884), p. 4.

17. Nicholas Wood, *A Practical Treatise on Railroads* (1825), pp. 45, 48.

18. T. C. Barker, 'The Beginnings of the Canal Age in the British Isles', in L. S. Pressnell, ed., *Studies in the Industrial Revolution* (Athlone, 1960), pp. 1–22, and 'The Sankey Navigation', *Transactions of the Historic Society of Lancashire and Cheshire*, 1948, C. 121–55.

19. Frank Mullineux, *The Duke of Bridgewater's Canal* (1959); Hugh Malet, *The Canal Duke* (Eccles & District Hist. Soc., 1961), esp. chaps. vi–ix; Herbert Clegg, 'The Third Duke of Bridgewater's Canal Works in Manchester', *Transactions of the Lancashire and Cheshire Antiquarian Society*, 1955, LXV. 91–103.

20. Malet, *op. cit.*, chaps xi–xv; Charles Hadfield, *British Canals; an Illustrated History* (Phoenix House, 1959 ed.), chap. iv; L. T. C. Rolt, *The Inland Waterways of England* (1962 ed.), chap. iii.

21. Quoted in Hadfield, *op. cit.* p. 36.

22. Sir Alexander Gibb, *The Story of Telford: the Rise of Civil Engineering* (Maclehose, 1936); L. T. C. Rolt, *Thomas Telford* (Longmans, 1958).

23. Hadfield, *op. cit.*, pp. 103–4.

24. For exact figures see Perkin, *Origins of Modern English Society*, p. 2.
25. Hadfield, *op. cit.*, pp. 165–73.
26. *Ibid.*, p. 132; Malet, *op. cit.*, pp. 157–60, Rolt, *Inland Waterways*, pp. 152–5.
27. C. R. Clear, *John Palmer* (*of Bath*), *Mail Coach Pioneer* (Blandford Press, 1955), Jackman, *op. cit.*, pp. 324–7.
28. *Ibid.*, pp. 234, 722–4.
29. *Ibid.*, pp. 266–8.
30. *Ibid.*, pp. 269–74; Rolt, *Telford*, chaps. iii, v, viii, ix.
31. Jackman, *op. cit.*, pp. 276–83; 'Roy Devereux' (Mrs. Rose McAdam Pember-Devereux), *J. L. McAdam: Chapters in the History of Highways* (Oxford University Press, 1936); R. H. Spiro, 'J. L. McAdam and the Metropolis Turnpike Trust', *Journal of Transport History*, 1956, II. 207–13.
32. Jackman, *op. cit.*, pp. 335–9, 345.
33. C. E. Lee, 'Early Railways in Surrey', *Transactions of Newcomen Society*, 1940–43, XXI, pp. 49–79, and *The Swansea and Mumbles Light Railway* (1954 ed.).
34. H. W. Dickinson and A. Titley, *Richard Trevithick* (Cambridge University Press, 1934), chap. iii; C. F. Dendy Marshall, *A History of Railway Locomotives down to . . . 1831* (Locomotive Publishing Co., 1953), chap. ii.
35. H. G. Lewin, *Early British Railways: a Short History of their Development, 1801–44* (1925), chap. ii; C. F. D. Marshall, *Locomotives*, pp. 29–33, 79–83, 105; L.T.C. Rolt, *G. and R. Stephenson*, (Longmans, 1960) chap. iv.
36. Simmons, *op. cit.*, p. 3.
37. G. S. Veitch, *The Struggle for the Liverpool and Manchester Railway* (Daily Post, Liverpool, 1930), pp. 53, 54.

Chapter Three

The Men who made the Railways

THE Railway Age began on 15 September 1830, the day on which the first modern railway, the Liverpool and Manchester, was officially opened. For the first time all the ingredients of the railway as we know it – or, rather, knew it, until electric and diesel traction took over from steam – were brought together: the double track of iron rails for the regular public conveyance of passengers and freight by steam-locomotive haulage between major cities, with all the accessories of stations, signals, bridges, tunnels, cuttings, embankments and trains of first-, second- and third-class carriages. The distinction of being the first modern railway has been claimed for other lines, notably the Bolton and Leigh Railway opened in 1828 and the Canterbury and Whitstable opened on 3 May 1830. But the former was essentially a feeder from Bolton to the Leeds and Liverpool Canal; it operated the usual mixed traffic, horse and steam, of most pre-1830 railways (including the Stockton and Darlington), and

it was not officially opened for passenger traffic until
June 1830, soon after which it became a branch of the
Liverpool and Manchester.[1] And the second, engineered
by Robert Stephenson in the intervals between supervis-
ing the locomotive works at Newcastle and helping his
father to build the Liverpool and Manchester, was a
small affair only six miles long and worked by stationary
engines for two thirds of the route.[2] The Liverpool and
Manchester operated on a modern scale from the first,
with steam locomotives (except for the one-mile tunnel
for freight down to the docks at Wapping, worked by a
stationary engine), regular passenger time-tables, and
over 1,000 passengers a day by 1831.

The official opening has long had its place in general
history, as the scene of the first and most famous of
public railway accidents, which had consequences for
national politics. The distinguished victim, William
Huskisson, was leader of the progressive wing of the
Tory party, the followers of the late prime minister,
George Canning, and had resigned from the Duke of
Wellington's government over its refusal to accept so
minor a measure of parliamentary reform as the en-
franchisement of Manchester. In 1830 the Reform crisis
had begun, sparked off by the French and Belgian Revolu-
tions and by the two-way split of the Tory party, between
the government and the Canningites on the left and the
High Tories on the right, incensed by Peel and Wellington's Catholic Emancipation Act of 1829 and by Peel
and Huskisson's earlier free trade measures. The government's main hope of survival and of keeping out the
reforming Whigs and Radicals was to heal the breach
with the Canningites, and according to some historians
the seemingly chance meeting between Wellington and

Huskisson at the opening of the railway was carefully staged to this end.

On the day the eight special trains carrying over 1,000 passengers set out to the cheers of 50,000 spectators from Crown Street Station in Liverpool, the Duke of Wellington and Huskisson together with Peel and other leading figures in a splendidly ornate coach with a crimson canopy surmounted by a ducal coronet, supported on gilded pillars 'so contrived as to be lowered when passing into the tunnel'. What passed between the duke and Huskisson and whether it would have led to a reconciliation and staved off the Reform Act we shall never know. At Parkside the engines stopped to take up water, and Huskisson and some others got out to stretch their legs. As they were returning to the train, the *Rocket* on its way back from watering bore down on them, and they scrambled back into the carriage, all except Huskisson, who had caught a chill at the old King George IV's funeral and was slightly paralysed down one side. He faltered with his hand on the door latch. The duke called out, 'Huskisson! Do get to your place! For God's sake get to your place!' But it was too late. Huskisson fell with one leg beneath the wheels. George Stephenson attached the *Northumbrian* to a single coach and rushed the victim to Eccles at thirty-six miles an hour for medical attention, but it was of no avail, and, having made his will with great fortitude, meticulously dotting the i's of his name, he died at the Vicarage near the line.

Meanwhile, Wellington refused to go forward from Eccles, but was persuaded by the Borough-reeves of Manchester and Salford that if he did not the peace of their towns would be broken. A million spectators were strung along the line, not all of them guided, in the

political excitement, 'by the most peaceful and orderly
spirit'. When they got to Manchester the trains had to
run the gauntlet of a hostile crowd, roaring opposition,
hurling stones and carrying banners with slogans such as
'Remember Peterloo!', and in Water Street Station they
were mobbed and forced to retreat without disembarking
their passengers. Unfortunately, most of the engines had
gone out to Eccles for water, leaving only three to haul
out one huge, composite train into the rainy night. With
the aid of two more locomotives, which joined them at
Parkside, they got it back to the Liverpool terminus by
ten o'clock and discharged the passengers. It seemed a
bad start to railways.[3]

It is symbolic that it should have begun in the midst of
the Reform crisis. Wellington's government resigned in
November, and there followed eighteen months of almost
continuous agitation and turmoil before the Great
Reform Act was finally passed. In spite of its very
moderate terms, which gave the franchise to the middle
class and a number of great industrial towns like Manchester and Birmingham but left a majority in the hands
of the counties and small boroughs controlled by the
landed upper class, this was the turning-point between
the old society dominated by the aristocratic man on
horseback and the new class society dominated by the
industrial capitalist. For the men who made the railways
were not merely creating a revolutionary means of
transport. They were helping to create a new society and
a new world. They were, as they themselves were aware,
men ahead of their time, visionary, energetic, self-reliant
individuals, scornful of difficulties, ruthless with rivals
and opponents, moving what they considered prejudice
and reaction as they moved mountains of earth and rock

to smooth the road into the future. They were typical representatives of the bustling, go-getting, self-confident, Victorian capitalist middle class.

Yet at the same time they were also products of the old society and its patronage system and upflow of new men. Of none was this truer than of George Stephenson himself, 'the father of the improved railway of modern times' as the inscription on his statue at St George's Hall, Liverpool, rightly claims. He was the very model of the Victorian ideal: the self-made man who rose from a humble cottage at Killingworth Colliery to make a fortune by native talent, hard work and the insight and determination to give the public what it wanted. Yet he was also a typical product of the old society: a village genius, like James Brindley or James Mill, who attracted the patronage of powerful landowners, in his case the 'Grand Allies' who dominated the Tyneside coalfield, Sir Thomas Liddell, the Earl of Strathmore and Stuart Wortley, who encouraged his engine-building, ordered his locomotives and supported his safety-lamp. Without their patronage he would have remained a clever but little-known colliery mechanic. His ambition, too, was that of every 'new man' in the old society, to buy an estate and join the landed gentry. 'I want to take thirty or forty thousand acres of land on the West Coast of England,' he wrote in 1837. And he ended his days in his country house, Tapton House, Chesterfield, near his Derbyshire coal mines and quarries.

No one man, of course, ever built a railway. So mighty an enterprise, greater in most cases than anything ever built in the country before, required an enormous range of talents and skills. It would take too long to describe all the men who made the railways – not merely the

engineers, contractors and 'navvies', but the lawyers,
parliamentary agents, shareholders, stockbrokers, surveyors, and so on – and the enormous problems, of
civil and mechanical engineering, legal, financial, mana-
gerial, and so forth, which they had to face. But we can
get some idea of them, at least in the early stages, from
the example of the Liverpool and Manchester. It is a good
example, except for one omission, the contractor: George
Stephenson, when he finally became the sole engineer,
preferred to be his own contractor, an arrangement
which in later enterprises would be considered unprofes-
sional and inefficient if not actually corrupt. And, given
George Stephenson's inferiority complex towards the
established civil engineers of the canal age and his
jealousy of any potential rival, it certainly led to a good
deal of friction between the men who built the first railway, some of whom were to be great railway builders in
their own right on far greater lines: his brilliant son
Robert, who so improved the locomotive that he clinched
its superiority over other forms of traction for nearly a
century and engineered the London to Birmingham and
other famous lines; Joseph Locke, who engineered the
Grand Junction to link the Liverpool and Manchester to
Birmingham, and went on to build the London to
Southampton and many of the great contractor Thomas
Brassey's railways; Charles Vignoles, who was sacked by
George Stephenson but went on to build the Midland
Counties railway from Rugby to Derby; and other great
civil and locomotive engineers, including William Allcard, John Dixon and Thomas Gooch, brother of the
famous Daniel Gooch, one of the greatest locomotive
designers of all; not to mention the 'Liverpool party' of
railway financiers, led by Joseph Sandars and Henry

Booth, who came to play a key part in railway development throughout the country.

It was, of course, the last group, the projectors, who took the initiative in building the railway. Joseph Sandars was a corn merchant and insurance underwriter who, with other Liverpool merchants and monied men, including Henry Booth, Lister Ellis, William Ewart and Sir John Gladstone, were incensed at the monopoly of transport to their principal market for corn and raw cotton by the allied waterways, the Bridgewater Canal and the Mersey and Irwell Navigation. Their minds had been turned towards an alternative by the self-appointed prophet of railways, William James of Henley-in-Arden, who advocated the application of the colliery tramroad system to public transport, and had been so impressed on a visit to Killingworth in 1821 by George Stephenson's engines that he agreed to sell them in return for a fourth share in the profits. In 1822 he persuaded Sandars and his friends to finance a survey for a line between Liverpool and Manchester, and carried this out with the aid of, among others, young Robert Stephenson. The Liverpool projectors enlisted the support of a committee of Manchester men, including great cotton men like John Kennedy and the two Birleys, and set about obtaining an Act of Parliament to enable them to set up a company, raise money from shareholders, buy the necessary land by compulsory purchase and build the railway. This cost two years of struggle against the opposition of the waterways, powerful landowners including the Marquess of Stafford, principal proprietor of the Bridgewater Canal, and the Earls of Derby and Sefton, across whose estates the railway would run, and for a time of the Corporation of Liverpool. The projectors' second survey, under

George Stephenson, was harried by the landowners' gamekeepers and tenants, and Stephenson and other witnesses before the Parliamentary Committee were exposed to bitter criticism. But eventually the opposition was overcome or bought off – the Marquess of Stafford bought 1,000 shares in the enterprise and obtained three seats on the board of directors – and they got their Act in June 1826.

Meanwhile, it was only by a long struggle that George Stephenson became chief engineer to the railway. William James, who had expected the post, overstretched himself by taking on too many projects, became ill and failed to complete his detailed plans and sections. George Stephenson was appointed to re-survey the line, but performed so pathetically before the Parliamentary Committee that the first Bill was lost, and the projectors engaged the Rennie brothers, sons of the famous canal engineer, to prepare a third survey and steer a new Bill through the Committee hearings. George Rennie was offered the post of consulting engineer, with J. U. Rastrick or George Stephenson under him as 'operative engineer', but he refused to act with either of them. The company, having by this time been impressed by the successful completion of the Stockton and Darlington, finally appointed Stephenson as engineer, subject to the advice of Josias Jessop as consulting engineer, which he then proceeded to ignore, up to the time when Jessop died in October 1826. Stephenson would brook no rivals, and he rapidly got rid of Charles Vignoles, the Rennies' assistant, and controlled the whole construction in three sections through his own assistants Joseph Locke, John Dixon and William Allcard with Thomas Gooch as chief clerk and draughtsman.

The work involved problems as difficult as any to be faced in later railway building. At the eastern end the line had to cross Chat Moss, an immense, black, oozy bog, in places over thirty feet deep, in which animals and men floundered and were drowned, and the drainage ditches continually caved in or filled up with peaty mud. Stephenson floated his railway across it on a continuous raft made of hurdles, brushwood and heather – a good example of how the rails spread the load over soft ground – and it proved to be the cheapest as well as the smoothest part of the line. The most difficult part was the embankment at the Manchester end, where the bog swallowed up thousands of tons of earth before the road-bed finally rose above the waters. At the western end of the line a very deep cutting through sandstone was required at Olive Mount and a tunnel under Liverpool from Edgehill down to the docks. The latter caused immense trouble. The pilot tunnel ran in places thirteen feet out of true, unexpected veins of soft blue shale and quicksand threatened to drown the workings, and water made it difficult to build the masonry lining. In between there were, besides cuttings and embankments and the two great inclined planes at Whiston and Sutton, sixty-three bridges and viaducts, including the nine arches (each spanning fifty feet) of the Sankey Viaduct and the small but remarkable skew bridges at Rainhill and elsewhere, for which the 'screw-thread' lines of masonry had to be traced on canvas stretched over the scaffolding. The rails themselves were of the new wrought-iron kind used on the Stockton and Darlington, laid for eighteen miles on massive stone blocks, but for thirteen miles over the embankments and Chat Moss on wooden sleepers of oak or larch. The stone for the Sankey Viaduct was

supplied by Thomas Brassey, then the young agent of a
Cheshire landowner. From this first contact with George
Stephenson he developed into the world's greatest railway
contractor, building over 4,000 miles of railways in
England, Europe, Persia, India, Australia and South
America.[4]

In spite of William James's and George Stephenson's
enthusiasm for steam locomotion, the question of the
form of traction was not settled until much of the line
was completed. Even horse traction, at least for mixed
working as on the Stockton and Darlington, was not
ruled out, but the real contest was between the locomotive, which was cheaper and more flexible, and the
stationary engine with cable haulage, which was thought
to be more reliable, especially on the gradients. In the
steep Edgehill tunnel a stationary engine was installed,
but over the rest of the line the contest was settled at the
famous Rainhill trials in October 1829, where the directors offered a prize of £500 for a locomotive of under
four and a half tons which could haul three times its own
weight over a distance of seventy miles at an average
speed of not less than ten miles an hour. At the trials the
other entries, notably Braithwaite and Ericsson's *Novelty*
and Timothy Hackworth's *Sans Pareil*, were completely
outclassed by Robert Stephenson's *Rocket*, the ancestor
of all modern locomotives, with multiple tubes carrying
the hot gases from the furnace through the boiler, and
twin pistons directly coupled to the driving wheels, which
proved capable of averaging 16 m.p.h. and could reach
speeds of over 30 m.p.h.

The novel sensation of travelling at such unprecedented
speeds is well described in a letter by Fanny Kemble the
actress, whom George Stephenson took for a trip on the

footplate of its more powerful sister, the *Northumbrian*, shortly before the opening of the railway:

You can't imagine how strange it seemed to be journeying on thus, without any visible cause of progress other than the magical machine, with its flying white breath and rhythmical, unvarying pace, between these rocky walls, which are already clothed with moss and ferns and grasses; and when I reflected that these great masses of stone had been cut asunder to allow our passage thus far below the surface of the earth, I felt no fairy tale was ever half so wonderful as what I saw. Bridges were thrown from side to side across the top of these cliffs, and the people looking down upon us from them seemed like pigmies standing in the sky.

Beyond the Sankey Viaduct the engineer opened the regulator to impress her, and succeeded:

The engine . . . was set off at its utmost speed, 35 miles an hour (swifter than a bird flies, for they tried the experiment with a snipe). You cannot conceive what that sensation of cutting the air was; the motion as smooth as possible too. I could either have read or written; and as it was I stood up, and with my bonnet off drank the air before me. The wind, which was strong, or perhaps the force of our own thrusting against it, absolutely weighed my eyelids down. When I closed my eyes this sensation of flying was quite delightful, and strange beyond description; yet strange as it was, I had a perfect sense of security and not the slightest fear.[5]

Thomas Creevey, M.P., friend of Lord Sefton and a passionate opponent of the railway, was less enthralled by his 'lark of a very high order', a five-mile trip on the railway in November 1829:

. . . the quickest motion is to me *frightful*; it is really flying, and it is impossible to divest yourself of the notion of instant

death to all upon the least accident happening. Sefton is convinced that some damnable thing must come of it; but he and
I seem more struck with such apprehension than others. . . .
The smoke is very inconsiderable indeed, but sparks of fire are
abroad in some quantity: one burnt Miss de Ros's cheek,
another a hole in Lady Maria's silk pelisse and a third a hole
in someone else's gown. Altogether I am extremely glad
indeed to have seen this miracle, and to have travelled in it.
Had I thought worse of it than I do I should have had the
curiosity to try it; but, having done so, I am quite satisfied
with my *first* achievement being my *last*.[6]

The thirty-four miles of the line were completed in
under four years, and George Stephenson and his assistant engineers had overcome all the enormous difficulties to do a remarkable job. But they had not done it
alone. The great majority of the men who made the railways were manual labourers, the 'navvies' who took
their name from the earlier 'inland navigators' who built
the canals, and who literally man-handled millions of
tons of earth and rock to exalt the valleys, make low the
hills and tunnel through the mountains, make straight
the crooked and the rough places plain. In strict usage
the navvies were the skilled labourers, the 'muck-shifters'
who dug the cuttings and heaped up the embankments,
carted away the spoil from the tunnels and generally
made and levelled the road-bed. There were also miners
to excavate the tunnels and the shafts to reach and
ventilate them, masons and bricklayers to line the tunnels
and approaches and build the bridges and culverts,
carpenters and blacksmiths to make scaffolding and
tunnel props and repair waggons and machinery such as
the horse gins which raised the buckets from the shafts,
and haulage men and lads looking after and leading the

horses. But it was the navvies themselves, the highly-paid getters or pickmen and the lesser-paid fitters or shovellers, who did the bulk of the work. They worked in gangs alongside a 'set' of trucks, two men to a truck. One would undercut with pick and shovel the side of the cutting, leaping out of the way as the 'lift' of earth and rock came down, and the other would shovel the spoil above his own head into the waggon, which was reckoned to hold two and a quarter cubic yards (and as many tons) of 'muck'. An average day's work was fourteen sets, so that each pair of navvies had to shift and lift over thirty tons a day. Each time they were full the waggons would be hauled away by a horse along the temporary railway track, usually to the next embankment, where they would be detached from the train and harnessed individually to a special tipping horse, trained to run them at a gallop to the edge of the bank, stepping smartly out of the way so that the waggon, halted by a baulk of timber, shot its contents down the bank. Where the next embankment was too far away, the 'muck' was laboriously raised by barrow-runs, lines of planks up the side of the cutting, up which the navvies ran their barrows with the help of a horse hauling on a rope which ran through a pulley-block at the top.[7]

All this was dangerous work. Paid by the piece – generally from $4\frac{1}{2}$d. to 6d. a cubic yard – the getters were tempted to undercut too big a lift at a time without paying a look-out at the top to shout a warning when the earth began to crack, and many of them were crushed by falling rock or suffocated in soft earth. The tippers might fail to fix the baulk of timber securely or might gallop the horse too fast, and send waggon, horse and sometimes driver hurtling over the brink. Most dangerous of all was the tunnelling, where falls of rock, runs of quick-sand or soft shale, and accidents to men riding the buckets up and down the access shafts were frequent. Four men were killed in the Edgehill tunnel under Liverpool, and in the notorious Woodhead tunnel on the Manchester to Sheffield line, built between 1839 and 1845, at least thirty-two men were killed and another 140 seriously injured. Some of the men were extraordinarily careless: they lit pipes near open barrels of gunpowder, and one on the Paris to Rouen line even blew on a fuse to make it go off, losing both eyes and both arms. But their employers were equally to blame, supplying defective equipment such as iron 'stemmers' to ram home charges of gunpowder, which struck sparks and set off premature explosions, or light-weight scaffolding or wooden packing for bridges and tunnels which gave way and sent men to their deaths. Unlike France, where the Code Napoléon enforced employers' liability for accidents at the rate of 5,000 francs (£200) for death and proportionate sums for disablement, in Britain there was no compensation for fatalities and a common-law claim for injuries only where the victim could prove negligence on the part of the employer, who might in law be the ganger or small subcontractor with small means of paying. Edwin Chadwick, the Poor Law official who championed the navvies, the Parliamentary Committee on the Railway Labourers of 1846, and even some railway directors with experience of the French system, thought that compensation should be compulsory and automatic, and pointed out that the total compensation on the Paris–Rouen railway had cost only £5,000, or one half of 1 per cent on the £1 million capital cost of the line.[8] But workmen's compensation was not introduced in Britain until the last years of the century, long after most of the railways had been built.

The theory was that the navvies were paid high wages to cover such risks. Their wages were certainly high compared with other labourers, averaging from 2s. 6d. to 3s. 6d. a day and occasionally higher, compared with farm labourers' wages of from 1s. 3d. in the south-west to 2s. 3d. in the north of England.[9] On the other hand, once trained and properly fed, they did two or three times as much work as the untrained labourer, and according to one railway engineer labour cost much the same all over the world, whatever the wages, since the higher-paid English navvies did so much more work than the lower-paid foreigners.[10] And their high wages were eaten into by the rents which they paid for their squalid huts, often made of turf, branches and straw, and the high prices they paid for food and other necessities in the truck (or ticket) shops run by the contractors or their agents, which often charged 10 per cent or more above the market rate. Working and living in such appalling conditions, there is little wonder that they drank and caroused themselves into a stupor in their 'randies' on pay days once a month or fortnight, and indulged in pitched battles between the English, the Scots and the Irish which the local rudimentary police forces found it impossible to suppress. Yet they were extraordinarily polite and respectful towards the missionaries who went among them to save their souls and their morals, and a doctor's daughter of Winchmore Hill near Enfield found to her surprise that 'their conduct was very orderly, and they can hardly be sufficiently commended for their behaviour'. They even spent part of their wages in 'keeping up with the Joneses', she noticed: 'On Sundays and holidays the men were, many of them, resplendent in scarlet or yellow or blue plush waistcoats and knee breeches.'[11]

Some 600 men built the Liverpool and Manchester railway. At the height of the 'railway mania' in 1847 there were over a quarter of a million engaged in construction, but for most of the main construction period – 1830 to 1870 – they averaged about 50,000.[12] Yet by 1851, the year of the Great Exhibition, they had managed to build nearly 7,000 miles of track, and most of the trunk lines were complete. As a result, you could travel between any two major cities in Britain in a few hours, instead of days by the old stage coach. Such a revolution in the speed of transport could not be without its effect on society. As Henry Booth, Treasurer of the Liverpool and Manchester and part-author of the *Rocket*, clearly foresaw,

. . . perhaps the most striking result produced by the completion of this Railway, is the sudden and marvellous change which has been effected in our ideas of time and space. Notions which we have received from our ancestors, and verified by our own experience, are overthrown in a day, and a new standard erected, by which to form our ideas for the future. Speed – despatch – distance – are still relative terms, but their meaning has been totally changed within a few months: what was quick is now slow; what was distant is now near; and this change in our ideas will not be limited to the environs of Liverpool and Manchester – it will pervade society at large.[13]

How it pervaded society at large in early Victorian Britain we shall see in the next chapter.

Further Reading

Jack Simmons, *The Railways of Britain: a Historical Introduction* (Routledge & Kegan Paul, 1961).

C. F. Dendy Marshall, *The Centenary History of the Liverpool and Manchester Railway* (Locomotive Publishing Co., 1930).

G. S. Veitch, *The Struggle for the Liverpool and Manchester Railway* (Liverpool Daily Post, 1930).

G. O. Holt, *A Short History of the Liverpool and Manchester Railway* (Railway and Canal Historical Society, 1965).

H. Pollins, 'The Finances of the Liverpool and Manchester Railway', *Economic History Review*, 2nd series, v, 1952, pp. 90–7.

L. T. C. Rolt, *George and Robert Stephenson* (Longmans, 1960).

Arthur Helps, *The Life and Labours of Mr Brassey* (1872).

C. F. Dendy Marshall, *A History of Railway Locomotives down to . . . 1831* (Locomotive Publishing Co., 1953).

C. Hamilton Ellis, *British Railway History: an Outline . . . 1830–76* (Allen & Unwin, 1954).

Terry Coleman, *The Railway Navvies* (Penguin, 1965).

Notes

1. Lois Basnett, 'The First Public Railway in Lancashire: the History of the Bolton and Leigh Railway, 1824–8', *Transactions of Lancashire and Cheshire Antiquarian Society*, 1950–51, LXII, 157–76.

2. R. B. Fellows, *History of the Canterbury and Whitstable Railway* (1930), esp. chap. viii; L. T. C. Rolt, *George and Robert Stephenson: the Railway Revolution* (1960), pp. 205–6.

3. This account of the opening and the subsequent account of the building of the railway are based on Henry Booth, *An Account of the Liverpool and Manchester Railway* (1830, Cass Reprint 1969); G. S. Veitch, *The Struggle for the Liverpool and Manchester Railway* (Daily Post, 1930); C. F. Dendy Marshall, *Centenary History of the Liverpool and Manchester Railway* (Locomotive Publishing Co, 1930; G. O. Holt, *A Short History of the Liverpool and Manchester Railway* (Railway and Canal Historical Society, 1965); and Rolt, *G. and R. Stephenson*, chaps. 5, 8, 9.

4. Arthur Helps, *Life and Labours of Mr Brassey* (1872), pp. 25, 161–6.

5. Margaret Armstrong, *Fanny Kemble, A Passionate Victorian* (Macmillan, 1938), pp. 107–9.

6. John Gore, ed., *The Creevey Papers* (Batsford, 1963 ed.), p. 255.

7. Terry Coleman, *The Railway Navvies* (Penguin, 1965), esp. chap. ii.

8. P.P. 1846, XIII, S.C. on Railway Labourers, Report, and Evidence; R. A. Lewis, 'Edwin Chadwick and the Railway Labourers', *Economic History Review*, 1950, 2nd series III, 107–18; Jack Simmons, 'The Building of the Woodhead Tunnel', in *Parish and Empire* (Collins, 1952), pp. 155–65.

9. Helps, *op. cit.*, p. 370; Coleman, *op. cit.*, pp. 66–7; A. L. Bowley, *Wages in the United Kingdom in the 19th Century* (1900), table at end.

10. John Hawkshaw, letter to Arthur Helps, 11 December 1871, in Helps *op. cit.*, p. 363.

11. S.C. on Railway Labourers, 1846, Minutes of Evidence, pp. 162–73. Coleman, *op. cit.*, chap. 5; Henrietta Cresswell, *Winchmore Hill, Memories of a Lost Village* (1912), in *ibid.*, p. 198.

12. Rolt, *G. and R. Stephenson*, p. 186; B. R. Mitchell, 'The

Coming of the Railways and Economic Growth', in M. C. Reed, ed., *Railways in the Victorian Economy* (David & Charles, 1969), p. 20.

13. Booth, *op. cit.*, pp. 89–90.

Chapter Four

The Great Connecter

On 2 May 1851 *The Times* reported:

There was yesterday witnessed a sight the like of which has never happened before, and which, in the nature of things, can never be repeated. . . . In a building that could easily have accommodated twice as many, twenty-five thousand persons, so it is computed, were arranged in order round the throne of our SOVEREIGN. Around them, amidst them, and over their heads was displayed all that is useful or beautiful in nature or in art.

It was, of course, referring to the royal opening of the Great Exhibition, that self-conscious symbol of the civilization created by the Industrial Revolution. The 19,000 exhibits, ranging from an earthenware water closet to a plaster statue of Shakespeare, from a many-bladed penknife to an express locomotive, and from a brass bedstead to the great hydraulic press which raised the tubes of Robert Stephenson's Britannia Bridge at

Menai, symbolized both the cultural and the economic success of Great Britain, the workshop, carrier, banker, insurer, and builder of railways of the world.

In tones of sublime euphoria *The Times* continued:

Above them rose a glittering arch far more lofty and spacious than the vaults of even our loftiest cathedrals. On either side the vista seemed boundless. . . . Some saw in it the second and more glorious inauguration of their SOVEREIGN; some a solemn dedication of art and its stores; some were most reminded of that day when all ages and climes shall be gathered round the throne of their MAKER; . . . all contributed to an effect so grand and yet so natural, that it hardly seemed to be put together by design, or to be the work of human artificers.

And some, including the authors of the *Official Catalogue*, saw in it a gigantic railway station. Under the marginal note, 'The present industrial position of England indicated by the building alone', they underscored the connection between the Crystal Palace and the construction industry developed by the railways:

It is by means of the experience acquired in the conduct of the vast engineering works which have of late years occupied the attention, and commanded the labours, of some of our most intelligent citizens, that this country has been enabled to bring to a perfect system this power of subordinating the supply of materials, and of eliciting, in similar works, that precise description of labour from every individual, for which his natural characteristics or education may have specially qualified him.[1]

Standing on a site of twenty-six acres, Paxton's gigantic conservatory was built from over 4,000 tons of iron, 400 tons of glass and 600,000 cubic feet of wood; it contained a million square feet of floor space and nearly a mile of

2. *Railways in 1851.*

exhibition galleries; the main nave was 264 feet wide and 1,848 feet long, twice the width and four times the length of St Paul's Cathedral; and it was built in six months by an army of over 2,000 craftsmen and labourers, aided by scores of ingenious machines for raising the cast-iron pillars and wrought-iron roof trusses, shaping and painting the window sashes, and glazing the roof. Like the railways, it was paid for by public subscription and the sale of tickets; was constructed by the same system of contract and subcontract; and (unlike them) it made a profit of over 100 per cent, which was devoted to founding the South Kensington museums.

The Great Exhibition, indeed, could not have occurred before the Railway Age, at least on so large a scale and with such spectacular success; not so much because of the difficulties of assembling the labour and materials and exhibits – for which the main railway companies 'agreed to afford additional accommodation for goods and passengers' – as of bringing together from every corner of the kingdom the six million visitors, equivalent to a third of the population of England and Wales, who peacefully filed through the Exhibition between May and October, without a window smashed or an exhibit stolen. This, in fact, was what impressed contemporaries most. To a generation which had lived – or thought it had lived – under the threat of revolution from the time of Peterloo (1819) until the last Chartist petition (1848) only three years before, the crowds of provincial working people who descended on London that summer were a symbol and a proof of the new-found social peace and political harmony of British society. As Charles Tomlinson, editor of the *Cyclopaedia of Arts* (1852–66) a magazine which grew out of the exhibition, put it,

The state of the Metropolis throughout the whole period of
the Great Exhibition will be remembered with wonder and
admiration by all. . . . Instead of confusion, disorder, and
demoralization, if not actual revolution, which were predicted
by some gloomy minds, instead of famine and pestilence con-
fidently predicted by others, London exhibited a great degree
of order, good-humoured accommodation of her crowds, and
power to provide for their wants. . . . Enormous excursion
trains daily poured their thousands. . . . Throughout the season
there was more of unrestrained and genuine friendship, and
less of formality and ceremonial than has ever been known. It
was like . . . a gigantic picnic . . . large numbers of workpeople received holidays for the purpose . . . 800 agricultural
labourers in their peasant's attire from Surrey and Sussex,
conducted by their clergy, at a cost of two and twopence each
person – numerous firms in the North sent their people, who
must have been gratified by the sight of their own handi-
work.

What was on show more than the exhibits was the
British people themselves in all their social variety and
their political acquiescence in the new industrial system.

In short, the Great Exhibition could not have been
held much before 1851 since it was only in the late 1840s
that the main trunk railways between London and the
provinces were completed – all, that is, but the Great
Northern, affording a more direct route to Doncaster and
the north-east, opened in 1852,[2] and the somewhat
superfluous second route to Manchester opened throughout on its own rails by the Midland in 1868. By 1850
practically every town of any importance in England,
though not in Wales and Scotland, was connected by
rail, if sometimes circuitously, with London (see Map 2).
The Royal Commission responsible for organizing the

exhibition, which included such eminent railway men as
Brunel, Cubitt and Robert Stephenson, took early steps
to get the agreement of the railway companies to run
cheap excursions, at single fare for the return trip, with
further abatements for distances over 100 miles. 'Subscription clubs' were organized to enable the working
class to pay the fare by instalments, and in the event the
third-class fare from Manchester and Leeds, normally
over 15s. single, was as low as 5s. return – a day's wages
for a craftsman, two days' for an urban labourer, and
well within the reach of all but the very poor. Contrast
this with the stage coach at its best: 35s. single for an
outside passenger, and no question of a day return, since
the journey took at least 19 hours.

The railways were the great connecter, linking up the
furthest corners of the country, and making one England
out of many. Their effects on passenger transport, and
therefore on society directly, were more profound than
those on the transport of freight, and therefore on industry and commerce. This was contrary to the expectations of the men who made the railways, who were more
concerned with breaking the waterways' monopoly of
the carriage of coal, corn, cotton and other bulky
materials. The Select Committee on Railways of 1844
remarked:

. . . from the immense superiority of the locomotive engine,
railway companies may be taken, for all practical purposes, to
possess a complete monopoly as far as regards the conveyance
of passengers. As regards the conveyance of goods, this is not
the case to the same extent, since railways are, in many cases,
exposed to effective competition from canals, and since the
saving of time does not give such a decided superiority over
the old modes of conveyance.[3]

Indeed, the canals, which had cost much less to build than the railways, were often more profitable, down to the middle of the century. While railway companies rarely paid dividends of more than 6 per cent, and often 3 per cent or less, some canals were paying from 8 to 30 per cent or more in 1838–9, and from 4 to 12 per cent in 1855, though in the non-industrial areas some paid no dividend at all.[4] Railway freight revenue did not overtake passenger receipts until 1852, but by 1867 the railways had eclipsed the canals as goods carriers and created a traffic which the latter could not have coped with. As the Royal Commission on Railways put it,

In considering the improvement of goods traffic, it is very difficult to institute any comparison with the past, because the introduction of the railway system has entirely altered all the conditions of that traffic, and has enabled industry and trade to spring up which, without railways, could have had no existence.[5]

Inland coalfields, such as the south Yorkshire and the east Midlands, expanded, and by 1867 for the first time more coal was carried to London by rail than by sea.[6] New iron-ore deposits, such as those of Cleveland and Lincolnshire, were worked on a large scale and, after Bessemer's invention of mass-produced steel in 1856, a great new industry came into being which both depended on railways for ore, coal and limestone and supplied them with a tougher and more reliable material for rails, locomotives and rolling stock. New factory industries arose in hosiery and lace, boot and shoe-making, machine-made screws and nails, pins and needles, pen-nibs and other metal goods, rubber goods and water-proof clothing, large-scale flour-milling and automatic biscuit-baking, and many other mass-produced consumer goods, as well as the engineering works to make the machines for them; and they could now be built wherever was most convenient, near the coal, the raw material, the labour or the market, since the railways could fetch and carry whatever else was needed. Steamships, mainly of iron, surpassed sailing ships in tonnage only in 1883, but long before that they were, with their superior speed, carrying more of the foreign and coasting trade of the United Kingdom – which, before it left and after it arrived at the ports, meant more work for the railways. Foreign trade more than trebled in value and increased much more in volume between the Great Exhibition and the end of the century, and most of it went to and from the sea by rail.[7]

No doubt much of this economic growth would have occurred if the railways had never been built. The canals were cheap, efficient and reliable carriers of goods, and the major contribution of the railways was not so much to lower freight charges – though they may have helped to keep them down in what was threatening to become an expensive monopoly service – as to quicken bulk transport and extend it to areas beyond the reach of canals. An American economic historian[8] has gone so far as to argue that the economic growth of the United States would not have been appreciably retarded in the absence of railways, and he may be right, not simply because of the existence of canals but because human ingenuity, given the vast opportunities of the booming American market, would no doubt have discovered an adequate substitute. But this kind of argument is the equivalent in economic history of 'What would have happened if Napoleon had won Waterloo?' – a speculation which does not repay the

historian's time spent on it. The railways did exist in
Britain, they did beat the canals and stage waggons, and
they did contribute enormously to the vast industrial
growth and rise of living standards of the Victorian age.
That something else – the 300-foot contour canal which
was suggested at the end of the century, or a steam road
vehicle such as was driven off the roads in the 1830s by
public opposition and the competition of the railways –
might have succeeded almost as well may be true, but
belongs to the world of fiction rather than history.

Whatever their effect on the transport of goods, there
can be no doubt at all about the impact of the railways on
the carriage of passengers. Here speed, convenience and
comfort were of the essence, time was money to business
and professional men, government officials and even
workmen travelling to work from cheaper houses in the
suburbs. As Sydney Smith put it,

Railroad travelling is a delightful improvement of human life.
Man has become a bird: he can fly quicker and longer than a
Solan goose. . . . Everything is near, everything is immediate –
time, distance and delay are abolished.

The conquest of time and space – that was the point.
Far more people travelled. The Liverpool and Manchester from the start carried twice as many passengers as
the old coaches had done, thus creating a new traffic.
By 1851 the railways were carrying 80 million passengers
a year (excluding season-ticket holders), by 1881 over 600
million, by 1901 over 1,100 million.[9] They carried them at
speeds which far exceeded those of the fastest stage
coaches: the *minimum* speed of 'parliamentary' trains
for third-class passengers under Gladstone's Railway
Act of 1844 was 12 m.p.h., and in practice most third-

class carriages came to be attached to ordinary trains, which maintained average speeds, including stops, in the 1850s of over 20 m.p.h., when expresses averaged nearly 40 m.p.h. Before the end of the century average speeds were approaching 40 m.p.h., while expresses were exceeding 50 m.p.h.

They carried their passengers in much greater comfort than the stage coaches could ever have hoped to attain on the uneven roads of nineteenth-century Britain. The first-class passenger was carried in comfort from the start. Charles Greville in 1837 decided on impulse to vary the London scene and 'run down to Knowsley', the Earl of Derby's house near Liverpool, via the new Grand Junction railway:

Nothing can be more comfortable than the vehicle in which I was put, a sort of chariot with two places, and there is nothing disagreeable about it except the whiffs of stinking air which it is impossible to exclude altogether. The first sensation is a slight degree of nervousness and a feeling of being run away with, but a sense of security soon supervenes, and the velocity is delightful. Town after town, one park and *château* after another are left behind with the rapid velocity of a moving panorama, and the continual bustle and animation of the changes and stoppages made the journey very entertaining. . . . Considering the novelty of its establishment, there is very little embarrassment, and it entirely renders all other travelling irksome and tedious by comparison.[10]

The 'chariot with two places' was the front compartment of a Grand Junction Royal Mail coach, built exactly like a road coach with three compartments (two of them for four passengers each) with a luggage rack on the roof and a high seat at the back for the guard. It was sprung, and had oil lamps on the outside. Over the years

the first-class passenger was always first with each development in comfort: sleeping cars ('bed-carriages') on
the London and Birmingham in 1838, 'footwarmers' on
the Great Western in 1856, Pullman coaches with steam
heating on the Midland in 1874, dining cars on the Great
Northern in 1879, gas lighting on the Metropolitan and
Great Eastern Railways in 1876–8, electric lighting on
the London, Brighton and South Coast in 1881, corridor
trains on the Great Eastern in 1891, and lavatories (to
which the second- and third-class passengers had access)
on the Great Western in 1892, all of which innovations
rapidly spread to other companies. At first the second-
class passengers were accommodated in very spartan
coaches, square boxes with wooden benches and often
with sides open to the weather, though even these were
more comfortable than clinging to the roof of a swaying
stage coach. After 1844, when third-class accommodation
was improved by law, the second class was improved by
competition, and the coaches were enclosed, with glass
windows, and increasingly sprung and lighted. Third-
class coaches were originally open trucks, often without
seats, and on some lines were attached only to goods
trains, but Gladstone's 1844 Act laid down that they
should be 'provided with seats and . . . protected from
the weather', in a manner satisfactory to the Board of
Trade. The board used its powers of withholding approval and of remitting duty on third-class passengers to
insist on fully enclosed carriages with provision for the
admission of light and air, which in the course of time
meant windows and ventilators.[11] Over the years the
comforts of the first class gradually extended to the
second- and third-class passengers. The gradual improvement of the track, with longer lengths of heavier-duty

rail, gave a smoother ride to all classes, and the introduction of spring buffers in the 1840s and of bogie-wheeled vehicles in the 1870s eventually became standard for all carriages. Towards the end of the century the Midland Railway in particular pioneered comfort for the third class, with upholstered seats and steam-heating, and raised the general standard by competition.

The railways also carried their passengers for the most part in greater safety than the road coaches, which were notorious for furious driving and frequent accidents. But as with air travel today as compared with the much more lethal roads, railway accidents were more spectacular, killed and maimed more people in one go, and struck the public imagination more forcibly. As with air accidents, too, there was the undoubted point that the lives of the travelling public were in the hands of largely unseen operators and were at the mercy of the efficiency or inefficiency, diligence or carelessness of anonymous manipulators, some of whom, such as construction engineers, maintenance mechanics and signalmen, would not themselves suffer the direct consequences of their misdeeds. Understandably, the public were alarmed by some early railway accidents, and the government was forced to take an early and continuous interest in railway safety.

In the early days brakes were rudimentary or non-existent, and the main way of stopping a locomotive was to put it into reverse – a manoeuvre which on the earliest engines required superhuman dexterity.[12] Boiler explosions, often caused by engine-drivers tying down the safety valve to build up a greater head of steam, were not infrequent. Signalling was often carried out by railway policemen with hand lamps and flags, and no means of knowing the whereabouts of trains they could not see, or what was happening at the next signal point. Traffic management was a matter of guesswork and the quick eyes and reactions of engine-drivers and guards, and with frequent engine breakdowns and other hold-ups any system of time-intervals between trains was apt to fail in preventing rear collisions. Passengers, too, were a frequent cause of accidents, climbing in and out of carriages in motion and on to the roofs much as they had done on the road coaches, but with more disastrous consequences. Most alarming of all, badly repaired engines could break down at speed, broken couplings leave breakaway carriages or waggons behind, broken wheels cause derailment, the track could give way, bridges collapse, embankments slip, cuttings cave in, and a host of other disastrous failures occur due to faulty engineering and workmanship by persons long departed and paid off.[13]

One of the earliest big railway disasters took place on the Great Western on Christmas Eve 1841, when a goods train, including two third-class carriages, ran into a landslip in Sonning cutting, and eight passengers were killed and seventeen injured. The crushed coaches had no spring buffers and were open-sided, with nothing to prevent their occupants being thrown out at any sudden stop or start.[14] The accident contributed to the movement for the reform of third-class travel which culminated in Gladstone's Act of 1844, already mentioned. Railway companies were already subject, of course, to parliamentary control, under the private Acts by which they were incorporated, and these contained a certain number of safety regulations, though they were difficult if not impossible to enforce. In 1840 a Railway Regulation Act was passed giving the Board of Trade various powers over the companies, including a right to call for returns of accidents involving personal injury, and the power of appointing inspectors to inspect new lines and to delay the opening by a month. 'Upwards of twenty-five fatal accidents' were reported to the new Railway Department of the Board of Trade in the first three months, and in spite of much opposition and criticism from the companies and from engineers like Brunel, the inspectors rapidly proved not only their fairness and impartiality in reporting on accidents and new lines, but also their creative ability in suggesting improved safety measures and better traffic management.[15]

Not all railwaymen were opposed to government supervision, and George Stephenson himself wrote in 1841 to the President of the Board of Trade, 'I am quite sure that some interference on the part of the Government is much wanted,' and went on to suggest a Board of Trade committee of railway engineers to vet improved plans for railway working, a speed limit of 40 m.p.h. on the most favourable lines and lower speeds on curves, uniformity of signals, self-acting brakes or, in the meantime, four brake coaches and two brakesmen per train, six-wheeled engines and carriages, government inspected and stamped wheels, springs and axles and government arbitration of disputes between companies.[16] Over the years most of these suggestions were put into practice. The Railway Department and its successors were able, under the very limited powers conferred by the various Acts before 1868, to persuade, cajole or bully the railway companies into adopting many safety devices and better methods of working, and improved technology made this easier. Fixed signals on posts (pivoted boards which could be swung at right-angles to the track to order a train to stop) had been introduced on the Liverpool and Manchester in 1834, and a disc (for 'go') and a bar (for 'stop') on the Great Western in 1841. In the latter year the London and Croydon introduced the familiar semaphore signal (horizontal for 'stop', lowered 45 degrees for 'proceed with caution', and lowered completely – in the early years into a slot in the post – for 'line clear') which, together with red, green and white lights for the same positions at night, became standard on most railways. 'Interlocking', a device by which two or more signals were prevented from conflicting with each other (e.g. by allowing two trains on different lines to proceed through the same set of points), was soon added, and in 1856 a foolproof mechanism was patented by which the signal arms, coloured glasses of the lamps and the points were all moved by the same lever.[17]

To keep trains apart and avoid rear collisions, the Liverpool and Manchester operated a time-interval system, maintaining the signal at stop for five minutes after a train had passed, and this became generally adopted. But while locomotives were still primitive and liable to break down, and even later where traffic was heavy, this was obviously inadequate. The introduction of Cooke and Wheatstone's electric telegraph (invented 1837) in the 1840s made it possible to know when the last train had left the section, and the 'block system' by which no train could enter a section until it was clear was introduced on the Yarmouth and Norwich in 1844. In spite of the support of the Board of Trade it spread only slowly, the companies being reluctant to go to the expense of wiring every signal box, and arguing perversely – not unlike the airways corporations today in relation to the

ultimate decision of the pilot – that it would diminish the
responsibility of the engine drivers.[18] The Board eventually had its way, and interlocking and block working
became general, but it was less successful with the 'communication cord' from the passenger compartments to a
bell on the footplate, which it decided to insist on after a
murder on the North London Railway in 1864, but
which awaited a more efficient system of continuous
brakes. After much experiment, a Royal Commission on
Railway Accidents settled on two systems of continuous
automatic brakes, the automatic vacuum and the Westing-
house air, which, especially after the 1889 Act that made
automatic brakes and other safety features compulsory,
gradually spread to most of the railway network – although standardization, using the vacuum brake, was
not achieved until the railways were nationalized in
1947. Continuous brakes solved the problem of the
'communication cord', which in the 1890s became the
familiar chain in a tube which itself applied the brakes.[19]
Other improvements in the last two decades of the century included 'lock-and-block' working, introduced on
the London, Chatham and Dover in 1882, by which the
signals and points were locked to the telegraph instrument itself; track circuiting, introduced by the same
company, by which the train's position was shown
electrically in the signal box; and automatic signalling,
introduced on the Liverpool Overhead Railway in 1893,
by which the train itself switched the signals to danger as
it passed.[20] The Board of Trade was also successful in
reducing the excessive hours of drivers, guards and
signalmen, a grievous cause of accidents which was
eventually removed by the Railway Servants' Hours of
Labour Act of 1893.[21] Although no system is proof

against human error and faulty materials, and great railway accidents were unavoidable from time to time, the railways by the later years of the Victorian age were remarkably safe, and certainly safer than the new forms of transport of the twentieth century.

As far as the roads were concerned the railways were the great disconnecter. The coaches could never have competed on speed, comfort or fares with the trains, and were cut off in their prime. The last stage coach left London, for Newmarket and Norwich, in 1846; the last one left Manchester in 1848; the very last in Britain disappeared in the north of Scotland when the Highland Railway opened in 1874. The Post Office took advantage of the railways from the start, using the Liverpool and Manchester from November 1830 and the Grand Junction and London to Birmingham as soon as they opened, and the Mail Coach Office was closed in 1854. The once-proud coaches with their splendid names and liveries were used to ferry passengers to and from the railway stations, or sold off as hen-coops or garden sheds. But in spite of the loud complaints of redundancy and unemployment for coachmen and horses, more horse-drawn vehicles than ever appeared on the roads, partly as feeders to the railways for both passengers and goods, partly with the need for more private carriages, hansom cabs and hackney carriages, and the ubiquitous horse omnibus, which accompanied increasing affluence and the growing size of towns.

Nevertheless, the main roads, only just brought to Telford and McAdam's standard by the time the railways came, inevitably decayed. The only thing that could have hoped to save them and competed successfully, in convenience if not in speed, with the railways, was the steam carriage, which with Walter Hancock and Goldsworthy Gurney in the late 1820s and 1830s reached a very promising stage of development, climbed hills steeper than any railway engine could tackle, and achieved speeds of 20 and even 30 m.p.h. in comparative safety. But they frightened the public, who preferred steam engines to be segregated from ordinary traffic, while the turnpike trusts, fearing for their road surfaces, charged them excessive tolls, and Parliament threatened to tax them out of existence.[22] In consequence, they were never allowed to compete sufficiently to achieve the kind of improved performance which benefited the railways. The personal horseless carriage had to wait until nearly the end of the century and for an alternative prime mover before it won a second chance. The turnpike trusts, meanwhile, had rejected their own salvation. They got into a vicious circle of debt, deteriorating roads, rising tolls and lower receipts, their gates and charges were clamorously opposed by the local people who were now their only users, many decayed and collapsed, and the rest were suppressed as their private Acts ran out by a Committee of the House of Commons, appointed annually from 1871, when there were still 854 trusts. They shrank by 1887 to fifteen, and the last one disappeared, in Anglesey, in 1895[23] – just in time, ironically, for the coming of the motor-car.

The canals survived better at first, as we have seen, some of them making profits of which the railways were envious. Some indeed, like the Bridgewater Canal, went on making substantial profits down to the present century, since on cheap and bulky loads where speed did not matter they could compete effectively, at least as long as bargees' wages were low enough, that is down to the First

World War. Many railway companies considered them a sufficient threat to buy them out, and with the exception of the Bridgewater, most of the canals from the North-West down to Birmingham and some important ones elsewhere, such as the Kennet and Avon from Bristol to Reading and the Witham Navigation from Lincoln to the Wash, passed into railway hands. The Trent and Mersey even turned itself into a railway company, the North Staffordshire or 'knotty', but continued to keep the navigation open, for coal and clay particularly, until recent years. But in general the canals were beaten by competition rather than by take-over bids and, like the turnpike roads, they were their own worst enemies, spending what money they had in fighting railway Bills instead of improving their service by standardizing draught, width and locks and by offering through tolls. By the time of the Parliamentary Committees of 1872 and 1882, the canals, with a few notable exceptions such as the Aire and Calder from Leeds to the Ouse or the Grand Junction which moved coal around London, had been decisively beaten.[24]

The great connecter had its most obvious effect on people. By 1862, when W. P. Frith painted his famous view of Paddington Station, nearly 10,000 miles of line were open, carrying 170 million passengers a year. What did the railways mean to some of the people in that crowded scene? The portly gentleman talking to the engine-driver – an early railway enthusiast, no doubt – is perhaps a commercial traveller. As Henry Booth, treasurer of the Liverpool and Manchester pointed out,

A great part of the inland trade of the country is conducted by the agency of travellers; and here, what a revolution in the whole system and detail of business, when the ordinary rate of travelling shall be twenty miles instead of ten, per hour. The traveller will live double times: by accomplishing a prescribed distance in *five* hours, which used to require *ten*, he will have the other five at his disposal. The man of business in Manchester will breakfast at home – proceed to Liverpool by the Railway, transact his business, and return to Manchester before dinner. A hard day's journeying is thus converted into a morning's excursion.[25]

By 1862 he could do a few hours' business in London and be back in time for supper. Add to that the new speed of delivery of orders, and one can see why industrial production multiplied six-fold between the opening of the first railway and the end of the century, and why national income per head (in real terms) more than doubled between the Great Exhibition and the death of Queen Victoria.[26]

Or take the engine-driver himself: the railways provided work for 65,000 engine-drivers and other railway workers in 1851, and for nearly as many again in railway construction, quite apart from the many thousands of coal-miners, iron and steel workers, engineers and mechanics, coach and waggon builders, and so on who supplied materials and equipment to the railways. The railwaymen themselves, as we shall see in Chapter Ten, were not always well-paid and were often over-worked, but in a world of insecurity and frequent unemployment they had good, steady jobs which they often kept for life.

Then there is the harassed lower-middle-class family below them in the picture, going on holiday for the first time perhaps. The railways brought holidays away from home within the reach of millions who could never have gone before, as we shall see in Chapter Eight. To the right of them, beyond the porter, is an upper middle-class family, seeing their boys off to school, younger brother with cricket bat clinging to mamma, manly older brother ready to take charge. Mamma need not worry: the public schools have been reformed by Dr Arnold of Rugby and other reforming headmasters, and are no longer the nurseries of vice and idleness of the old society, but seminaries of Christian gentlemen, statesmen, civil servants and empire-builders, made more accessible to the growing business and professional classes by the railways. And what of the proud father? He looks rather like Matthew Arnold, son of the famous headmaster, and one of the new, professional, cultivated civil servants, appointed an inspector of schools in 1851. What could the travelling government inspectors of the Victorian age, of schools, factories, poor law, public health, police, and, indeed, railways – the heralds of the revolution in government and the intervention of the state in the lives of ordinary people – have done without the railways? Matthew Arnold wrote much of his poetry – 'The Strayed Reveller' or 'The Scholar-Gipsy' perhaps? – on the train, as well as his incisive criticism in *Culture and Anarchy* of the new society created in part by the railways.

The rich man arguing with the cabby about the fare, his binoculars already slung for the races, is perhaps a politician – he looks like Lord Robert Gascoyne-Cecil, later as Marquess of Salisbury to be foreign secretary and prime minister. The railways brought national politicians for the first time face to face with their supporters outside their own constituencies. Before the railways came the voters knew national leaders only at second hand, through the newspapers. At the opening of the Liverpool and Manchester the crowds craned forward calling out 'Which is the duke?', so little did they know the appearance of the prime minister. In the 1860s Gladstone was beginning that stumping of the country, making speeches at mass meetings of middle-class reformers and working-class 'Lib-Labs', which was to make him 'the people's William'.[27] The railways contributed an important element to the politics of mass democracy.

Next there is the soldier kissing his plump baby good-bye – joining the army was no longer like going into exile. And war itself was becoming mechanized. In the Crimea Thomas Brassey and Sir Morton Peto built a railway – the first seven miles of it in twelve days – from the dockside to the front line, which was more than the Russians had to theirs from Moscow.[28] And in Britain the existence of railways meant that the government could concentrate its troops in a few garrison towns, and withdraw from the industrial areas the seeming 'army of occupation' which had been so provocative a cause of political unrest and class conflict in the years of threatened revolution from 1815 to 1848. By the later years of the century, the years of imperialist fervour, soldiers actually became popular heroes in Britain – a remarkable change from the age of the Chartists.

The wedding party at the next compartment are in the height of fashion for 1862, wide crinolines, small poke-bonnets, voluminous shawls. Fashions now travelled faster than ever, and 'keeping up with the Joneses' was even more the national pastime. Social emulation can be seen in the width of the skirts and the style of the bonnets across all the classes depicted on Paddington Station.

But what is happening at the last compartment? Police officers arresting a criminal. Crime, no doubt, found uses for the railway, in operating in one area and disposing of the loot in another, and in pilfering from the railways themselves, but so did the police, whose long arm was now lengthened and could with the aid of the railway and the telegraph cut off the swiftest get-away. Certainly, there was a striking reduction in the amount of crime in the second half of the nineteenth century.[29] While this had many causes – improved living standards, more settled town life, better elementary education, an improved penal code, police force and prison management, and more efficient government generally – the railways made an important contribution beyond the mere catching of criminals. For they reinforced the self-confidence of government, their psychological security, the knowledge that they could cope swiftly and efficiently with outbreaks of crime and violence, and were no longer so dependent on the panic decision of local magistrates which had proved so disastrous in crises such as Peterloo in 1819. Once the main lines had been built there were no more Peterloos in Britain. Confident of their power to keep order in the remotest corners of the country, the government could relax its old repressive grip – and found to its surprise that a repressive grip was no longer needed.

The most significant departure on Paddington Station in 1862 is the least noticeable one: the working-class group in the background on the left. Working people had long travelled long distances to new jobs – how else could the Industrial Revolution have happened? But now travelling to a new job in a far-away place was no longer like emigrating to a different continent; the migrants were not cutting themselves off for ever from their families and friends, and Rowland Hill's penny post of 1840, another by-product of the railways, brought letters within the reach of all. Most of all, the railways helped to concentrate the growing population in the great towns and cities. To quote the pessimistic John Ruskin, who disliked 'the ferruginous temper . . . which . . . has changed our Merry England into the Man in the Iron Mask',

all along the iron veins that traverse the frame of our country, beat and flow the fiery pulses of its exertions, hotter and faster every hour. All vitality is concentrated through those throbbing arteries into the central cities; the country is passed over like a green sea by narrow bridges, and we are thrown back in continually closer crowds upon the city gates.[30]

By 1851, for the first time in any country, more people lived in the towns than in the countryside. What the railways connected most of all, as we shall see in the next chapter, were the new towns of the Railway Age.

Further Reading

Asa Briggs, *1851* (Historical Association, 1951).

Jack Simmons, *The Railways of Britain: an Historical Introduction* (Routledge & Kegan Paul Ltd., 1961).

C. Hamilton Ellis, *British Railway History: an outline . . . 1830–77* and *1877–1947* (Allen and Unwin, 1954, 1959).

J. B. Snell, *Early Railways* (Weidenfeld & Nicolson, 1964).

M. C. Reed (ed.), *Railways in the Victorian Economy: Studies in Finance and Economic Growth* (Newton Abbot, 1969).

L. T. C. Rolt, *Red for Danger: a History of Railway Accidents and Railway Safety Precautions* (Bodley Head, 1955).

Henry Parris, *Government and the Railways in Nineteenth-Century Britain* (Routledge & Kegan Paul, 1965).

Notes

1. *The Great Exhibition of Works of Industry of All Nations: Official Description and Illustrative Catalogue* (1851), I. 50.
2. The Great Northern nevertheless provided excursions to the Great Exhibition, at 5s. return from Yorkshire, running into London over another company's rails.
3. Parliamentary Papers, 1844, XI, Appendix 2.
4. J. H. Clapham, *An Economic History of Modern Britain* (Cambridge, 3 vols., 1963 ed.), I. 81, II. 201.
5. Parliamentary Papers, 1867, XXXVIII. lxv.
6. B. R. Mitchell and Phyllis Deane, *Abstract of British Historical Statistics* (Cambridge, 1962), p. 113.
7. *Ibid.*, pp. 218, 223, 283; for the effect of railways on economic growth generally, see Reed, ed., *op. cit.*, esp. paper 1, B. R. Mitchell, 'The Coming of the Railways and United Kingdom Economic Growth'.
8. R. W. Fogel, 'A Quantitative Approach to the Study of Railroads in American Economic Growth', *Journal of Economic History*, 1962, XXII. 163–97.
9. Mitchell and Deane, *op. cit.*, pp. 225–6.
10. C. C. F. Greville, *A Journal of the Reign of Queen Victoria from 1837 to 1852* (3 vols., 1885), I. 11.
11. Henry Parris, *Government and the Railways in Nineteenth-Century Britain* (Routledge & Kegan Paul, 1965), pp. 93–9.
12. L. T. C. Rolt, *George and Robert Stephenson* (Longmans, 1960), pp. 135–6.
13. L. T. C. Rolt, *Red for Danger: a History of Railway Accidents and Railway Safety Precautions* (Bodley Head, 1955), *passim*.
14. *Ibid.*, pp. 228–30.
15. Parris, *op. cit.*, esp. chap. ii.
16. Letter from George Stephenson to Rt. Hon. Henry

Labouchere, President of Board of Trade, 31 March 1841, in Rolt, *Red for Danger*, Appendix I, pp. 217–18.

17. Jack Simmons, *The Railways of Britain: an Historical Introduction* (Routledge & Kegan Paul, 1961), pp. 160–2.

18. *Ibid.*, pp. 162–4; Parris, *op. cit.*, pp. 186–201.

19. Parris, *op. cit.*, pp. 215–18.

20. Simmons, *op. cit.*, p. 166.

21. Parris, *op. cit.*, pp. 225–6.

22. Jackman, *History of Transportation* (Cass, Reprint, 1964), pp. 333–5; Anthony Bird, *Roads and Vehicles* (Longmans, 1969), pp. 167–74.

23. Clapham, *op. cit.*, II. 206–7.

24. *Ibid.*, II. 198–201.

25. Booth, *op. cit.*, pp. 90–1.

26. Mitchell and Deane, *op. cit.*, pp. 271–2, 367.

27. Cf. John Vincent, *The Formation of the Liberal Party, 1857–68* (1966), pp. 211–35.

28. Helps, *op. cit.*, pp. 216–17.

29. J. J. Tobias, *Crime and Industrial Society in the 19th Century* (Batsford, 1967), pp. 187–92 and *passim*; K. K. Macnab, 'Aspects of the History of Crime in England and Wales, 1805–60' (Ph.D. thesis, University of Sussex, 1965).

30. John Ruskin, *Seven Lamps of Architecture* (1849).

Chapter Five

New Towns for Old

NEW towns for old – that was what the Railway Age was to give to Britain: new, much bigger and, in spite of the enormous social problems of poverty, squalor, disease, crime and public disorder which they were to bring with them, towns which in the end were better built, better governed and healthier to live in than those it inherited from the old society. The railways themselves did not of course make the new towns – or, at least, not many of them: Crewe, Swindon, Wolverton and a few others – but contributed powerfully to the founding of many others as diverse as Middlesbrough, Fleetwood and Eastbourne, and they played a critical part in that general concentration of population in the great towns of which Ruskin and other critics of industrial society complained.

It was of course the Industrial Revolution which made both the railways and the new and much larger towns of what the Victorians themselves called 'the age of great cities'.[1] Urbanization, the agglomeration of population in large 'nodules' not immediately dependent on agriculture and other rural occupations, is one of the best measures of economic growth, since it can only occur where a relatively decreasing proportion of a society can feed a relatively increasing one engaged in industry, trade and other services. The process of industrialization or development requires the transfer of population from agriculture, forestry and fishing to industry, commerce, transport and the professions (including government).[2] Although it is possible, as in Britain in the eighteenth century, for a considerable amount of industry to be carried on in the countryside, in the cottages of domestic outworkers and in rural water-mills, even there the organization of industry, the supply of materials and the marketing of the products tends to increase the size of the towns. Eighteenth-century England already had a larger proportion of the population living in the towns than any other European country – about a quarter by 1801 compared with a fifth in France, perhaps a sixth in Germany, a tenth in Austria-Hungary, and a fourteenth in Russia.[3] The truly rapid growth of the towns, however, came only with the general advent of the steam engine in the nineteenth century, first of all with the general application of steampower to factory production which released the mills from dependence on water power and concentrated industry itself in the towns; and, secondly, with its application to transport, which confirmed and intensified this concentration.

The first cause began to operate before the railways came, and the towns grew at an unprecedented rate in the early nineteenth century, most rapidly of all in the second quarter when steam power was becoming general in textiles and the basic metal industries and when the main-line railways were being built. In 1801 there were only fifteen towns in England and Wales with over 20,000 inhabitants, and only London (865,000) had over 100,000. By 1851 there were sixty-three, including eight with over 100,000, and for the first time in any country more than half the population lived in towns.[4] In the decade before the railways came, 1821–31, the population of Sheffield grew by 41 per cent, that of Birmingham by 42 per cent, of Manchester by 45 per cent, Liverpool by 46 per cent, Leeds by 47 per cent and Bradford by no less than 66 per cent. Bradford, which grew eight-fold between 1801 and 1851, had one mill at the beginning of the century; by 1841 it had sixty-seven.[5] The tall chimneys of the densely packed, smoky, industrial towns were a new feature of the early Railway Age.

The railways themselves added both to the smoke and to the congestion. As Robert Vaughan foresaw in 1843,

the new and speedy communication which will soon be completed between all the great cities in every great nation of Europe, will necessarily tend to swell the larger towns into still greater magnitude and to diminish the weight of many smaller places, as well as of the rural population generally in social affairs. Everywhere we trace this disposition to converge upon great points. It avails nothing to complain of this tendency as novel, inconsiderate, hazardous. The pressure towards such an issue is irresistible, nor do we see the slightest prospect of it ceasing to be so.[6]

Between 1851 and 1891 the urban population grew from 50 to 72 per cent of the total. The number of towns in England and Wales with over 20,000 inhabitants increased from sixty-three to 185, and their share of the population from 35 per cent to 54 per cent, while those with over 100,000 increased from eight to twenty-four

and from 21 per cent to 32 per cent. Meanwhile, the
smaller towns grew less rapidly than the national average,
and the population of the rural areas declined absolutely,
so that the degree of concentration in the larger towns
was intensified, as Vaughan had forecast. Thus the growth
of the larger towns was greater in the decade when the
main lines were completed, 1841–51, than in the previous
one, and this was most noticeable in those towns most
affected by the railways – London, the major ports, and
the iron towns of South Wales, the midlands and the
north-east – where cheap transport of raw materials and
the increased demand for railway iron worked together.[7]
In Scotland, similarly, the towns with over 20,000 inhabitants increased from five in 1801 to nine in 1851 and
to seventeen in 1891, and the urban population surpassed
the rural in 1851, and reached two thirds of the whole by
1891. Glasgow, indeed, which concentrated all the
activities of a great port, textile, engineering and shipbuilding centre, came to constitute a larger proportion of
Scotland's population than London did of that of
England and Wales, rising from 5.1 per cent in 1801 to
19.4 per cent in 1891, as against London's 9.7 per cent to
14.5 per cent.[8] In both countries the railways were helping, in Ruskin's words, to throw back the people in continually closer crowds upon the city gates.

Not all these towns were new in site and name, though
they were nearly all new in size and the conditions and
problems of social life. Even ancient and economically
moribund cities like Exeter and Norwich grew more than
threefold during the century. About seventy towns,
however, were new in every sense, although their names
were sometimes borrowed from an older village or small
town nearby. Even before steam power was applied to it,

the factory system often created industrial colonies which
occasionally grew into small towns, like Arkwright's
Cromford, David Dale's New Lanark or Oldknow's
Mellor, and the canals and mines sometimes created new
communities, like the Duke of Bridgewater's head-
quarters at Worsley, the trading estate which grew up
around the Grand Junction Canal's terminal basin at
Paddington, or the coal town and harbour of Maryport
which Humphrey Senhouse named after his wife.[9] Most
individually founded industrial colonies, however, of
which there were many, were, with notable exceptions
like Lord Leverhulme's Port Sunlight, too small to
become towns in their own right, and either remained
villages or were swallowed up by the expansion of
neighbouring towns.[10]

Where a completely new industrial town grew up on a
virgin site it was likely to be the creation of a number of
industrialists acting in conjunction with one or more
local landowners. The Derbyshire cotton town of Glossop,
for example, grew up around a group of rural water
mills at the crossroads of two turnpikes, one from south
Derbyshire to the West Riding built in 1792 and the
other the new Snake Pass road from Manchester to
Sheffield opened in 1821. The initiative in planning and
developing the new town was taken by the squire of
Old Glossop, Bernard Edward Howard, from whom in
the early years it took its name of Howardtown. In 1815
the squire inherited from a distant cousin the Dukedom
of Norfolk, and with the resources of that vast inheritance
behind them he and his sons laid out the streets, built
the town hall, two churches, schools, shops, the gasworks
and waterworks and even, when the Manchester and
Sheffield Railway was being built close by, constructed a

mile-long branch line from the junction at Dinting Vale and sold it to the railway company. The millowners, meanwhile, were also busy, building cottages, rival churches and chapels, schools, reading-rooms and, later in the century, a hospital, nurses' home, library, public baths and park. Both landowners and some of the millowners, notably the Sidebottoms, had interests in the Manchester, Sheffield and Lincolnshire Railway, during the building of which, especially of the Woodhead tunnels between 1839 and 1852, Glossop became a centre of excitement and riot on the navvies' pay-days. And the Howards and Sidebottoms also had interests in Sheffield, where the latter came to have a share in some of the largest iron and steel works and the former owned the ground and planned most of the Victorian expansion of the city.[11]

The railway companies were among the largest enterprises of the nineteenth century, however, and could create industrial colonies far larger than could any individual firm. Most famous of the railway company towns was Crewe, built by the Grand Junction Railway (later the London and North-Western) on a virgin site in the Cheshire parish of Monks Coppenhall near to their railway junction, which took its name from Lord Crewe's Hall and township on the other side of the line. The new town was the result of the decision of the company's board of directors to transfer their locomotive repair works from Edge Hill at Liverpool to a more central position. As John Moss, the chairman, put it,

the company had found it advisable to remove their great works for the whole line to that place; ... the men around him had, no doubt, by coming there, dissevered many ties of kindred and affection and deprived themselves of many of the enjoyments of more populous localities; but . . . he and his brother directors were anxious to make them as comfortable as lay within their power.[12]

The company was as good as its word and, besides the houses, built a church and a school, paid the curate and schoolmaster, provided a medical doctor at a cost of 1d. a week for a single man and 2d. a week for a family, and two company policemen to keep order, supplied mains water, emptied the ash-pits, cess pools and privies, let cottage gardens and allotments and organized a savings bank for the employees.[13] The company houses were rented at from 2s. to 4s. 3d. a week according to size and amenity (apart from nine at 7s. a week for the 'superior officers'), yielding 4 to 5 per cent on the capital, which was about half the usual rate for the period, and according to an account in *Chambers's Journal* in 1846 were model dwellings with gardens, 'capacious' rooms, tiled floors, and cheap gas supplied by the company. The same journal reported four years later:

The general appearance of Crewe is very pleasing. The streets are wide and well-paved; the houses are very neat and commodious, usually of two stories, built of bricks, but the bricks concealed by rough-cast plaster, with porches, lattice windows and a little piece of garden-ground before the door. . . . The accommodation is good, and it would be difficult to find such houses at such low rents even in the suburbs of a large town.[14]

The population of Crewe, only 203 in 1841 before the new town was built, grew from 4,571 in 1851 to 42,074 in 1901. During that period the community developed other industries and interests, acquired a Local Board (1860) and borough status (1872), and gradually, though not without a row of national dimensions which attracted the attention of Gladstone in the 1880s, escaped from the tutelage of the railway company.[15]

Wolverton was a similar, if smaller, railway town on the same line, planned by the Grand Junction's sister company, the London and Birmingham, before the two merged to form the London and North-Western in 1847. It was described in 1849 by Sir Francis Head, when the population was 1,405, as

a little red-brick town composed of 242 little red-brick houses – all running either this way or that way at right angles – three or four tall red-brick engine chimneys, a number of very large red-brick workshops, six red houses for officers – one red beer-shop, two red public-houses, and, we are glad to add, a substantial red school-room and a neat stone church, the whole lately built by order of a Railway Board, at a railway station, by a railway contractor, for railway men, railway women, and railway children; in short, the round cast-iron plate over the door of every house, bearing the letters L.N.W.R., is the generic symbol of the town.

Here again the company supplied most of the amenities: gas, water, church, school-house, free reading-room and library, and 130 allotments at trifling rents.[16]

Swindon, or New Swindon as it was originally called to distinguish it from the decaying Wiltshire market town nearby, was created almost simultaneously with Crewe and Wolverton, by the Great Western Railway, which in 1840 decided to build its main locomotive repair works there, a convenient mid-point in their system where the easy gradients of the Thames valley changed to the hilly country of the West and required trains to change engines. Old Swindon had less than 2,000 inhabitants. New Swindon was designed to accommodate 2,000 workmen and their families, plus a large number of engine-drivers and firemen. In fact, as the company under the dynamic drive of Daniel Gooch, the locomotive superintendent and later chairman, came to manufacture its own locomotives and rolling stock and even its own iron and steel, employment at the works rose to 4,000 by 1875 and 14,000, plus 5,000 footplatemen, by 1905, the local population rising accordingly. The Great Western did not have so good a reputation for its houses and amenities as the L.N.W.R., and the first estate was close-packed and overcrowded, but it provided churches, schools and other necessary public buildings and all the facilities of a typical company town.[17]

There were other towns built or at least called into larger existence by railway companies, such as Carnforth, which owed its development as an iron and locomotive centre to the rail junction linking the Furness haematite iron ore with Yorkshire and south Lancashire coke; Grimsby, whose fishing industry owed its rapid growth to Sir Edward Watkin and the Manchester, Sheffield and Lincolnshire Railway; and Fleetwood, the product of Sir Peter Hesketh-Fleetwood and his Preston and Wyre Railway's over-ambitious plan for a holiday resort, port and fish-dock.[18] Perhaps the greatest of the company towns in which a railway played the leading role was Barrow-in-Furness. A tiny village of 150 inhabitants before the Furness Railway opened to export iron ore from there in 1847, and still a small town of only 3,135 in 1861, it then exploded to 8,176 in 1864, 37,000 in 1875, and 57,712 in 1891. This was due to the opening in 1859 of the ironworks and the addition of steel-making from 1865, together with the associated docks and, from 1897, the shipbuilding yards. The railway, the steelworks, the docks and much else in the town were controlled by the same group of directors, including the Dukes of Devonshire and Buccleuch, H. W. Schneider and Sir James Ramsden. The Furness Railway built the church, the town and market halls, the police offices, the gasworks and waterworks, the schools, the mechanics' institute, and many of the houses, and laid out the streets on a spacious grid-iron plan which is still more than adequate to the needs of the automobile age. Some of the houses, and especially the barrack-like flats built for the immigrant Clyde shipbuilding workers in the 1890s, are small, inconvenient and ugly, but are still too substantial to abandon.[19]

Middlesbrough, the most spectacular of the brand-new towns of the nineteenth century, was also a railway creation, but soon outgrew its parentage. Joseph Pease and his fellow directors of the Stockton and Darlington bought the solitary farm on the site there in 1829 and planned a new port on deeper water six miles nearer the sea than Stockton. The population rose steadily from 154 in 1831 to 5,463 in 1841 and 7,431 in 1851, as the Quakers' symmetrical little town arose around their modest town hall and the parish church for which they provided the land. But the railways might have strangled 'the infant Hercules', as Gladstone was to call it in 1862, for when the main lines came into action it was cheaper to send out the inland coal by rail than by sea. What saved and, indeed, enabled Middlesbrough to triumph was another group of capitalists, led by Henry Bolckow and John Vaughan, who after years of search discovered vast deposits of iron ore on the seaward slopes of the Cleveland Hills and founded the local iron and steel industry. The first blast-furnace was blown in in 1851, and within ten years there were forty, owned by some of the most famous names in iron and steel. The population grew to 19,416 in 1861, 55,934 in 1881 and 91,302 in 1901. Bolckow, a model employer who made it his hobby 'to improve the conditions of my workpeople, to see what good tenements, and good schools, and just wages paid in a fair manner, and the encouragement of civilizing pursuits would do to elevate their character', became the first mayor on the town's incorporation in 1853. At the Jubilee celebrations in 1881 that marked the half-centenary of the town's foundation, Joseph Cowen, the famous radical editor of the *Newcastle Chronicle*, descanted on 'the story, the marvellous story, of its rise', in which he found a fitting symbol for the economic, technological and cultural progress of the Victorian age.[20]

There were other, and more surprising, towns which owed their rise to the railways. Windermere did not exist before the railway reached there from Kendal in 1847.[21] Eastbourne was planned and largely built by the same Duke of Devonshire who developed Barrow and Buxton, from the opening of the railway in 1849.[22] Older resorts, such as Brighton, Blackpool and Scarborough, boomed when the railways came, for the trains could carry as many visitors in a week as the stage coaches in a year. But the impact of railways on holiday-making is another story, to be told in Chapter Eight.

The great majority of towns, of course, and especially the large cities, were not called into existence or rapid growth by a single landowner, industrial firm or railway company. They were much too complex and manifold creations for that. Even the greatest of them, however, were profoundly affected by the intrusion of the railway which, as a recent historian of Victorian cities, Dr John Kellett, has laconically expressed it, 'did not perform its service within the existing framework of social overhead capital'. In other words, the railways could only operate effectively if they profoundly changed the physical character of the cities they invaded, tunnelling under them, cutting through them, or building great viaducts to reach their goal, a terminal station as near the city centre as possible.

By 1890 the principal railway companies had expended over £100,000,000, more than an eighth of all railway capital, on the provision of terminals, had bought thousands of acres of central land, and undertaken the direct work of urban demolition and reconstruction on a large scale. In most cities they had become the owners of up to eight or ten per cent of central land, and indirectly influenced the functions of up to twenty per cent. The plans of British towns no matter how individual and diverse before 1830, are uniformly super-inscribed within a generation by the gigantic geometrical brush-strokes of the engineers' curving approach lines and cut-offs, and franked with the same bulky and intrusive termini, sidings and marshalling yards.

On the ground, the great viaducts, bridges and stations still dominate the skyline of some of our cities, and carve into separate and sharply demarcated areas the business and shopping centre, the run-down slums and low-grade trades beside the inner urban lines, and the Victorian and Edwardian suburbs down the line. In Glasgow, Liverpool, Manchester, Birmingham and London the railways played by far the largest part in shaping the Victorian city, in demolishing slums and redeveloping the central area, in causing new industries and new slums to develop in once fashionable residential areas and new residential areas to grow further out, and in generally accelerating and intensifying the trends towards urban renewal and segregation of the social classes which were already going on at such a pace there and in most other Victorian cities.[23] Horse-buses, beginning in London in 1829, horse-trams, successfully launched there only in the early 1870s, and electric battery trains, tried experimentally in the 1880s, contributed to the congestion and social segregation, as did the first, shallow, steam underground railway, the Metropolitan of 1863, and the deep, electric 'Tube' of 1890, as we shall see in Chapter Nine. Meanwhile, there can be no doubt of the revolutionary impact of the railways on even the greatest of Victorian cities.[24]

There were slums, squalor, disease, poverty, crime and prostitution in the cities and larger towns long before the railways came and long before the tall chimneys of the steam-powered factories arrived in the early nineteenth century, and eighteenth-century death-rates were undoubtedly higher than those of the Victorian age. Nevertheless, the enormous growth of towns created enormous social problems, especially of public health. Much of the ground which had been gained by the bodies of 'improvement commissioners' which had paved, drained, watered and lighted over 300 towns was rapidly lost. As Edwin Chadwick, the great public health reformer, put it in 1842, 'Such is the absence of civic economy in some of our towns that their condition as to cleanliness is almost as bad as that of an encamped horde, or an undisciplined soldiery.' The wynds of Edinburgh and Glasgow and the cellar dwellings of Liverpool, Manchester, Leeds and large parts of London, contained 'more filth, worse physical suffering and moral disorder than Howard describes as affecting the prisoners' in the unreformed gaols of the previous century.[25]

In the 1830s and 1840s the sheer pace of town growth

threatened to engulf the inhabitants with the diseases of
dirt and overcrowding. Cholera epidemics, due to infected water supplies, broke out in 1831–2, 1848–9, 1854
and 1867, and frightened town and central governments
into taking preventive measures. Typhus, the flea-borne
'fever' which carried off many children and others, was
endemic throughout the period, and broke out from time
to time in epidemics, especially in years of distress and
unemployment such as 1826–7, 1831–2, 1837 and 1846.
Tuberculosis, consumption, or phthisis as it was called
at the time, was the greatest killer of all, and was always
present. In addition, 'summer diarrhoea' and other
gastric disorders due chiefly to unhygienic feeding methods
carried off large numbers of babies. All these and many
other causes of disease and death increased with the
rapid growth of towns, and death-rates, after falling
steadily for eighty or a hundred years, began to rise
again, especially in the towns, in the second quarter of
the nineteenth century when the towns were growing
fastest. Moreover, not only were death-rates considerably
higher in the towns than in the countryside – 26.2 per
1,000 compared with 18.2 per 1,000 in 1831–9 – but they
were much higher in the packed town centres than in the
suburbs – 35.2 per 1,000 in 'inner Manchester' in 1840
compared with 28.6 in the inner suburb of Ardwick and
15.8 in the outer suburb of Broughton.[26] This meant that
death came earlier and more frequently to the working
and lower middle classes than to their betters, and to all
classes in the towns than in the country. Thus the average
age of death for mechanics and labourers and their families in 1837 was seventeen years in Manchester compared
with thirty-eight in Rutland, for tradesmen and their
families it was twenty in Manchester compared with

forty-one for farmers and shopkeepers and their families in Rutland, and for professional people and gentry and their families it was thirty-eight in Manchester compared with fifty-two in Rutland. On the face of it, it was twice as dangerous for a poor man to live in a large city as in the country, and wealth gave no advantage to the rich townsman over the poor countryman.[27]

This last fact, when it became known, was a powerful incentive to improve the health of towns. It became known, along with many other unpalatable facts, through the famous *Report on the Sanitary Condition of the Labouring Population* in 1842, by Edwin Chadwick, Secretary of the Poor Law Commissioners, which stirred up a great agitation by the Health of Towns Association and led on to a Royal Commission and the first general Public Health Act of 1848. The latter, in spite of its establishment of the General Board of Health with compulsory powers to set up local boards wherever the death-rate rose above 23 per 1,000, was not so great a success as was once thought, and it required further major legislation, in 1866, 1872 and 1875, before the problem was brought under control and death-rates began to decrease again decisively.[28] Yet behind and even before the general legislation there were forces at work attempting, not without success, to create new, clean towns out of the old dirty ones. Local citizens, in continuation of the self-help and mutual aid which had characterized the improvement commissioners of the eighteenth century, got together to stir up the new or newly reformed town councils, and in some places to obtain private Acts which anticipated most of the reforms of the general Public Health Acts.

In Manchester, for example, the new Borough Council

of 1838 took over the powers and property of the Police
Commissioners, including the gasworks and street
lighting in 1843, and procured the Manchester Police and
Improvement Acts of 1844 and 1845, under which it
compelled the owners of rented houses to equip them
with enclosed privies and ash-pits and prevented the
building of further back-to-back houses and cellar
dwellings. It also bought out the inadequate Waterworks
Company, built new reservoirs in Longdendale, and
piped water to most of the houses. It closed down the
old insanitary open markets and built new ones under
cover, provided two of the first public parks in the
country in 1846, and the first municipal free library in
1852. Later, the Manchester and Salford Ladies Sanitary
Reform Association, founded in 1862, began the system
of home visiting of the sick and of expectant and nursing
mothers which anticipated the health visitors of the
Welfare State, and the Manchester Improvement Act of
1867 became 'the rootstock from which has sprung the
whole slum clearance legislation of the country'.[29] In
this way the town which had repelled and horrified visitors
like Engels and Faucher in the 1840s as what Asa Briggs
has called 'the shock city of the age', became the pioneer
of public health and housing reform and of many other
amenities of modern urban life.

In all this Manchester was not alone. Many other
towns and cities went ahead of and beyond what they
were forced to do by law to clean up and improve their
physical surroundings. Liverpool obtained a Sanitary
Act in 1846 and in the next twelve years paved 258 new
streets, built 146 miles of new sewers and reconstructed
old ones, provided public baths, wash-houses and
public conveniences, and adopted a town plan for the

reconstruction of streets and the provision of public parks. London, which was excluded from the Public Health Act of 1848, had its main drainage reconstructed between 1855 and 1865 by the Metropolitan Board of Works, which built the Embankment and the great catchment sewer beneath it to end the previous fouling of the Thames. Before it was replaced by the London County Council in 1888 the Board had cleared fifty-nine acres of densely packed slums and rehoused many thousands of their inhabitants. Glasgow and Edinburgh set up City Improvement Trusts in 1866 and 1867 with statutory powers of slum demolition and street reconstruction. Most celebrated of all, though by no means the earliest in the field, Joseph Chamberlain's Birmingham in the 1870s cleared and reconstructed the central city area around its new thoroughfare, Corporation Street.[30] All these schemes except the last, which coincided with it, anticipated the legislation of 1875, the great consolidating Public Health Act and the Artisans' Dwellings Act, under which decent standards of public health, water supply, sewerage and house building were made compulsory.

Meanwhile, many smaller towns, which could not afford the expense of private legislation and grandiose improvement schemes, had lobbied and petitioned the central government for powers to clean up and improve themselves. Even in the 'era of localism' between the abolition of the Board of Health in 1858 and the establishment of the Local Government Board in 1871, when the only central public health authorities were the largely advisory Medical Department of the Privy Council under the progressive but frustrated Sir John Simon and the Local Government Act Office under the dilatory and

dilettante Tom Taylor, some progress was made. The
1866 Act 'conferred on the central executive a coercive,
interfering and even superseding power the like of which
Chadwick had never possessed', notably of compelling
inspection of dangers to public health and forcing the
local authorities to do something about them.[31] Even
more important were the demands from local authorities
themselves upon the reluctant and overworked Local
Government Act Office for the inspection and approval of
water supply and drainage schemes. In the thirteen
years of its existence the Office mounted over 1,200 local
inquiries, approved over 1,600 schemes at a cost of more
than £7,000,000, issued 350 Provisional Orders and
promoted thirty-four parliamentary Bills, and in nine
cases superseded the local authority altogether. All
this state intervention, far from provoking 'irritation on
the part of the local authorities', had been 'as a rule,
eagerly called for and warmly welcomed by the ratepayers'.[32]

None of this meant that the new and greatly enlarged
towns of the Railway Age were cleaned up and improved overnight. The problems were too vast for that,
and the expense of clearing slums and rebuilding central
areas was astronomical. The Birmingham redevelopment
scheme far exceeded its estimated net cost (after resale of
building sites) of £500,000 for forty-three acres, Glasgow
lost £1,500,000 on redeveloping eighty acres and London
£1,600,000 on fifty-nine acres. As the disillusioned
Chairman of the City of London Commissioners of
Sewers commented on two small improvement schemes,
'If we had given every man, woman and child £100 or
£150 to start them in life elsewhere, it would have been
cheaper to the ratepayers.'[33] Death-rates remained

stubbornly high until the 1870s, and after that only gradually declined; by the end of the century they were often still twice as high in the slum areas as they were in the outer suburbs and the countryside. But, considering the scale of the problem, it was perhaps remarkable that they declined at all. It can be claimed for the Victorians that they were the first to begin to solve the problems of living together in great cities. By the end of the century most towns in Britain had a clean water supply, main drainage, paved and lighted streets, public baths, wash-houses and conveniences, not to mention public parks, recreation grounds and libraries. If they still had – as many still have – too many slums and depressing rows of terrace cottages without baths or indoor lavatories, they were at least no longer the 'encamped hordes' of the 1840s. The railways, no doubt, added to the noise, congestion and smoke pollution of the towns, but they also helped in the task of urban renewal. The cheap Bedford bricks, Welsh slate, Baltic timber, Scottish granite paving stones and Medway or Peak District cement poured into all the towns by rail – a great loss to local vernacular building styles, but a great gain to healthy housing. To this extent the railways themselves helped to exchange new towns for old.

There is more to life than cleanliness and survival, however, and the new industrial towns of Victorian Britain have often been accused of being cultural deserts, with none of the spontaneous joys of the old villages nor the more civilized pleasures of traditional towns. This belief is based on a double ignorance: ignorance of the older way of life in the villages and smaller towns, where apart from the occasional fairs and saints' days almost the sole permanent institution for pleasure or pastime

was the local pub, and ignorance of the new way of life
in the industrial towns, where in addition to an in-
ordinate number of pubs a remarkable collection of social
institutions appeared at an early stage of their existence.
It is of course true that the rise of the industrial town
coincided with the decline of fairs and saints' days, as
the shops and more regular markets of the industrial
economy undermined the first, the discipline of the
factory system undermined the second, and the puritanical
onslaught of what I have called elsewhere the 'moral
revolution', better known as 'the rise of Victorianism',
reduced both to a shadow of their former importance.[34]
During the first half of the nineteenth century most fairs
either disappeared or were transmuted from their important economic functions of supplying 'long-term'
consumer goods and hiring rural workers into mere
'wakes' and collections of catch-penny sideshows and
amusements, while the number of saints' days maintained
as holidays was similarly reduced, in the case of the
Bank of England from forty-seven in the eighteenth
century to eighteen in 1830 and a mere four in 1834.[35]

Fairs and saints' days were the casualties of the collision between the old and new ways of organizing
business, and could not have survived in their old form
in the new industrial society, to which they were in-
appropriate. But that is not to say that the new industrial
towns were not capable of creating their own institutions
of culture and amusement. On the contrary, they were
much more so than the old villages and smaller towns,
since they had the numbers and resources to support a
much greater variety of them. First in the field were the
middle-class literary and philosophical societies, beginning with the Birmingham Lunar Society formalized

in 1780 but which can be traced back to 1765, the Manchester Literary and Philosophical Society founded in 1781 and that of Derby in 1784.[36] These and many others eleswhere grew out of the spontaneous interest of the new middle-class business and professional men in the science and literature of the day. Later the same kind of men created the statistical societies of the 1830s, beginning with Manchester, Liverpool and London, which investigated every social problem of their towns from poverty, housing and education to 'moral statistics' and crime.[37] In between they played a large part in the movement from the 1820s to found mechanics' institutes, beginning with London, Manchester and Glasgow, which were designed to provide similar intellectual fare for the skilled working class. The fact that they were gradually taken over by lower-middle-class clerks, shopkeepers and the like, and became devoted to literature and the arts rather than science and technology, does not alter the point that they were popular institutions which filled a cultural and intellectual need.[38] All these came to rely on the railways for visiting lecturers, conferences and other contacts, and later, from the 1870s, the university extension movement founded a widespread system of adult education on part-time lecturers travelling by rail from Cambridge.[39]

Meanwhile, the working classes developed their own social institutions, of many different kinds, also increasingly dependent on the railways for regional and national organization: the friendly societies, which met their need for mutual aid in sickness, old age and death as well as for convivial company in health and high spirits; the trade unions, which gave similar support at work and in unemployment and which, until 1824, had been suppressed in the old society; a large variety of political and similar debating clubs, from the Owenite 'halls of science' to radical reading-rooms and Chartist classes; co-operative societies which from the 1820s to the 1840s put retailing and production second to the founding of utopian Socialist communities; not to mention the numberless kinds of Methodist sects, spiritualist, Chartist and other churches in which working men could take the lead as class leaders, elders and lay preachers. To these and similar 'serious' institutions we shall return in the next chapter.

The 'frivolous' institutions of town life, those called into existence for pleasure and entertainment, were always – and understandably – more popular with the majority of inhabitants, whose free time was so short and therefore so precious. In the factory towns twelve- to fifteen-hour working days, six days a week, were normal in the first half of the nineteenth century, and even after the Ten Hours Act of 1847 (strictly, ten and a half hours under the 'no relays' Act of 1851) the working day in textiles, including meal-times, spanned twelve hours (eight on Saturdays). Only the exceptional man, dedicated to self-education, politics or religion, wanted to spend his few leisure hours in 'serious' pursuits. As so morally upright a magazine as *Good Words* approvingly remarked in 1866, in 'A Plea for Music in Common Life',

To prove that recreation is more in demand than mental culture by those who toil we have only to contrast the slight progress made by Mechanics' Institutes, their lectures, classes and libraries, with the number of popular Music Halls and Concert Rooms that are being opened throughout the Kingdom, till there is scarcely a town of any consideration that has not a place of this kind.[40]

Almost every pub – and there were astonishing numbers of public houses and beer shops, 227 in Preston in 1834 for a population of 33,000, 311 in Blackburn in 1854 for one of 46,000 – had its 'free and easies', evenings devoted to spontaneous concerts by volunteer singers with a few professional accompanists. The *Northern Monthly* declared in 1862:

It is not in concert halls, though professedly devoted to music for the million, that one finds the real working classes, or learns what is the sort of musical entertainment that has the greatest attraction for the lower strata of the 'people'. It is the singing saloon [of the public house] that is characteristically theirs.

There were, however, hundreds of organized choirs for more formal music making, many of them attached to factories, and utilizing the brief mealtimes for practice. The Privy Council Committee on Education reported in 1841 that 'In the northern counties of England choral singing has long formed the chief rational amusement of the manufacturing population', and it went on to instance other areas, such as Norfolk.[41] It was given a large boost by the Tonic Sol-Fa movement, developed by Sarah Ann Glover and the Rev. John Curwen in the 1840s, which enabled otherwise untutored amateurs to sing ambitious works like Handel's *Messiah* at sight. The brass band movement, boosted by the railways and the invention by Adolph Sax of piston-valve instruments, was the special delight of northern industrial workers, and great contests were mounted at Belle Vue, Manchester, from 1853, Hull from 1856, Sheffield from 1858, and the Crystal Palace, London, from 1860, at which famous bands like Black Dyke Mills, Accrington and the Leeds Railway Band competed for prizes.[42]

The theatre, with its high prices and too early start for most factory workers, was at first a middle-class preserve, perhaps deliberately so: an amateur actor looking back from the 1880s to the Bolton theatre of 1824 objected to 'the present overdone system of cheapening prices and reducing the quality of the plays by overtasking the energies of the actors and filling the houses with factory lads and girls for whom theatres were never intended'.[43] But not all actors and managers agreed, still less the factory lads and girls, who in the next few decades, with shorter hours and increasing wages, thronged the galleries, especially where the half-price system after the interval operated. The Victorian theatre evening was a feast, usually with a curtain-raiser, music and dancing before the interval, so that the half-price late-comers still saw the main play. For those who could not afford even this there were 'penny gaffs' or back-street theatres, where amateurish performances, with 'flash dancing' and smutty songs, could be seen for a copper.[44]

It would take too long to catalogue all the pastimes and entertainments of the Victorian town: the dance-halls, billiard rooms, bowling greens, football and cricket matches and, later in the century, tennis and golf clubs, and of course prostitution and the ubiquitous brothels. If cock-fighting, bull-baiting, dog-fighting, bare-fisted prize-fighting and many other cruel sports were suppressed in the 1830s and 1840s, other pastimes took their place, such as boxing under the Marquis of Queensberry's rules from 1867, the Football Association Cup competition from 1872, and the Rugby League from 1895. Enough has been said, however, to show that 'the insensate industrial town' is a myth concocted by modern intellectuals who either do not know or do not like the pleasures of the majority of town-dwellers of the last century – or, for that matter, of this.

Whether the quality of life in the large towns of the Railway Age was better or worse, culturally or morally, than in the villages and small towns of the eighteenth century it is impossible to say. All that is certain is that it was different. By their very size the new towns changed the character and structure of society. In the small communities of the old society rich and poor lived cheek by jowl, and the poor had little opportunity to combine successfully against the squire or master. In the new towns, for better or worse, employers and employed were increasingly segregated in different areas, and there pressed together into mutually hostile classes. In the next chapter we shall trace the rise, largely in the towns, of the new class society.

Further Reading

Asa Briggs, *Victorian Cities* (Odhams, 1963).

William Ashworth, *The Genesis of Modern British Town Planning* (Routledge & Kegan Paul, 1954).

H. J. Dyos (ed.), *The Study of Urban History* (E. Arnold, 1968).

G. M. Young (ed.), *Early Victorian England* (Oxford, 1934), Vol. I, Chapters 3 and 4.

J. R. Kellett, *The Impact of Railways on Victorian Cities* (Routledge & Kegan Paul, 1969).

T. C. Barker and Michael Robbins, *A History of London Transport*, Vol. I: *The Nineteenth Century* (Allen & Unwin, 1963).

W. H. Chaloner, *The Social and Economic Development of Crewe, 1780–1923* (Manchester, 1950).

L. V. Grinsell *et al.*, *Studies in the History of Swindon* (1950), esp. H. B. Wells, 'Swindon in the 19th and 20th Centuries', pp. 93ff.

J. D. Marshall, *Furness and the Industrial Revolution* (Barrow, 1958).

N. J. Frangopulo (ed.), *Rich Inheritance: a Guide to the History of Manchester* (Manchester Education Committee, 1962).

S. E. Finer, *The Life and Times of Sir Edwin Chadwick* (Methuen, 1952).

R. A. Lewis, *Edwin Chadwick and the Public Health Movement, 1832–54* (Longmans, 1952).

Royston Lambert, *Sir John Simon, 1816–1904, and English Social Administration* (Methuen, 1963).

E. D. Mackerness, *A Social History of English Music* (Routledge & Kegan Paul, 1964).

Stella Margetson, *Leisure and Pleasure in the Nineteenth Century* (Cassell, 1969).

Notes

1. Robert Vaughan, *The Age of Great Cities* (1843).
2. Cf. Colin Clark, *The Conditions of Economic Progress* (Macmillan, 1960 edition), p. 492.
3. Depending, of course, on how towns are defined; cf. A. F. Weber, *The Growth of Great Cities in the Nineteenth Century* (1899, Cornell Reprints, Ithaca, N.Y., 1963), pp. 40–7, 71, 82, 95, 101, 107.
4. *Ibid.*, pp. 43, 46.
5. Asa Briggs, *Victorian Cities* (Odhams Press, 1963), pp. 81, 139.
6. Vaughan, *op. cit.*
7. Weber, *op. cit.*, pp. 46–7, 53–4.
8. *Ibid.*, p. 59.

9. H. J. Dyos, ed., *The Study of Urban History* (Edward Arnold, 1968), pp. 264–5; Edward Hughes, *North Country Life in the Eighteenth Century*, II (Oxford, 1965), p. 22.

10. Cf. J. D. Marshall, 'Colonisation as a Factor in the Planting of Towns in North-West England', in Dyos, ed., *op. cit.*, pp. 215f.

11. H. J. Perkin, 'The Development of Modern Glossop', in A. H. Birch, *Small Town Politics* (Clarendon Press, 1959), chap. ii.

12. W. H. Chaloner, *The Social and Economic Development of Crewe, 1780–1923* (Manchester University Press, 1950), p. 48.

13. *Ibid.*, pp. 44–8, 52, 55, 56, 61, 64.

14. *Ibid.*, p. 48.

15. *Ibid.*, chaps. v, vi, vii, and appendix 9.

16. Sir F. B. Head, *Stokers and Pokers, or the London and North Western Railway* (1849, Cass Reprint 1968), pp. 81–3, 89–91.

17. H. B. Wells, 'Swindon in the 19th and 20th Centuries', in L. V. Grinsell *et al.*, *Studies in the History of Swindon* (1950), pp. 93f.; D. E. C. Eversley, 'The Great Western Railway and the Swindon Works in the Great Depression', in Reed, ed., *op. cit.*, pp. 111f.

18. J. D. Marshall, *Furness and the Industrial Revolution* (Barrow, 1958), pp. 254–5, 393–4; A. Harris, 'Carnforth, 1840–1900: the Rise of a North Lancashire Town', *Transactions of Historic Society of Lancashire and Cheshire*, CXII, 1960, pp. 105f.; J. H. Sutton, 'Early Fleetwood, 1835–47', (unpublished M.Litt. dissertation, University of Lancaster, 1968).

19. Marshall, *Furness*, Part II; S. Pollard, 'Barrow-in-Furness and the Seventh Duke of Devonshire', *Economic History Review*, 2nd Series, VIII, 1955, pp. 213–21.

20. Briggs, *Victorian Cities*, pp. 247–82.

21. J. D. Marshall and M. Davies-Shiel, *The Industrial*

Archaeology of the Lake Counties (David & Charles, 1969), pp. 216–17.

22. J. H. Powell, *Powell's Popular Eastbourne Guide* (1863); William Ashworth, *The Genesis of Modern British Town Planning* (Routledge & Kegan Paul, 1954), p. 39.

23. J. R. Kellett, *The Impact of Railways on Victorian Cities* (Routledge & Kegan Paul, 1969), pp. 1, 2 and *passim*.

24. T. C. Barker and Michael Robbins, *A History of London Transport*, I, *The Nineteenth Century* (Allen and Unwin, 1963), pp. 1, 20–2, 99, 183–8, 299, 300–3; J. R. Day, *The Story of London's Underground* (London Transport, 1963), pp. 1–6.

25. Edwin Chadwick, *Report on the Sanitary Condition of the Labouring Population of Great Britain* (1842, ed. M. W. Flinn, Edinburgh, 1965), pp. 116, 277.

26. M. W. Flinn, Introduction to Chadwick, *op. cit.*, pp. 3–17.

27. Chadwick, *op. cit.*, p. 223; as Mr. Wood, who supplied the figures, warns, they were somewhat affected by migration and the consequently larger proportion of old people in Rutland and of children in Manchester.

28. Cf. S. E. Finer, *The Life and Times of Sir Edwin Chadwick* (1952), Books v, vii, viii; R. A. Lewis, *Edwin Chadwick and the Public Health Movement, 1832–54* (1952), *passim*; Royston Lambert, *Sir John Simon, 1816–1904, and English Social Administration* (1963), *passim*.

29. N. J. Frangopulo, ed. *Rich Inheritance: a Guide to the History of Manchester* (Manchester Education Committee, 1962), pp. 56–60, 241 (quoting a later Town Clerk of Smethwick).

30. Ashworth, *op. cit.*, pp. 62–3, 64, 94–5, 97–9; Briggs, *Victorian Cities*, chap. v.

31. Lambert, *op. cit.*, pp. 386–90.

32. R. Lambert, 'Central and Local Relations in Mid-Victorian England: the Local Government Act Office, 1858–71', *Victorian Studies*, 1962, VI. 120f.

33. Ashworth, *op. cit.*, pp. 97–9.

34. Perkin, *Origins of Modern English Society*, pp. 273f.

35. G. M. Young, ed., *Early Victorian England* (Oxford University Press, 1934), I. 179.

36. R. E. Schofield, *The Lunar Society of Birmingham* (Oxford, 1963), p. 17; F. Nicholson, 'The Literary and Philosophical Society, 1781–1851', *Memoirs of the Manchester Literary and Philosophical Society*, LXVIII, 1923–24, pp. 97f.; Eric Robinson, 'The Derby Philosophical Society', *Annals of Science*, IX, 1953, pp. 359f.

37. T. S. Ashton, *Economic and Social Investigations in Manchester, 1833–1933* (Manchester, 1934), chap. i; *Annals of the Royal Statistical Society, 1834–1934* (1934), chap. i, which also gives details of the founding of other societies.

38. J. W. Hudson, *History of Adult Education* (1851); Mabel Tylecote, *The Mechanics' Institutes of Lancashire and Yorkshire before 1851* (1957); Thomas Kelly, *George Birkbeck* [founder of the movement] (1957); J. F. C. Harrison, *Learning and Living, 1790–1960* (1961), pp. 57–89.

39. Harrison, *op. cit.*, chap. vi, 'Universities and the Railways'.

40. I owe this reference, and several more below, to Mr. M. B. Smith, M.Litt. student at the University of Lancaster, on the subject 'The Development of Popular Entertainment in the Lancashire Cotton Towns, 1830–70'.

41. *Minutes of Committee of Council on Education 1840–41* (1841), p. 46; quoted by E. D. Mackerness, *A Social History of English Music* (Routledge & Kegan Paul, 1964), pp. 154–5.

42. Mackerness, *op. cit.*, pp. 157–69.

43. James Clegg, ed., *Life and Recollections of John Taylor* (Bolton, 1883), cited by M. B. Smith.

44. Henry Mayhew, *London Labour and the London Poor* (4 vols., 1861–62), I. 40–2, and information from M. B. Smith on Lancashire cotton towns.

Chapter Six

The New Class Society

THE new class society which came to maturity in the large new towns of the Railway Age can be seen in microcosm in Ford Madox Brown's *Work*, painted in 1852.[1] It may not be great art, but it is excellent social history, putting flesh and blood, and perhaps even more tellingly, clothes, on the bare occupational statistics of the 1851 Census. At the top of the picture are the top-hatted, equestrian upper-class gentleman and his lady, the landed gentry who still held great influence in social and political life. The man on horseback still dominated the countryside and many of the small towns, where the new class society had yet to come into existence and the old society of patronage and deference to the squire and parson still held sway. In spite of the Great Reform Act of 1832, he still dominated Parliament, for the House of Lords remained a powerful body and, since a majority of the seats in the Commons still belonged to the counties and the smaller towns, landowners formed a majority of

the M.P.s.[2] Their majority in the Commons lasted down
to the 1880s, and even after that the early age at which
they entered Parliament and acquired invaluable experience in office enabled them to maintain a majority in
the Cabinet until 1906.[3] The difference after the first
Reform Act and increasingly after the second and third
in 1867 and 1884 was that they now had to woo the
votes of the other classes instead of taking them for
granted – or, perhaps, for purchased.

The class whose opinions came to matter most, and
who therefore set the pace and the policies in politics and
the ideas and values in morality and intellectual life, was
the urban middle class, represented in Brown's painting
by two groups. The crinolined ladies on the left, with
their parasols, ribboned bonnets and silk pelisses, can be
taken to represent the business middle class, the industrialists, merchants and bankers – presumably, their
husbands are at the factory or the office, for it is the
middle of the working day. The middle-class gospel of
work was the most important of their ideas, and duty was
a hard taskmaster. Their other leading ideas, self-help,
competition, free trade, *laissez-faire* (no state intervention), buying cheap and selling dear, and scorning delights and living laborious days so as to amass a fortune,
all helped to keep their noses to the grindstone. In a
sense their womenfolk lived for them, scorning domestic
or paid work as beneath their station and dignity, and
employing servants to ensure them complete leisure. Yet
nor were they idle, for the Nonconformist conscience
required them to be busy with charitable works, and
especially with educating the working classes in religion
and morality. Chief among the virtues they preached was
temperance: one of them carries a tract, 'The Hodman's

Haven, or Drink for Thirsty Souls'. (The thirsty hodman nearby is downing a pint.)

The other middle-class group, on the right, the intellectuals characteristically leaning on the fence – said to be Thomas Carlyle, at once the scathing critic and the prophet of the new industrial society, and Professor F. D. Maurice, the Christian Socialist and advocate of co-operative production – represent the professional middle class, who were the thinkers and critics of society and who increasingly came to offer a different point of view from that of the businessmen. They equally believed in hard work and competition, but the hard work and competition of talent, merit and education rather than the factory and the market place. And when they saw economic competition and *laissez-faire* threatening the lives of factory children, the health of towns, pure food or the education of the people, they were much more ready than the businessmen to call in the state to redress the balance. As the state and the economy expanded and required much larger numbers of civil servants, government inspectors, doctors, lawyers, teachers, engineers, and so on, they became an increasingly important and influential class, and one which has been much underrated in most histories of the period.

The painter, too, belongs to this class, and is expressing his own ideal, of work as at once the burden and the ennobler of man. On the gilt frame is inscribed the text 'In the sweat of thy face shalt thou eat bread'. At the centre of the picture stand the labourers in all the dignity of labour, the sole source of wealth according to the professional economists of the age. Even the work has a moral significance: they appear to be mending a sewer. But moral comments abound, in the sleeping tramps, the well-dressed lounger, the sandwich-board carriers, the ragged urchins at play, even the pampered whippet and the eager mongrel eyeing each other suspiciously – a symbol of the contrast between idle wealth and poverty, idle as well as laborious, which pervades the picture. There is also the contrast within the working class between the labourers in the middle and the craftsman on one side, uppish, well-dressed with fancy waistcoat and bow tie, and copy of *The Times*, and on the other the ragged, barefooted, shamefaced flower-seller, representing the depressed and degraded poverty of Mayhew's street-folk and Marx's *lumpenproletariat*.

Here, then, are all the layers of the new class society of the Railway Age. But why was it new? And how did it come into existence? It was new because the modern class system as we know it only emerged during the Industrial Revolution. The very word 'class' in its modern sense of a small number of mutually hostile layers in society only came into general use, as Asa Briggs has shown, in the last years of the eighteenth and the early years of the nineteenth. centuries[4] It was a new word for a new phenomenon. Before that, in the small towns and villages of the old society, there was little elbow-room for class organization, and class institutions like trade unions and political societies had little chance of succeeding against the overwhelming power of the squire, the parson, the merchant and the master manufacturer. The old society had its own structure, of some forty statuses from the nobility and gentry down through the merchants and yeomen to the husbandmen, craftsmen and 'labouring poor', which were 'ranks' or 'orders', steps on a social scale rather than groups organized in mutual competition or antagonism. In so far as rival groups existed, they consisted of the 'great functional interests', the landed interest, the fund-holding interest, the major professions, the various groups of merchants trading to different countries and organizing the different manufactures. In all these the leaders claimed to represent everybody within the interest, from the landlord, judge or master manufacturer down to the lowest labourer, copying clerk or working manufacturer (as the handworker was then called). The interests competed with each other for government favour, as when the General Chamber of Manufacturers in 1784 successfully opposed the Irish merchants and defeated Pitt's Irish trade treaty.[5]

Within each interest, as within each small town and village, paternalism and patronage were supposed to operate, the higher members fostering the welfare and employment of the lower. But paternalism was Janus-headed, and had a stern, disciplinary face as well as a smiling, benevolent one, and any kind of class activity, like a strike or political protest, was labelled 'insubordination' and suppressed. Strikes, machine-breaking riots, political riots and the like, did of course break out from time to time, but they did not generally lead to the kind of permanent class organization, trade union or political movement, in which class truly exists, and most of the riots and protests of the eighteenth century were 'interest' actions, against the bakers for selling dear bread, against the Irish for undercutting wages, or against the religion or politics of the traditional sects or parties, such as the Roman Catholics in the Gordon Riots of 1780, or the Whigs and Tories in the Sacheverell Riots of 1710 or the 'Wilkes and Liberty' Riots of 1768–75. Class antagonism was latent rather than overt, and the chief way in which it expressed itself was in religion, where the dislike of the aristocracy and gentry by the few merchants, craftsmen and yeomen farmers of the middle ranks who could afford to be independent of the dependency system took the form of dissent from the established Church. And even there the Dissenters, with their Whig patrons and lobbying of the landed Parliament and government for 'complete toleration', were more a part of the interest system than they were an anticipation of class. Class politics in the modern sense certainly did not exist: as the late Richard Pares has said, 'the distribution of political power between the classes was hardly an issue in politics before 1815'.[7]

The Industrial Revolution was to change all this. In the large new towns the old society and its traditional social control by the landlord, parson and master broke down, and the middle and working classes, pressed together in large numbers, asserted their independence and hostility to the landed class and to each other. Engels wrote in 1844:

The cities first saw the rise of the workers and the middle classes into opposing social groups. It was in the towns that the trade union movement, Chartism and socialism all had their origin.[8]

Sir Walter Scott noticed the change a quarter of a century earlier. In 1820 he deplored 'the unhappy dislocation which has taken place between the employer and those in his employment', and blamed it on the new technology:

Much of this is owing to the steam engine. When the machinery was driven by water, the manufacturer had to seek out some sequestered spot where he could obtain a suitable fall of water, and then his workmen formed the inhabitants of a village around him, and he necessarily bestowed some attention, less or more, on their morals and on their necessities, had knowledge of their persons and characters and exercised a salutary influence as over men depending on and intimately connected with him and his prospects. This is now quite changed; the manufactures are transferred to great towns, where a man may assemble five hundred workmen one week and dismiss them the next, without having any further connection with them than to receive a week's work for a week's wages, nor any further solicitude about their future fate than if they were so many old shuttles.

Thus the workers were 'entirely separated from the influence of their employers, and given over to the management of their own societies, in which the cleverest and most impudent fellows always get the management of the others, and become bell-wethers in every sort of mischief'.[9]

Yet it would not be true to say that the birth of class was entirely due to the steam engine and the new towns. Quite apart from these, industrialism and its opportunities for new wealth, in the form of increased rents from agricultural land, mines and urban property, had induced the landed ruling class to embrace new attitudes towards society and their responsibilities, which undermined their old paternalism and provoked the emerging middle and working classes to protest. This was what Thomas Carlyle called 'the abdication on the part of the governors'.[10] In the last years of the eighteenth century the landed aristocracy and gentry, partly under the influence of Adam Smith and similar opponents of state interference, began to give up their old paternal responsibilities for fixing wages and prices and ensuring the welfare of the people. In the hungry years of the 1790s, when the French Revolutionary Wars and bad harvests raised the price of bread to famine level, the government and the magistrates refused to apply the wage- and price-fixing clauses of the 1563 Statute. The most they would do was to introduce the Speenhamland system of poor relief in aid of wages, making up the wages of farm labourers in the south of England to subsistence level according to the price of bread.[11] At the same time they refused to allow the workers to try and raise their own wages, and passed the general Combination Acts of 1799 and 1800 which repeated the traditional old society ban on trade unions and speeded up the operation of the law against them. When the industrial workers, from the textile weavers of Scotland and Yorkshire down to the journeymen millers of Kent, petitioned for the laws regulating wages to be applied, Parliament responded in 1813–14 by repealing the wages and apprenticeship clauses of the 1563 Statute.[12]

At the same time, under the influence of Joseph Townsend and Thomas Malthus, a campaign was mounted against the Poor Law itself, the last defence of the wage-earner against starvation, which reached a crescendo in 1817 when a Committee of the House of Commons recommended its abolition, but was over-ruled by the government and the House of Lords. The campaign continued until 1834, when it culminated in the New Poor Law and its denial of relief to the unemployed outside the workhouse.[13]

The final straw, which offended the middle class as well as the workers, was the Corn Law of 1815, by which the landlords, according to middle-class critics like James Mill and Ricardo, set out to maintain the high corn prices and rents of wartime into the peace at the expense of the rest of the community.

All this seemed to prove to middle-class and working-class radicals alike that the ruling class was governing in its own selfish interest, and wanted to have its cake and eat it: to abandon its old paternal responsibilities (which the working class deplored and the middle class welcomed) while at the same time demanding its old paternal privileges (which both equally condemned). Their response was to emancipate themselves completely from the paternal dependency system, to create their own class organizations to safeguard their own rights and interests, and to demand a share in government. Since class inheres in class conflict and in the more or less permanent institutions created to sustain it, it was in the ensuing class struggles over parliamentary reform, Chartism, the Repeal of the Corn Laws, the legalization of trade unions, factory reform, the New Poor Law, and the rest, that the modern classes came into existence.

Parliamentary reform has a long ancestry, going back through Fox, Paine and the 'English Jacobins' of the 1790s to 'Wilkes and Liberty' in the 1760s. But Reform in the old society was not a class movement. It began as a straightforward example of old society politics, of the Whig 'outs' against Tory 'ins', both sides mobilizing their dependants and clients among the middle ranks and lower orders, including the riotous mobs drawn from the urban artisans and the labouring poor.[14] Even in the Revolutionary 1790s the Reformers were an interest group rather than a class movement: the supposedly middle-class Society for Constitutional Information was under the patronage of the aristocratic Friends of the People, and in turn patronized the London Corresponding Society, which was a group of independent shop-keepers and craftsmen rather than proletarian wage-earners. Perhaps they would in time have turned into specifically middle-class and working-class bodies, but they were suppressed by traditional old society means, the Church-and-King mobs, organized by aristocrats and loyalist merchants and lawyers, but consisting of patriotic artisans and labourers.[15]

It was not until the French Wars were over, and patriotism ceased to reinforce dependency in defence of the old order, that Reform became a class movement. Then, in the five years after Waterloo, the first nation-wide working-class political movement of modern times swept the country, in a series of mass meetings for universal manhood suffrage. The great radical leaders William Cobbett and Orator Hunt set out to channel all working-class discontents, brought to boiling point by the un-employment and high bread prices of the post-war slump, into one great political movement. The government, especially the home secretary, Lord Sidmouth, obsessed by fears of revolution and misinformed by spies, found treason plots and threats of revolution everywhere. A Cruikshank cartoon of 1817 shows Sidmouth, Canning and Castlereagh discussing with the spies, Reynolds, Castle and Oliver, a suitable reward for their services in supplying the bulging 'Green Bag' of seditious plans and papers on the table.

There were, however, some real plots. At the Spa Fields meeting in 1816 Arthur Thistlewood and other followers of Thomas Spence, the harmless land reformer, led away a contingent in a somewhat ridiculous attempt to storm the Tower of London. In 1817, misled by a call for a general uprising emanating from Oliver the spy, Jeremiah Brandreth, the 'Nottingham Captain', led an army of poor Derbyshire framework knitters in 'the Pentrich Revolution'. More dangerously, in 1820 Thistlewood and the Spenceans in 'the Cato Street conspiracy' plotted to murder the Cabinet at dinner in the Earl of Harrowby's house, but were betrayed by a government informer. The vast majority of working-class radicals however were not revolutionaries, but genuine Reformers who sought improvement of their lot through constitutional change.[16]

The movement culminated in the great meeting at St Peter's Fields, Manchester, on 16 August 1819. The magistrates, led by the young, effeminate and inexperienced Mr Hulton of Hulton Hall, vacillated before ordering the arrest of Orator Hunt in the midst of a crowd of peaceful working men with their wives and children, variously estimated at from 30,000 to 150,000, but most probably about 60,000. Mr Nadin, the Deputy Constable (professional police chief) of Manchester, who had been pelted with cobble stones by rioting Reformers at White Cross the week before, refused to do so without military aid. The magistrates sent the Yeomanry, the local part-time cavalry of gentlemen-amateurs, to assist him and his men. They got stuck in the crowd, panicked, and began to slash about them with their sabres. The magistrates sent in the professional cavalry, the Hussars, to rescue them, and in the words of one of them, Lieutenant Jolife, 'By the time we had arrived at the end of the field, the fugitives were literally piled up to a considerable elevation above the field.' Eleven people were killed and over 500 injured. No doubt not all the reformers at Peterloo were guiltless of violent intent: the

Stockport contingent in particular were prepared to defend their flags and banners with 'nature's ammunition, brickbats, stones, and mud', as they had done at a previous meeting. But the great majority who brought their wives and children in their Sunday best did not come to make a revolution or even to provoke a riot. The undoubtedly 'good intentions' which some recent historians have found in the magistrates, police and soldiers – what authority *wants* to get involved in a blood-bath of this kind? – resulted in death or injury for a large number of innocent men, women and children, and hurt feelings on the part of Mr Hulton at the ensuing public condemnation.[17]

Whatever the rights and wrongs of the occasion and the disparity in consequences for the two sides, Peterloo became a legend for the parliamentary reformers and for generations of working-class radicals. It was condemned by *The Times* and by many Whig aristocrats and Liberal businessmen who had previously held aloof from the Reform Movement, and it marked the real beginning of the joint movement of the middle- and working-class radicals which culminated, with the aid of the Whigs, in the great Reform Act. In that movement, of course, it was the middle class who increasingly took the lead, with the Benthamite civil servant, James Mill, and Francis Place, the radical tailor, organizing, in collusion with the Whig government, a 'threat of revolution' at the London end, and Thomas Attwood, the unorthodox banker, and Joseph Parkes, the radical newspaper editor, in Birmingham, organizing the joint middle- and working-class political unions which helped to bully Parliament into reforming itself.[18]

The Reform Act, with its narrow property franchise

and imperceptible change in the politicians, did not satisfy the working-class radicals, especially when the new Parliament passed the unpopular New Poor Law and refused to grant the factory reformers' Ten Hours' Act. At first they shifted to industrial action. The trade unions had been granted a bare toleration by the repeal of the Combination Acts in 1824–5, and a vigorous movement began – or emerged from illegal obscurity – with such nationwide organizations as John Doherty's Federation of Cotton Spinners of Great Britain and Ireland, 1829, and his National Association for the Protection of Labour, 1831, an unsuccessful precursor of the T.U.C.[19] After the failure of Reform on their terms, many working-class radicals turned their hopes to unionism, and especially to general unionism, or the union of the whole working class not merely for the protection of wages but also for social and political ends.

One idea, inspired by Robert Owen, the successful cotton-mill owner turned pioneer Socialist, was for the whole working class to opt out of the competitive capitalist system and supply each other with the necessities of life through a system of 'labour exchanges' in which goods were exchanged for tickets valued at so many hours of labour. Another, inspired by an old Regency radical cobbler named William Benbow, was for a short cut to the millennium by means of a 'sacred month' or general strike which would bring the capitalist system to a halt, to be peacefully taken over by the workers. These ideas and others were brought – or muddled – together in the Grand National Consolidated Trade Union of 1834, which claimed half a million members, but collapsed after a premature general strike in support of 'the Derby turn-out' against a wage cut.[20]

Its only success was the massive campaign it mounted, including a mammoth meeting in Copenhagen Fields, London, against the transportation for swearing an illegal oath of the 'Tolpuddle martyrs', the six Dorsetshire farm labourers who had formed an affiliated union. The campaign united the movement and was successful in getting the sentence reversed and the labourers brought back from Australia, but it did not enable the union to survive.[21] Trade union advance lay along another line, in the craft unions for the highly paid skilled workers, who built up brick by brick strong local, regional and finally national organizations, the 'new model unions' of the mid-Victorian period which, by controlling apprentice-ship and therefore entry to their crafts, were able to maintain a high living standard for their members.[22]

Some of the energy released by the collapse of general unionism, especially in the north of England, went into the campaign against the New Poor Law and the 'bas-tilles', as the new large workhouses were called. It was not a purely working-class movement, but was led by Tory radicals like Henry Fielden, the Yorkshire mill-owner, and the Rev. J. R. Stephens, the fiery Methodist preacher. In some areas, such as Todmorden, where Fielden led the opposition, it became impossible for the 'three Bashaws of Somerset House', the Commissioners of the Poor Law Board, to set up a local board of guardians and build a workhouse. In the long term this campaign was successful, in that under the Outdoor Relief Regulation Order, 1852, the central government abandoned its policy of refusing relief to the unemployed outside the workhouse as far as the industrial towns were concerned, though this was mainly due to the impractica-bility of operating it in modern economic conditions of boom and slump, when the workhouse was alternately too large and too small for the purpose.[23] In the short term, however, the agitation merged with two others: the factory reform movement and Chartism.

The factory agitation for shorter hours and better conditions for children, adolescents and ultimately for women workers was also led by Tory radicals, Michael Sadler, Richard Oastler, Henry Fielden and Parson Bull, together with the aristocratic Lord Ashley. This alliance was, on the part of Sadler and Ashley at least, a conscious attempt to revive the paternalism of the old society in the context of industrialism, on the basis of common opposition by the landed upper class and the working class to what they considered the selfish individualism of the industrialists. It was of immense importance for the future, since upon it Disraeli and other Tory leaders were to base the revival of the Conservative party and its appeal to a large minority of the working-class vote, but in the meantime Ashley and his followers met frustration from both parties and both Houses of Parliament. It took until 1847 to achieve the Ten Hours Act, for textile factories only, and until 1851 to make it effective by banning 'relays' or shift work.[24] Until then, from the working-class point of view the movement was one more proof of the need for united action to attain redress of their grievances, and for a further reform of Parliament to make their voice effective.

The paths of agitation thus all led back to parliamentary reform. In 1836, when all other movements seemed to have failed, the radical cabinet-maker, William Lovett, of the London Working Men's Association, with the aid of Francis Place drew up 'the People's Charter', demanding universal manhood suffrage, vote by ballot,

equal electoral districts, annually elected Parliaments,
payment of and no property qualification for M.P.s.
Chartism became a great mass movement. Vast mass
meetings were held throughout the country, national
conventions were held in 1839 and annually from 1842
to 1848, claiming all the moral if not the legal authority
of a democratic Parliament, and three great petitions
signed by millions of supporters were presented to the
Westminster Parliament in 1839, 1842 and 1848. It was
all to no avail. The movement became divided between
the 'moral force' wing, led by Lovett and middle-class
sympathizers like Thomas Attwood the Birmingham
banker, which believed in constitutional methods, and
the 'physical force' wing, led by the Irish lawyer-journalist
Feargus O'Connor and Bronterre O'Brien, which was
prepared to threaten revolution. The latter captured the
movement and alienated the moderates, who drifted
away into educational, temperance and similar reform
movements, but became itself divided, notably over
Feargus O'Connor's 'Land Plan', a scheme to escape
from industrialism by the resettling of working men in
villages of peasant smallholders. After the last great
petition campaign of 1848, when the government called
O'Connor's bluff and exposed the hollowness of his
threat of revolution, the movement dwindled away in the
milder economic climate of the 1850s.[25]

The great rival of Chartism for mass support from 1838
to 1846 was the Anti-Corn Law League, 'that uniquely
powerful instrument in the forging of middle-class
consciousness', as Asa Briggs has called it.[26] It was not
the only middle-class agitation in the two decades after
the Great Reform Act. There was also the Dissenters'
campaign against the Anglican Church, its parochial

church rates, privileged position in education, and the establishment itself, which reached a crescendo in 1847 when they tried, and failed, to get their own, independent, M.P.s elected to Parliament.[27] Even the anti-Corn Law agitation was in part an attack by the Dissenters on the Church and its tithes as well as on the landlords and their rents. Since dissent was increasingly powerful in the middle class, it was sometimes difficult to distinguish between the two, and both the religious and the economic grievances helped to unite the middle class in opposition to the landed ruling class. The Anti-Corn Law League concentrated attention on a single, easily understood grievance, but one with enormous implications for society. The landlords, they claimed, abused their monopoly of political power to increase their own incomes at the expense of the other classes; the Corn Laws not only raised the price of bread but prevented foreigners from selling us grain and earning the sterling to buy our manufactured goods, and thus depressed trade and caused unemployment of capital and labour. The lucid arguments of Richard Cobden and the passionate rhetoric of John Bright not only united the middle class but persuaded Sir Robert Peel of the justice of their case. In 1846, under duress from the Irish potato famine, Peel capitulated, and repealed the Corn Laws at the expense of splitting the Tory party and wrecking his government.[28] Yet his courageous sacrifice was justified by events. Not only did trade revive without depressing agriculture, but the middle class came to accept the leadership of the aristocratic parties and the justice of their government. Repeal was the most important step on the way to harmony between the aristocracy and the middle class.

The working class, too, came to accept the political,

social and economic system, at least for a long generation. The repeal of the Corn Laws and cheap bread, reviving trade and wages, the Ten Hours Act of 1847 and the general feeling that the government was no longer against them, all contributed to a profound change of attitude on the part of the working class. This was partly due to what has been mistakenly called 'mid-Victorian prosperity' which replaced the supposedly depressed and 'hungry forties'. In fact, 'prosperity' was an illusion due to rising prices, which made money profits rise and wage increases (which might not mean much in real terms) easy to come by. But people are as well off as they feel, and when the money in their pockets increases (even though its value rises less), they feel that they are swimming with the tide, and that the economic system is on their side.

Yet there was more to the new harmony between the classes than the euphoria produced by mild inflation. Society in Britain had passed between 1815 and 1848 through a generation of class conflict which had been all the more violent for being new. The political riots, machine-breaking and violent strikes on the one side and the armed repression and harsh justice on the other, had been due to a trial of strength between the new classes demanding redress of their grievances and a ruling aristocracy which denied their right to exist as classes with their own institutions and leaders. As long as the latter regarded any kind of class organization in old society terms as insubordination to be violently suppressed, violent reaction was inevitable from the other side. Only when all three sides accepted each other's right to exist and were prepared to negotiate rather than fight could violence end and a viable class society come into existence. This was the real achievement of early Victorian England.

The railways played an important part in the rise of class and the process of social pacification. On the one hand, they enabled class movements like the trade unions and the Anti-Corn Law League to organize on a nation-wide scale, to send visiting delegates and speakers to all parts of the country, and to arrange regional and national conferences. The first Chartist Convention of 1839, for example, met in London and Birmingham soon after the completion of the Grand Junction and London and Birmingham Railways. On the other, they enabled the government and the politicians to see for themselves what was going on instead of relying on spies and in-formers, to engage in persuasive and mutually educational dialogue with the people in the localities, and to hold troops in reserve instead of quartering them provocatively in the industrial towns to be used at the behest of panicky local magistrates. The change in policy and effectiveness can be seen in the difference between Peterloo, over which the government could only retrospectively and reluctantly defend the use of troops by the magistrates, and the Chartist crises of 1839 and 1842, in which the government itself, through General Sir Charles Napier in charge of the Northern District, could control the move-ment of troops. By 1848 the army was 'seated like a spider in the centre of its web, on the diverging lines of iron road'.[29] With the self-confidence which this gave the government against any threat of a general rising, it very rarely chose to use it.

What we see in Ford Madox Brown's painting of 1852, therefore, is a viable class society, in which the different classes have learned to live with each other and tolerate one another's existence. But it was not a society in which all classes were equal in influence any more than in wealth and status. One class in particular dominated the political ideas and moral values of the age. In spite of its retention of the reins of office in central and local government, that class was not the landed aristocracy, which had long been converted to the new morality and the new political economy. It was the capitalist middle class, which by a long process of education and propaganda had managed to impose its beliefs in free trade, competitive individualism, *laissez-faire*, the gospel of work and the puritan morality of the 'Nonconformist conscience' upon the rest of society. The 'spirit of the age' in mid-Victorian England was the spirit of the capitalist middle class.

That spirit was not without challenge, from several different directions. The working class, chiefly through the trade unions, continued to press for reform, of factory hours and conditions (culminating in the general Factories and Workshops Acts of 1867, 1871 and 1878), of the legal relations between employer and employed (achieved by the modification and repeal of the unequal Master and Servant Acts in 1867 and 1875), and for the parliamentary franchise (which they effectively received in the towns with the Household Suffrage Act of 1867). The landed class, through its control of Parliament, passed these reforms, and also set limits to irresponsible business enterprise through such legislation as the Alkali Act of 1863, to prevent the destruction of the countryside by acid vapour from chemical works, and the Adulteration of Foods Acts of 1860, 1872 and 1875. The professional middle class offered the biggest challenge of all, for the civil servants and government inspectors played a large part in undermining the principle of *laissez-faire* in matters of public health, education and factory reform from within, while writers and thinkers like Thomas Carlyle, Matthew Arnold, John Ruskin and John Stuart Mill began to question the spirit of the age from without.

Nevertheless, at least until the 1880s, the capitalist middle-class ideal of an individualist, competitive society without undue interference by the state survived intact, and was the norm from which any kind of interference on behalf of the weak or underprivileged was the exception, to be accepted only under protest and for the most compelling reasons. In that society the capitalist businessman was the uncrowned king, or at least the power behind the throne. And yet his is the one figure missing from Ford Madox Brown's painting. Who should we put there to represent him? George Stephenson, 'the father of the improved railway of modern times', the very epitome of the self-made, hard-working capitalist of the Industrial Revolution? But Stephenson was already dead, and in his place there stood a new type of capitalist, the great company director who manipulated money rather than things, and instead of attacking the landed class joined it on equal terms or bought its services on company boards – men such as George Hudson, the 'railway king', who at the peak of his power in 1849 controlled companies worth £30 million, covering a quarter of the countries' railway mileage and most of the strategic main lines to the north.

Dr Thomas Arnold, the headmaster of Rugby, saw railways as heralding the downfall of the aristocracy. Of the London to Birmingham Railway which ran past his school he said, 'I rejoice to see it and think that feudality is gone for ever. It is so great a blessing to think that any one evil is really extinct.'[30] He was right, but for the wrong reasons. Feudality in the sense of the domination of society by a landed ruling class was gone, or going, but it was to be replaced by another aristocracy, an aristocracy of big business – or, rather, by a plutocracy in which the old aristocracy of land merged with the new one of capital. And the railways heralded this transition as they did so much else. For the railways were the pioneers of big business, of the great joint-stock company in which a few tycoons and professional managers controlled vast capitals and huge labour forces, far greater than anything controlled by either the old feudal aristocrats or by individualist, owner-managing capitalists of the Industrial Revolution. The great railwaymen were the precursors of the business magnates of today. They did not fit into the simple class system of mid-Victorian society, and they were to do as much as anyone to undermine and transform it. In the next chapter we shall consider the effect on society of the railways as big business.

Further Reading

Harold Perkin, *The Origins of Modern English Society, 1780– 1880*, Chapters 6–9.

Edward Thompson, *The Making of the English Working Class* (Gollancz, 1963).

J. R. Poynter, *Society and Pauperism: English Ideas on Poor Relief, 1795–1834* (Routledge & Kegan Paul, 1969).

George Rudé, *The Crowd in History, 1730–1848* (Wiley, 1964).

Joseph Hamburger, *James Mill and the Art of Revolution* (Yale University Press, 1963).

Norman McCord, *The Anti-Corn Law League, 1836–46* (Allen & Unwin, 1958).

Mark Hovell, *The Chartist Movement* (Manchester U.P., 1925).
Asa Briggs (ed.), *Chartist Studies* (Macmillan, 1962).
Henry Pelling, *A History of British Trade Unionism* (Macmillan, 1963).

Notes

1. In the Manchester City Art Gallery.
2. Norman Gash, *Politics in the Age of Peel* (Longmans, 1953), chap. iii.
3. H. J. Laski, *Studies in Law and Politics* (1932), chap. viii; W. L. Guttsman, *The British Political Élite* (MacGibbon and Kee, 1963), p. 78.
4. Asa Briggs, 'The Language of "Class" in early 19th-century England', in A. Briggs and J. Saville, eds., *Essays in Labour History* (Macmillan, 1960).
5. *Plan of the General Chamber of Manufacturers* [1784], in Birmingham Public Library.
6. Cf. G. Rudé, *The Crowd in History, 1730–1848* (Wiley, 1964), chaps. ii-iv.
7. R. Pares, *King George III and the Politicians* (Clarendon Press, 1953), p. 3.
8. F. Engels, *The Condition of the Working Class in England* (trans. W. O. Henderson and W. H. Chaloner, (Blackwell, 1958), pp. 137–8.
9. Sir W. Scott, *Familiar Letters* (1894), II, 78.
10. *Chartism* (1839), chap. vi.
11. Cf. J. R. Poynter, *Society and Pauperism: English Ideas on Poor Relief, 1795–1834* (Routledge & Kegan Paul, 1969), chap. iii.
12. S. and B. Webb, *History of Trade Unionism* (Longmans, 1950 ed.), pp. 56–8.
13. Poynter, *op. cit.*, chap. vi.
14. Cf. Rudé, *op. cit.*, pp. 55–7.

15. Cf. Austin Mitchell, 'The Association Movement of 1792–93', *Historical Journal*, 1961, IV, 56f.

16. R. J. White, *Waterloo to Peterloo* (Heinemann, 1957), pp. 141–3, 152–61, 162–75, 189–90.

17. *Ibid.*, chap. xv; F. A. Bruton, *Three Accounts of Peterloo* (Longmans, 1921); Donald Read, *Peterloo: the Massacre and its Background* (Manchester University Press, 1958); Robert Walmsley, *Peterloo: the Case Re-opened* (Manchester University Press, 1969).

18. Cf. Joseph Hamburger, *James Mill and the Art of Revolution* (New Haven and London, Yale University Press, 1963), esp. chap. iv.

19. G. D. H. Cole, *Attempts at General Union* (Macmillan, 1953), chap. iii.

20. *Ibid.*, chaps. xiv, xv; W. H. Oliver, 'The Consolidated Trades' Union of 1834', *Economic History Review*, 2nd series, XVII, 1964, pp. 77–95 (which shows a paid-up membership in April 1834 of only 16,000).

21. Cole, *op. cit.*, chaps. xvi–xviii; Oliver, *loc. cit.;* *The Martyrs of Tolpuddle, 1834–1934* (T.U.C., 1934).

22. Cf. H. A. Turner, *Trade Union Growth, Structure and Policy: a Comparative Study of the Cotton Unions* (Allen and Unwin, 1962), book III, chap. 1.

23. S. and B. Webb, *English Poor Law Policy* (1910), p. 90.

24. M. W. Thomas, *The Early Factory Legislation* (Leigh-on-Sea, Thames Bank Publishing Company, 1948); J. T. Ward, *The Factory Movement, 1830–55* (Macmillan, 1962); J. C. Gill, *The Ten Hours Parson* (S.P.C.K., 1959) and *Parson Bull of Byerley* (S.P.C.K., 1963), chap. vi.

25. Mark Hovell, *The Chartist Movement* (Manchester U.P. 1925); Asa Briggs, ed., *Chartist Studies* (Macmillan, 1962).

26. Briggs, 'Language of "Class" ', *loc. cit.*, p. 59.

27. R. G. Cowherd, *The Politics of English Dissent . . . from 1815 to 1848* (Epworth Press, 1959), pp. 153–63; N. Gash, *Reaction and Reconstruction in English Politics, 1832–52* (Oxford University Press, 1956), pp. 86–8, 100–6.

28. Norman McCord, *The Anti-Corn Law League, 1836–46* (Allen and Unwin, 1958), esp. chap. viii.

29. F. C. Mather, 'The Railways, the Electric Telegraph and Public Order during the Chartist Period, 1837–48', *History*, XXXVIII, 1953, pp. 40f., and 'The Government and the Chartists', in Briggs, ed., *Chartist Studies*, pp. 372f.

30. A. P. Stanley, *The Life and Correspondence of Thomas Arnold* (1877), II. 388.

Chapter Seven

The Railway as Big Business

BIG business on the scale we know it today began with the railways in the nineteenth century. The giant joint-stock company with its capital of millions of pounds held in small shares by the general public – the characteristic institution of modern business – was pioneered by the railways half a century before it became at all general in most other industrial fields. Before the railways came most enterprises, with a few exceptions like canals, docks, water companies, turnpike trusts and a very few mining and trading companies, were owned by individuals, families or partnerships. Until 1825, in fact, the joint-stock company was illegal under the Bubble Act of 1720 except where Parliament specially sanctioned it, which it was very loath to do. From 1825, until the Companies Acts of 1856–62, which finally introduced the modern limited liability company, shareholders were in effect partners in the enterprise, and liable if it failed for its debts to the full extent of their goods and chattels. Not surprisingly, few people were willing to invest on these terms without having some say in the running of the company. And even when limited liability by registration was introduced, it did not become very common outside banking, insurance, mining and the public utilities like gas and water until the 1880s. In 1885 the total paid-up capital invested in railways was £816 million, as against £495 million in all other companies.[1]

The railways, each with its own separate Act of Parliament, were created from the start as large joint-stock companies with limited liability. This was inevitable from their very size. The main principle of the Industrial Revolution was a rise in the scale of organization, in the case of manufacturing from the domestic workshop with its handful of workers and £2 to £3 worth of equipment to the factory worth from £20,000 to £200,000 with fifty to 300 workers and £40–£50 of machinery per worker.[2] In this rise in scale the railways went still further. The average mortgage debt (loan capital) of a turnpike trust when the railways came was £6,300 and it employed perhaps a score of tollkeepers, road-repair men, and the like. The average canal in 1825 had a capital of £165,000, and employed a few score lock-keepers and maintenance men. The average cost of constructing twenty-seven railways opened between 1830 and 1853 was nearly £2 million, and the average labour force in 1851, excluding construction workers, was upwards of 2,500.[3] Moreover, the real unit of production (of passenger and ton miles) on the roads was the stage coach or waggon with two men, on the canals a pair of barges worked by a family, but on the railways, where the system of private vehicles paying tolls soon broke down, it could be nothing less than the whole system of the company, with its station staff, signalmen, mechanics and gangers as well as the footplatemen and guards. Indeed, through-working of trains soon required the whole railway network, or a large part of it, to be worked as a unit, and this led to the setting up in 1844 of the Railway Clearing House, to allocate the revenue from fares and freight charges between the companies whose rails and rolling stock served the through traffic. But this no more limited the autonomy of the member companies than the Bank Clearing House on which it was modelled, and the real unit of financial control and management remained the railway company, which continued to grow by extension and amalgamation. By 1858 the average authorized capital of the eighty-nine largest railways in Great Britain was £3.6 million, and that of the largest company (the London and North-Western) was £43.8 million.[4] By 1909 the average capital of the twenty remaining main-line companies was £52 million, that of the three largest, the Midland, the L.N.W.R. and the G.W.R., £193 million, £125 million and £96 million respectively.[5]

The shares in these vast concerns were at first very large, like those of the canals and other early companies, and the shareholder was still called a proprietor and thought of as a partner, if a limited and sleeping one. The shares in the Liverpool and Manchester were set at £100; in 1826 some 308 shareholders held 4,233½ of them. The Marquis of Stafford, proprietor of the Bridgewater Navigation, held 1,000, but two thirds of the rest were held by 141 smaller shareholders in blocks of from ten to 107.[6] But in most later railways the shares were smaller, £50, £25, £10 or less, and could be bought quite easily by small investors – especially as most of the shares in a new railway were not 'paid up' but 'light' shares on which a deposit, generally of about 10 per cent, had been paid, the rest merely being promised for when later 'calls' were made for part or all of the total value. The shares came to be bought and sold on the Stock Exchange, until then devoted mainly to government funds, where they soon came to dominate the hitherto exiguous market in company securities. In 1830 only four of the 205 companies named in the *Course of the Exchange* were railways; by 1844 the sixty-six railways out of the 755 companies quoted had the largest single block of paid-up capital, £47 million, compared with the 417 joint-stock banks' £26 million, and by the end of the 'railway mania' in 1847 the railways' capital had risen to over £200 million.[7] At the same time stock exchanges began in the provinces, notably in Manchester, Liverpool, Birmingham, Leeds, Glasgow and Edinburgh, where company securities, and especially railway shares, came to be more important than government stock, particularly from the 'railway mania' of 1845–7.

Thus the railways played the leading role in enlarging the investment market and in bringing into it large amounts of money and large numbers of investors hitherto untapped. As one historian has put it, 'The buying and selling of shares, unimportant before the coming of the railways, was an essential part of the Victorian commercial structure.'[8]

The growth of the joint-stock company and the buying and selling of shares had important consequences, not all of them good, and the railways pioneered not only the virtues of big business in large-scale and efficient organization but also its vices. Among these were speculation in shares, amounting at times to feverish gambling, on a scale big enough to entail a financial panic and a national slump; a widening gap between the ownership of companies and their management, with consequent opportunities for the directors to mismanage and make private profit from the shareholders' property; and the irresponsible power of these giant companies in relation to their customers, their employees and even the government of the country. Being first in the field, the railway companies were open to all the temptations of an unregulated competition in avarice and speculation; but they were also the whipping boys of public indignation and the guinea-pigs for the first experiments in parliamentary control and the development of modern company law.

There had, of course, been plenty of speculative investment booms before the railways came, from the South Sea Bubble of 1718–20 to the 'canal mania' of the 1790s. But the three great railway booms of 1824–5, 1836–7 and 1845–7 involved more people and larger sums of money, and they certainly had a larger effect, for better or worse, on the national economy and on the physical appearance of the country. In 1824–5 schemes amounting to a total expenditure of nearly £22 million were put forward, and most of the later main lines were actually projected, though very few were proceeded with. In 1836, thirty-five railway Acts were passed, twenty-nine of them for new lines covering 994 miles at an estimated cost of £17,595,000.[9] In the third and greatest boom, the 'railway mania' of 1845–7, the sky was the limit. In November 1845, when the whole capital investment in existing railways amounted to £71 million, *The Times* estimated that the cost of 620 new railway schemes (not counting 643 other companies which had not yet registered their prospectuses) came to £563 million, equivalent to over two thirds of the National Debt. In April 1846

Sir Robert Peel told the House of Commons that 519 railway Bills were actually under consideration, involving a capital expenditure, apart from loans, of £230 million.[10] The rush to get rich quick, to buy shares – or rather to put down one's name for them without paying, or to pay only the 10 per cent deposit usually called for before a company got its Act with the intention of selling them quickly on the rising market – produced a bubble of speculation. The Chairman of the Railway Clearing House described the mania with understandable exaggeration:

The subtle poison of avarice diffused itself through every class. It infected alike the courtly and exclusive occupant of the halls of the great and the homely inmate of the humble cottage. Duchesses were even known to soil their fingers with scrip, and old maids to inquire with trembling eagerness the price of stocks. Young ladies deserted the marriage list and the obituary for the share list, and startled their lovers with questions respecting the operations of bulls and bears. The man of fashion was seen more frequently at his broker's than at his club. The man of trade left his business to look after his shares; and in return, both his shares and his business left him. In short, 'madness ruled the hour,' and brought the country to the very verge of fiscal ruin.[11]

The bubble could not fail to burst when it became apparent that there was not enough money in the country to pay for all these schemes, still less for the quick profits hoped for from the inflated value of the shares, and the high cost of construction, as prices of land, labour and materials soared by competition, cut back the hope of high dividends. In 1846 the Bank of England was forced to raise the bank rate to stop the drain of gold and credit, the price of shares came tumbling down, and thousands of shareholders found themselves holding paper scrip worth much less than they had paid or promised for it, often with money they had not got. The slump which followed the crash was only saved from being catastrophic by the construction of the railways which survived, employing over a quarter of a million workers directly, and many more in manufacturing iron, locomotives and rolling stock for them.

The greed and gullibility of the investing public gave enormous scope to the unscrupulous company promoter. Schemes were projected and companies formed which were never intended to build railways, but merely to collect deposits from shareholders, sell off the directors' shares at a premium, and then wind themselves up at a cost in lawyers' and accountants' fees which absorbed the original deposits. The directors of even *bona fide* companies became adept at manipulating the share market, by advertising the names of well-known engineers and bankers, not always with their permission, by publishing optimistic forecasts of high dividends, by employing agents to buy shares with the company's money so as to bolster up the price, and, most obvious and tempting trick of all, by paying dividends on the existing shares out of capital, sometimes before a penny of revenue had been earned. The best of directors were under the temptation to extend existing lines, build branches, locomotive works and the like, so as always to have a construction account, preferably with fresh capital coming in, out of which to pay dividends, or at least to 'balance out' the profits from year to year so as to keep the dividend steady. And the worst could steer the company's spending towards the purchase of land, equipment or materials, often at inflated prices, in which they had a private interest, or even quite blatantly vote themselves or their friends blocks of shares as a reward for unspecified services.[12]

All this was possible because the law in the early stages, and for most purposes until the Regulation of Railways Act, 1868, was so vague, particularly in relation to accounting procedures. Railway companies before 1844 were generally required by their Acts to keep 'proper Books of Account', but little was said about their form, or auditing, or the presentation of balance sheets. Legislation in 1844–5 required them to appoint a book-keeper, balance the books from time to time and issue an exact balance sheet exhibiting a true statement of the capital stock, property, credits and debts of the company, and 'a distinct view of the profit or loss' in the preceding half-year, and have them audited by shareholders not holding office in the company.[13] But the companies resisted any form of government audit, and defeated Gladstone's attempt to impose it in 1884, when even so upright a railway chairman as George Carr Glyn of the London and North-Western denounced the interference of the state with the right of the shareholder to look after himself.[14] Thus, unlike in the matter of safety in which, as we saw in Chapter Four, it felt itself bound to interfere, the government contented itself with requiring a copy of the balance sheet and certain other railway statistics. Hence the railway companies were free, subject to the unlikely challenge of a majority of their shareholders, to put out what accounts they liked in whatever form, charging items of income and expenditure indiscriminately to capital or revenue, making as much or as little allowance for depreciation and betterment of their equipment and property as they wished, and generally making it almost impossible for the shareholders, still less the government, to know what was going on and whether they were being fairly treated.

In this situation there were opportunities for fraud on the grand scale, and there were famous cases of embezzling and absconding railway officials, like that of Leopold Redpath, registrar of the Great Northern Railway, who was transported for life in 1857.[15] But far more important than criminal activity was the immorality and sharp practice of those who kept within the law. Most notorious of these was George Hudson, the York draper who became 'the railway king' of the 1840s.[16] Hudson was the very epitome of the self-made man of the early railway age – except for the legacy of £30,000 which enabled him to make his transition from shopkeeper to railway company promoter: bluff, genial, rough in speech and manners, overbearing in business negotiations, ruthless with rivals and opponents, careless, it was said, of the safety of passengers and the welfare of employees, and cavalier, to say the least, in his dealings with other people's money. He knew nothing about the technology of railways, but a great deal about finance and the psychology of investors, and in his defence it can be said that he merely manipulated men more avid for profit but less able in its pursuit than himself.

Hudson's base was the York Union Bank, which he founded in 1833 with the aid of his political ally and patron, Sir John Lowther, leader of the York Tories, and its invaluable connection with the powerful Glyn's Bank in London, owned by George Carr Glyn, chairman of the London and Birmingham Railway, the largest at that time, and other lines. He began in a small way with a scheme in 1833 for a railway from York to Leeds, but in

1835 a chance meeting with George Stephenson enabled him to link up with the latter's North Midland Railway from Derby to Leeds. Next he took a lease of the rival Leeds and Selby line, and forced the Selby and Hull line into submissive co-operation by buying out their steam-tug rivals on the Ouse and Humber. Having raised the York and North Midland dividend to 10 per cent – out of capital, his enemies said – and made a reputation as a wizard of railway management who could conjure dividends out of the air, he was called in to perform his magic on the North Midland. This he did by dismissing staff and reducing salaries and wages to the point of inefficiency where breakdowns and accidents occurred. From this base he proceeded to blackmail the rival Midland Counties and Birmingham and Derby Junction companies – by threatening to cut off one or the other's through traffic to the north – into an amalgamation, in the formidable Midland Railway (1844), which in turn rapidly annexed the Leicester and Swannington, the Sheffield and Rotherham, and, under the nose of the Great Western, the Bristol and Gloucester, and then pushed out branches to Lincoln and Peterborough on the line of advance to London of Hudson's hated rival, the Great Northern.

Meanwhile, in 1841 Hudson brilliantly solved the impasse into which Pease and the Quakers of Stockton and Darlington had got themselves with their Great North of England railway, by persuading the eight companies whose lines it crossed to form a separate company, under his control, to complete the line between Darlington and Newcastle. He further extended the line to Edinburgh by floating the North British Railway and the Newcastle and Berwick (1844–5). Finally, on his reputation

alone, he was called in to restore the fortunes of the
ailing, elephantine Eastern Counties Railway (1845). By
the end of 1848 Hudson was master of companies worth
£30 million, covering 1,450 out of the 5,007 miles of
railway open to traffic, stretching from Berwick in the
north down to Bristol in the south-west, Maryport in the
north-west, Yarmouth and Colchester in the east, and
London to the south. During the 1840s, and especially
during the 'railway mania' which he helped to foster, he
had been courted by the aristocracy and business community alike, who had flocked to his West End house,
Albert Gate, had been admitted to the company of the
Queen and Prince Albert, joined the Tory leadership on
the front bench of the House of Commons, and was the
generally acknowledged spokesman of the railway
interest at a time when the railway interest was a force in
the land.

But he overreached himself. The collapse of the railway
boom destroyed the rising market which kept his shareholders happy and uncritical, and the ensuing depression
undermined the profits required to support the vital
dividends. Hudson tried to maintain them by the old
expedient of paying dividends out of capital, but in the
new situation of business pessimism it no longer worked.
Share prices slumped. He had made many enemies by his
sharp business practice, including the powerful 'Liverpool
party', whose leadership in railway finance he had
snatched, and their ally Edmund Denison of Doncaster,
whose Great Northern Railway, shortening the route to
the north and avoiding Hudson's lines, he had opposed
tooth and nail. They were ready to pounce.

Ironically, it was a deal with the latter which proved
his downfall. To rescue the Great Northern from finan-

cial difficulties and bolster his own original company, he allowed it running rights over the York and North Midland rails, thus providing a shorter route to the north-east and Scotland than that via Rugby. This infuriated the shareholders of the outflanked Midland Railway, the one company in his empire over which he was not absolute dictator; the Liverpool party formed a committee of inquiry, and in April 1849 he was forced to resign from the board. This started the rot in his other companies. Committees of inquiry in the York and North Midland and the York, Newcastle and Berwick found the accounts 'in such a muddle that it was impossible to unravel them completely', but sufficient proof that Hudson had doctored the books to improve the balance sheets, had paid dividends out of capital, had bought and sold Great North of England shares on behalf of the companies and pocketed the difference, and had made contracts in his private capacity with the companies to his personal profit. A similar inquiry in the Eastern Counties Railway found that he had manipulated the books and paid out of capital dividends amounting to £514,714 on a profit of £225,141. His alleged illicit profits and defalcations added up to the astounding total of £598,785. By June 1849 he had been forced to resign all his railway chairmanships. Pursued by lawsuits by his old companies and hounded by creditors, he fled abroad in 1855. After numerous unsuccessful attempts to restore his fortunes and political influence, he ended his days in 1871 on an annuity of £600 a year, raised by subscription among his friends.

Hudson was only the most notorious of the company floaters and speculators who thrived in the uncertain state of the law and the dubious commercial morality of

the early railway age, and he was by no means the worst.
He claimed, with some plausibility, that he had never
broken the law, and that he was persecuted for his failure
to fulfil the golden expectations he had raised in the
minds of investors who did not much care where the
dividends came from as long as they came but who
refused to forgive him when they did not. He was made
the scapegoat for a whole class of men whose practice
was no better, and to his credit and their relief he did not
drag others down with him in his fall as he might easily
have done. In his defence it has often been said that,
though careless of the means, he had a vision of the great
public end he wished to achieve, an efficient, national
railway network which would provide the country with
cheap transport to the benefit of everybody. Whether or
not this was true, his policy of amalgamation into large
area units free from cut-throat competition did pave the
way for a rational and workable system, but it was also
meant to increase the wealth and power of George
Hudson. To paraphrase a modern American big businessman, 'What was good for the country was good for
George Hudson.' His cavalier attitude to money and his
plausible if naïve inability to keep his personal finances
separate from those of his companies suggest that he was
less interested in wealth for its own sake than in power,
and this too is characteristic of the modern business
tycoon. Hudson's crime was not that he cheated, nor
even that he was found out, but that he failed to hold on
to power.

Other railway magnates wielded power just as ruth-
lessly, and more successfully. In the decade after Hudson's eclipse the most ruthless and successful was
Captain Mark Huish, who as manager of the London and

North Western was the most powerful man in the railway industry.[17] These were the years of the 'battle of the gauges', when the standard (4 feet 8½ inch) gauge companies led by the L.N.W.R. were at war with the Great Western Railway and its allies, which were trying to extend Brunel's heroic broad (7 feet) gauge into what they considered their territory. In theory this battle was settled by the Gauge Act, 1846, which forbade the construction of non-standard-gauge railways, but it made an exception for extensions to the existing broad gauge in the west, and in practice the Great Western and its allies were able to pursue a forward policy in the whole area of the west midlands, with ambitions as far north as Warrington and Birkenhead. The gauge war, moreover, was only the most dramatic of a series of struggles between major networks, to settle the frontiers of their empires and their shares of the lucrative through traffic by means of running rights over other companies' rails.

The L.N.W.R., with its central position along the industrial spine of the country from London through the Midlands to Lancashire, found itself in conflict on both sides, not only with the G.W.R. but also with the Midland and the Great Northern to the east and north, both of which aimed at outflanking the L.N.W.R.'s near-monopoly of through traffic between London and the north. Huish's business methods had been learned in a hard school when, as secretary of the Grand Junction, he had used the threat of a 'mixed gauge' deal with the Great Western to force the London and Birmingham into an amalgamation on favourable terms, and so made himself virtual dictator of the L.N.W.R. at its formation in 1846. He immediately set about turning those adjacent companies he could bully or cajole, with threats to cut off

or agreements to extend running rights, into protector-
ates or subservient allies which he could use as agents of
his implacable hostility against those he could not. In
this way he was able to win over the Midland, the
Manchester, Sheffield and Lincolnshire, the North
British, and the Edinburgh and Glasgow, against the
Great Northern, and to put stop-blocks on the latter's
junctions at Leeds, Wakefield, Retford, Grimsby and
Edinburgh. He evaded an arbitration award by Gladstone in 1857 for those lines over which joint running still
operated, tempting passengers by cut-rate fares to re-
book instead of buying through tickets. And he and his
allies were not above violent confrontations, with block-
ing engines and gangs of platelayers armed with picks
and shovels, to prevent rival trains from crossing their
rails.

   In the end Huish could not prevent the Great Northern
from reaching London, and running faster and more
comfortable trains from King's Cross (1852) to Edinburgh. Nor on the other side could he prevent the Great
Western from reaching the Mersey, though at the cost of
an extremely bitter battle. This was the battle with the
G.W.R.'s standard-gauge allies, the Shrewsbury and
Birmingham, the Shrewsbury and Chester, and the
Birkenhead, Lancashire and Cheshire Junction, which
between them were to connect the G.W.R. at Birmingham
with the Liverpool ferries at Birkenhead. Huish threatened and bribed the three companies and packed their
shareholders' meetings with his nominees, but the two
Shrewsbury companies defied him, leased the Birkenhead
line jointly with the G.W.R. in 1851, and finally amalgamated with the latter in 1854 – a defeat which began
the decline and led to the ultimate dismissal of Huish in

1858. There were other battles between the L.N.W.R. and the G.W.R., in Oxford, Wolverhampton, Worcester, South Wales, and elsewhere, but enough has been said to show the autocratic temperament and dictatorial methods of Captain Huish.

He was not alone in this second phase of railway construction in the 1850s and 1860s, when the big companies were rounding off their empires and mopping up the borderlands in between. Huish's ally, James Allport of the Manchester, Sheffield and Lincolnshire and later of the Midland, John Parson of the Oxford, Wolverhampton and Worcester, the West Midland and various London railways, Robert Jacomb-Hood and John Craven of the London, Brighton and South Coast, Captain Laws of the Lancashire and Yorkshire, and many more, were of similar fighting spirit and dubious practice.[18] This generation of aggressive frontiersmen and empire-builders was succeeded, however, by another breed of big businessmen – proconsuls and bureaucrats who knew how to run empires and extract profit from them without the necessity for going to war. Their prototype was perhaps Sir Richard Moon, Huish's successor as dictator of the L.N.W.R., though he did not become chariman until 1861. Cold, steely, aloof and incorruptible, he preferred to rule by fear rather than persuasion, but he was just the man to pull together the biggest and most sprawling of railway empires and make not only the largest joint-stock corporation in the world, but one of the soundest, most efficient and respected. He ruled it with his iron rod for no less than thirty years. Under him equally despotic and efficient deputies carried out his orders: William Cawkwell, the general manager, George Findlay, the chief traffic manager, and Francis Webb, the

chief mechanical engineer, who ran the largest railway
works in the world and the adjacent town of Crewe like a
viceroy, until his intimidation of his workmen to vote for
the Conservatives attracted the attention of Gladstone in
the 1880s.[19]

In similar mould was Sir Daniel Gooch, the brilliant
locomotive superintendent of the Great Western who
rose to be chairman from 1865 until his death in 1889.
Having left the company in disappointment at its
management in 1864, to lay the first Atlantic cable from
Brunel's *Great Eastern*, he was called back to put it on its
feet again. It fell to him to abandon the costly aggressive
policies which had brought it so low, 'to avoid all further
obligations with new lines and extensions, to make as far
as possible friendly relations with adjoining companies,
and to cut down all capital expenditure to a minimum'.
He was a strict puritan, a master of reprimand, and a
terror to those who disobeyed. Under his severe régime
the company recovered, the broad gauge was abandoned,
and the expansion, chiefly by amalgamation, began
again, to make the Great Western in its turn the biggest
railway company in the world.[20]

The transition to bureaucratic management was not
instantaneous, and there were notable exceptions and
survivals. The greatest of the late-Victorian railway
magnates was Sir Edward Watkin, son of Absolom
Watkin of the Anti-Corn Law League, who had become
secretary of a railway company (the Trent Valley) at the
age of twenty-six, had soon been absorbed into Huish's
empire as his pupil and lieutenant, and had become his
ally as general manager of the Manchester, Sheffield and
Lincolnshire. This he turned into a base for a great
empire of his own, deserting his old ally for an arrange-

The old society before the railways came: the landed gentleman and his lady abroad in their carriage and pair (George Stubbs' "The Phaeton", by kind permission of the National Gallery).

The "lower orders" making hay. Note that, unlike continental peasants, English farm labourers wore clothes recognizably similar to those of their "betters" above (George Stubbs' "Haycarting", by kind permission of the Trustees of the Lady Lever Collection).

Pre-railway transport:

A stagecoach, and

roadmakers on a turnpike road (from W. H. Pyne's
Microcosm, 1808).

Pre-railway transport: two scenes on the Regent's Canal.
The junction at rural Paddington.

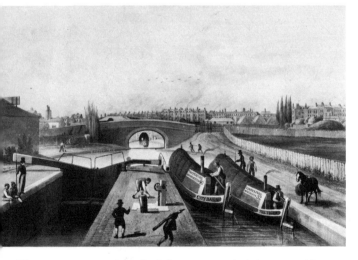

The eastern entrance to the Islington tunnel. A horse could
pull half a ton on an eighteenth-century road, up to 50 tons
(usually a pair of barges) on water. (By kind permission of
the British Waterways Museum, Stoke Bruerne, near
Towcester).

The coming of the railways:

the first train into Grimsby, 1848.

A use for railway arches: the able-bodied poor breaking stone
for roads in the labour yard at Bethnal Green, 1868 (from
the *Illustrated London News*, 15 April 1848 and 15
February 1868).

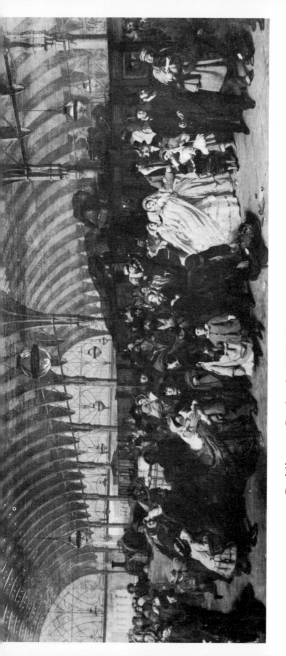

Paddington Station in 1862 (W. P. Frith's "The Railway Station", by kind permission of Royal Holloway College, Englefield Green). This famous painting, with its microcosm of the new railway-travelling public, is extensively referred to in Chapter 4, "The Great Connecter".

Life in the new towns: cellar dwellings in Manchester in the 1830s. Exterior.

Interior (by kind permission of the City Librarian, Manchester Public Libraries).

The new class society: Ford Madox Brown's "Work", 1852 (by kind permission of the Director, Manchester City Art Gallery). This brilliant commentary on mid-Victorian society is extensively referred to in Chapter 6, "The New Class Society".

The building of the railways:

a cutting near Whitby in the 1880s. There are few actual photographs, as distinct from artists' impressions, of Victorian railway building. This and the following eight photographs were taken by Frank M. Sutcliffe (1853-1951), an indefatigable photographer of late nineteenth and early twentieth century Yorkshire (reproduced by kind permission of Mr. W. Eglon Shaw, The Sutcliffe Gallery, Whitby).

Entrance to Grinkle tunnel near Easington on the Whitby-Middlesbrough line: steam replacing the horse as the work progresses.

Entrance to Kettleness tunnel, built to replace the dangerous cliff-edge route on the same line.

Building the brick piers of the railway viaduct over the River Esk near Whitby, c. 1882.

The men who made the railways: a group of navvies and craftsmen at the Esk viaduct.

The men who ran the railways: the station staff outside the goods office, Whitby Town Station, 1888.

Whitby Market, 1884. A typical town scene in late Victorian England.

Water-sellers in Whitby, c. 1880. In spite of the Public Health Acts, mains water was still absent from some streets of many towns until the end of the century.

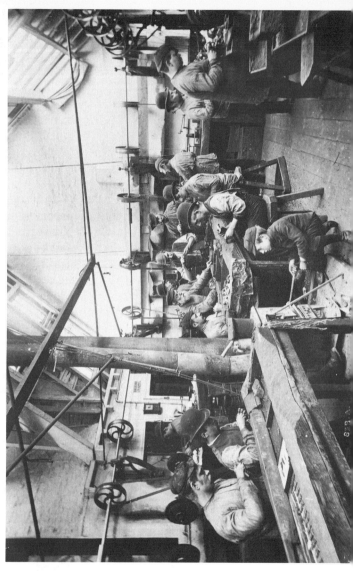

A late Victorian factory: jet workshop, Whitby, c. 1890,
where local stone was worked into trinkets and ornaments.

ment with the Great Northern which gave him running rights to London, and acquiring the chairmanships of the South-Eastern and the Metropolitan Railway (the first Underground), not to mention the presidency of the Canadian Grand Trunk Railway. At the Metropolitan in the 1870s he inherited a feud with J. S. Forbes, the equally stubborn head of the rival Metropolitan District Railway, which spilled over into competition for the Continental traffic between Watkin's South-Eastern Railway and Forbes's London, Chatham and Dover. He had grandiose plans to link Manchester to Paris via London, by means of his companies (the northern one transformed into the Great Central and extended to Marylebone in 1899) and the Channel Tunnel, for which he actually began to dig the pilot tunnel under Shakespeare Cliff, until the defence-minded government stopped him in 1882. His restless and extravagant scheming, which included a Dublin–Galway ship canal, a major port at Dungeness and an imitation of the Eiffel Tower at Wembley, only came to an end in 1894 when he suffered a stroke at the age of seventy-five. Watkin was a transitional figure between the age of Hudson and Huish and that of Moon and Gooch, a buccaneer in the world of the bureaucrats. He was survived, in both senses, by his suave and charming rival Forbes, who lived to see the war between their Kentish companies settled on terms favourable to both in a joint working agreement.[21]

The great railway magnates of the late Victorian age moved on a different plane from that of their fathers' generation. Like Watkin, Richard Potter was the son of a Manchester cotton merchant, who became chairman of various railway companies, including the Great Western (before Gooch), and president of the Canadian Grand

Trunk (after Watkin). As his daughter, the Fabian Beatrice Webb, shows, he belonged to a new race of international capitalists, travelling along his railways in his own private coach, and negotiating contracts with the Emperor Napoleon III.[22] George Carr Glyn, chairman of the London and North-Western, was such another, son of a London banker and Lord Mayor, but moving in still more exalted circles as a friend of Gladstone, father of the Chief Liberal Whip and, as Lord Wolverton, one of the first industrial peers.[23] Thomas Brassey we have already seen building 4,500 miles of railway, 1,700 of them in Britain and the rest in Europe, Canada, the Crimea, Australia, the Argentine and India – one mile for every twenty in existence in the world in 1870.[24] He was followed by other great contractors, who did not stop at railways, docks and bridges: Sir John Aird, who gas-and-watered London, Rotterdam, Amsterdam, Copenhagen, Berlin, Archangel and Moscow, and went on to build the original Aswan Dam on the Nile; Weetman Pearson, Lord Cowdray, who built railways in Spain, tunnels under New York, modernized Mexico under the dictator Porfirio Díaz, and founded the Mexican Eagle Oil Company; and Sir John Norton-Griffiths, who built railways, docks, roads and dams all over Africa and South America.[25]

These men became civil engineers and developers to the world, international capitalists who talked on equal terms with heads of state. Their activities contributed to the domination by Britain of the Victorian world economy. During the Victorian age 35 million tons of iron and steel rails were exported, plus the locomotives, rolling stock, signalling equipment, the engineers and many of the skilled men to build a large part of the world's railways. They added to the favourable balance of payments, and to the enormous growth of overseas investments and credit, which grew from £110 million in 1830, when the railway age began, to £4,000 million in 1914. Half of that huge balance went to pay for the First World War, and the other half for the second. Thus in a sense the profits of the railway age helped Britain to survive the military holocausts, if not the economic struggles, of the twentieth century.

The big businessmen who helped to make Britain the workshop, banker, insurer, carrier and civil engineer of the world were also the heralds of a new type of capitalism and a new sort of society, as different from the economy and society of their fathers as theirs had been from the old society of the eighteenth century. The cotton merchants, factory-owners and ironmasters of the Industrial Revolution were big men in their world, but they were still in the main smaller than the great landowners, who still dominated politics and social life. They were also owner-managers of family businesses, closely involved in their day-to-day running, and tied to the particular industrial town in which they lived. As active managers and creators of material wealth, they considered themselves morally superior to the 'idle class' of leisured, landed gentlemen, and opposed them in such agitations as parliamentary reform and the Anti-Corn Law League. The much bigger type of capitalist created by the rising scale of organization pioneered by the railways was on an entirely different plane, controlling, if not necessarily owning, masses of corporate capital far greater than even the greatest of the landowners, living a cosmopolitan life in trains, luxury liners and grand hotels across the globe traversed by their enterprises, and vying in wealth and

style of life with presidents and emperors. It was, significantly, while the railways were being built that the big
capitalists overtook the great landowners in wealth and
numbers. In 1850 there were under 2,000 businessmen
earning profits of £3,000 a year or more, compared with
the (fairly static) 2,500 great landowners in the 'Modern
Domesday' Returns of the 1870s with rentals (excluding
London property) of that size. By 1880 there were over
5,000 such businessmen. And if 866 landlords had over
£10,000 and seventy-six over £50,000 a year, the corresponding numbers of businessmen had risen from 338 to
987 and from twenty-six to seventy-seven.[26]

The new big businessmen, however, did not seek to
eject and replace the great landowners in social influence
and political power. Unlike their owner-managing
fathers, they had no need to be jealous, and as receivers
of interest and profits from enterprises too vast to be
seen and managed personally they felt great affinity for
the owners of great estates, whose manners and way of
life attracted them. They therefore joined forces with
them, in society, in politics, and even in business, where
titled directors were an asset to any board. While railwaymen like Richard Moon, Daniel Gooch and Edward
Watkin became baronets, or even peers, like George Carr
Glyn, Lord Wolverton (1869) and Brassey's son (1886) –
and were followed by brewers like Allsopp, Guinness
and Bass, ironmasters like Guest, machine manufacturers like Armstrong and Cunliffe-Lister, and even
shopkeepers like W. H. Smith's widow – 167 peers, a
quarter of the peerage in 1896, became directors of companies.[27] Meeting frequently in the boardroom, the
House of Lords, in London 'society' and in each other's
country houses, they formed a new plutocracy, distinct

from the old landed gentry and old industrial middle class.[28] By the Edwardian age, when the king could 'go boating with his grocer' in Sir Thomas Lipton's yacht, the plutocracy had come into its own.

Big business, of course, had other implications than the rise of a new plutocracy. The great companies needed others to run them efficiently besides the great capitalist at the top: managers, engineers, accountants, and lawyers, besides an army of clerks and skilled and unskilled workers. The managers and professional men contributed to the enormous growth of the salaried middle class which is so important a feature of modern society, and to the 'professionalization of industry' which goes under the name of 'managerialism'. The 'organization man', 'the man in the grey flannel suit', the professional manager who gives his life and loyalty to the company in return for a secure salary, steady promotion, and the ultimate hope of a seat on the board, began with men like Daniel Gooch and Francis Webb in the railway age. The railway companies also pioneered secure employment for wage-earners, long-service awards such as gold watches, holidays with pay, and even pensions. For they prided themselves on being good employers, of the paternal if despotic kind. However, as we shall see in Chapter Ten, their despotism often outweighed their paternalism, particularly towards the mere idea of trade unionism, and in the thirty years before the First World War they also had the misfortune to pioneer some of the worst features of modern industrial relations, and to attract the intervention of the government. But that is another story, to which we shall return after we have dealt with two other effects of the railways in their prime: on holidays for the masses and on the growth of suburbia.

Further Reading

C. Hamilton Ellis, *British Railway History: an Outline . . . 1830–76* (Allen & Unwin 1954) and *1877–1947* (Allen & Unwin 1959).

R. S. Lambert, *The Railway King, 1800–71: a Study of George Hudson and the Business Morals of His Time* (Allen & Unwin 1934).

M. C. Reed (ed.), *Railways in the Victorian Economy* (David & Charles, 1969).

O. S. Nock, *North Western: a Saga of the Premier Line of Great Britain, 1846–1922* (Ian Allan 1968).

O. S. Nock, *The Great Northern Railway* (Ian Allan 1958).

E. T. MacDermot, *History of the Great Western Railway* (2 vols. in 3, G.W.R.Co. 1927–31).

C. H. Grinling, *History of the Great Northern Railway* (Allen & Unwin 1898).

   G. Dow, *Great Central* (Locomotive Publ. House 1959).

C. Hamilton Ellis, *The Midland Railway* (Ian Allan 1953).

Notes

1. Cf. B. C. Hunt, *The Development of the Business Corporation in England* (Cambridge, Mass., 1936); G. Todd, 'Some Aspects of Joint-Stock Companies, 1844–1900', *Economic History Review*, 1932, IV. 46–71; Clapham, *Economic History of Modern Britain*, II. 133–45, III. 201–13.
2. For sources, see Perkin, *Origins of Modern English Society*, p. 109n.
3. S. and B. Webb, *Story of the King's Highway* (1913), p.

224; *Quarterly Review*, 1825, XXXII. 170–1; H. Pollins, 'A Note on Railway Constructional Costs, 1825–50', *Economica*, 1952, XIX. 407.

4. Ernest Carter, *An Historical Geography of the Railways of the British Isles* (Cassell, 1959), pp. 296–8.

5. G. R. Porter, *The Progress of the Nation* (ed. F. W. Hirst, 1912), p. 552.

6. H. Pollins, 'The Finances of the Liverpool and Manchester Railway', *Economic History Review*, 1952, Second Series, V. 92.

7. M. C. Reed, 'Railways and the Growth of the Capital Market', in Reed, ed., *Railways in the Victorian Economy* (Newton Abbot, David and Charles, 1969), pp. 162–83.

8. *Ibid.*, p. 183.

9. John Francis, *A History of the English Railway: its Social Relations and Revelations, 1820–45* (1851, David and Charles Reprint, 1967), I. 135, 283.

10. *The Times*, 17 November 1845; C. Hamilton Ellis, *British Railway History: an Outline . . . 1830–76* (1954), p. 158.

11. Kenneth Morison, quoted by Francis, *op. cit.*, II. 174–5.

12. Cf. Francis, *op. cit.*, I. 296–8, II. 175–80.

13. H. Pollins, 'Aspects of Railway Accounting before 1868', in Reed, ed., *op. cit.*, pp. 138–61.

14. Francis, *op. cit.*, II. 7n.

15. D. Morier Evans, *Facts, Failures and Frauds* (1859), chap. ix; Reed, ed., *op. cit.*, p. 139.

16. What follows is based mainly on R. S. Lambert, *The Railway King, 1800–71: a Study of George Hudson and the business morals of his time* (1949), *passim*, and Ellis, *op. cit.*, pp. 97–100, 108–10, 157–8, 164–75.

17. For Huish, see Ellis, *op. cit.*, pp. 104–5, 182, 184–220, 234–8.

18. Cf. Ellis, *op. cit.*, esp. part II, chap. ii, 'The Warring Companies'.

19. O. S. Nock, *North Western: a Saga of the Premier Line of Great Britain, 1846–1922* (1968), chap. viii; Ellis, *op. cit.*,

pp. 238–9, 411–12; Ellis, *British Railway History ...
1877–1947* (1959), pp. 17–20; Chaloner, *Crewe*, pp. xx,
42, 72–6, 135–66, 217–18, 244–7, 308–10.

20. E. T. MacDermot, *History of the Great Western Railway*
(1927–31), esp. II, chaps. i–iii, ix; Ellis, *1877–1947*, pp.
32–40.

21. Ellis, *1830–76*, pp. 177–8, 197–8, 235–7, 306–9; *1877–1947*,
part I, chap. iii, 'The Watkin Empire'.

22. Beatrice Webb, *My Apprenticeship* (Longmans, 1950), pp.
2–10, 56–63.

23. F. M. L. Thompson, *English Landed Society in the 19th
Century* (Routledge & Kegan Paul, 1963), p. 61.

24. Arthur Helps, *Life and Labours of Mr Brassey* (1872);
Charles Walker, *Thomas Brassey: Railway Builder*
(Frederick Muller, 1969).

25. R. K. Middlemas, *The Master Builders* (Hutchinson,
1963).

26. John Bateman, *The Great Landowners of Great Britain
and Ireland* (1880), p. 491; Schedule D assessments from
Leone Levi, *Wages and Earnings of the Working Classes*
(1885 ed.), as interpreted by Perkin, *Origins of Modern
English Society*, p. 431.

27. F. M. L. Thompson, *English Landed Society in the Nineteenth Century* (Routledge & Kegan Paul, 1963), pp.
264–5.

28. Cf. Webb, *My Apprenticeship*, pp. 37–49, 102–12.

Chapter Eight

A Day by the Sea

No less than big business, modern holidays were a product of the Railway Age. Until the railways came, as far as holidays were concerned there were, with very few exceptions, only two classes of people, those who were on holiday all the time and those who almost never took a holiday in the sense we understand of a period of a week or more away from work and home. For one class, the leisured aristocracy and gentry and a few 'fundholders' (rentiers) and retired merchants on their way to becoming gentry, life was one long holiday – as long as we accept that leisure is not idleness and that holidays can sometimes be strenuous and constructive. From harvest, when they collected their rents, until Christmas they would spend at home on their estates, hunting, shooting, fishing, visiting each other's houses for dinners, house parties, balls, political or other intrigue, and similar bucolic pleasures. From the New Year until late spring, if they were rich enough, they would spend in London, attending the Court, Parliament, the law courts, the theatres, coffee

houses and pleasure gardens, and enjoying each other's
company in all the social delights of the 'Season'; if they
were not so rich they would enjoy similar if less exalted
pleasures in the county town, where the Quarter Sessions,
the Assizes, and the assembly rooms fulfilled a similar
function. And the summer they would spend at an inland
spa such as Bath, Harrogate or Buxton, or, increasingly,
at a seaside resort such as Brighton or Scarborough, if
they did not go abroad to a foreign capital or watering-
place.

For what distinguished the aristocracy and gentry from
the rich city men and lawyers was not the size of their
income, which might indeed be smaller, but the fact that
it was unearned and enabled them to do as they pleased
with their time. What they liked to do might sometimes
look like hard work, from national or local government
in which they were all interested, to writing poetry or
novels like Lord Byron or Jane Austen, experimenting
with science like Henry Cavendish, with agriculture like
the Earls of Leicester, with industrial production like
Lord Dundonald, or even with aeronautics like Sir
George Cayley, but they were essentially amateurs and
did it because they liked it, like modern mountaineers or
summer school attenders. The great majority spent their
time in less creative occupations, eating, drinking,
gambling, wenching, field sports and the social round –
which was the unchallenged prerogative of a leisured
class, on holiday all the year round.

It was the third and most completely leisured phase of
their existence which was the nearest thing to a holiday
in the modern sense – the root stock, as it were, from
which the modern holiday developed.[1] It began as a
holiday from over-indulgence, taken at a mineral-water

spa for medicinal reasons, to give their systems a chance
to recuperate from the excessive eating and drinking of
the rest of the year. Mineral-water springs, for drinking
and bathing in, were originally for the genuinely sick of
all social levels: Bath and Buxton were mentioned in the
Poor Law Act of 1572 as places of resort for the sick
poor. During the sixteenth and seventeenth centuries
there was, under Continental influence, a great revival in
the belief in the therapeutic value of taking the waters,
and hundreds of springs with different mineral properties,
from the chalybeate (iron-bearing) waters of Tunbridge
Wells and Scarborough to the purgative (magnesium
sulphate) waters of Epsom, were discovered. Scarborough waters were claimed in 1669 by Dr Robert
Wittie to be 'good against diseases of the head, as the
Apoplexy, Epilepsie, Catalepsie, Vertigo', of the nerves,
lungs and stomach, asthma, scurvy, leprosy, 'the
Jaunders both yellow and black', and were 'a most
Sovereign remedy against Hypochondriack Melancholly
and Windiness'.[2] Others, such as those of Tunbridge,
Bath and Wellingborough, were prescribed for feminine
disorders and especially as an aid to fecundity.

To some of these spas, notably Tunbridge Wells, great
personages like Lord North in James I's reign and Queen
Henrietta Maria, wife of Charles I, came for treatment,
and drew after them other fashionable people who came
more for the company than for the treatment. By
Charles II's reign hundreds of courtiers and followers
attended the king and queen on their visits to Bath,
Tunbridge Wells and Epsom, many of them 'solely to
amuse themselves in good company'. Diversions and
amusements were organized to entertain them, masques
of water-nymphs at Tunbridge Wells, horse races at

Epsom, 'music, plays, promenades, balls, and perpetual amusement' at Bath, which became 'more fam'd for Pleasure than for Cures'. Under Richard Nash, its famous Master of Ceremonies from 1705 to 1758, Bath became the queen of watering places, and an annual visit there was as compulsory for the fashionable aristocracy and gentry as the London Season itself. It became a sort of aristocratic holiday camp, in which the visitors were forced by an elaborate code of rules, drawn up by Nash in 1707, to be sociable and to mix, visit and dance with each other on terms, within the age's limitations of rank and precedence, of equality.[3]

Many other spas thrived, too, and at one of these, Scarborough, in the early eighteenth century the transition took place to sea bathing. Some of the medical men, and especially the apostle of cold bathing, Sir John Floyer, had noted that 'since we live on an Island, and have the sea about us, we cannot want an excellent Cold Bath, which will preserve our Healths, and cure many Diseases, as our Fountains do'.[4] Some practitioners, like Dr Richard Russell, the later popularizer of Brighthelmstone, or Brighton, recommended drinking it as well as bathing in it, as a cure for practically every known disease from consumption to gonorrhoea.[5] Scarborough had the double advantage of a chalybeate spring discovered in 1626, and a good bathing beach. Setterington's well-known panorama of Scarborough in 1735 shows people of fashion on horseback, a sedan chair and a coach and six on the beach, and others bathing naked in the sea, some of them from a 'bathing machine' at the water's edge. In the later eighteenth century, sea bathing vied with drinking the waters at an inland spa as an aristocratic pastime. George III bathed regularly at

Weymouth to the accompaniment of fiddles. His son, the Prince of Wales, and Mrs Fitzherbert made Brighton more fashionable than Bath. The rejected Princess of Wales favoured Worthing next door, and their only daughter, Princess Charlotte, gave Southend an early burst of fame when sent there by the royal physicians at the age of five in 1807. By the early nineteenth century the inland spas were decidedly giving place to the seaside resorts as places of rest, recuperation, diversion and entertainment for the leisured rich.[6]

Continental travel, with its much greater demands on time and expense, also necessarily began with the same class. Some of them went to Baden, Spa or Montpellier for their health, some to Paris, Geneva, Rome and other capitals for their political and cultural enlightenment, and many in their youth made the Grand Tour of Europe under a 'bear-leader' or tutor, which from the late seventeenth century to the French Revolution became the favourite finishing school for the heirs to great estates. The last, of course, was much more than a holiday, and lasted many months or even years, but it established the taste for foreign travel, sight-seeing and the collection of works of art, as well as the acquisition of foreign languages and friendships, which might lead on to repeated visits. In one respect the Continental holiday could be an escape for the English gentleman from the pressures of debt or the law or both, as many found, from eighteenth-century Catholic recusants like the Blundells of Ince to Beau Brummell or George Hudson, the 'railway king'. Continental living costs, especially if you lowered your standards as you could not do at home, were considerably cheaper. But cheapness is relative to income, and Continental holidays, voluntary or enforced, were beyond the means of any but the leisured class.[7]

For the other class, all the rest from the merchant or industrialist down to the farm labourer or domestic weaver, holidays away from home and work were practically unknown. A few, like William Hutton, the Birmingham warehouseman and topographer, who made a hobby of visiting places like Blackpool and Scarborough and writing them up, or Charles Lamb, the India Office clerk who spent his single week's holiday per year visiting his literary friends, managed to get away from it all occasionally, and in the later eighteenth century the richer business and professional men began to emulate the gentry by visiting Bath, Brighton and other spas and resorts. But for the great majority a holiday was what its name implied: a holy day, a saint's day, a single day set aside for religious worship, a fast or festival of the Church, an additional Sunday, as it were, when work stopped to enable people to attend services and only incidentally to allow them to relax and enjoy themselves.

The number of these saints' days varied a good deal from one part of the country to another, but it was nowhere small, and the total amount of time off from work (the modern week-end excepted) was greater for most workers than today. The Bank of England, which was followed by most businesses in London, closed on forty-seven days in 1761, forty-four in 1808, and forty as late as 1825.[8] Outside London, in a largely rural and small-town society where agriculture was the main occupation and followed the rhythm of the seasons and most industry consisted of domestic or workshop crafts in which people worked at their own pace, odd days off were not disruptive and could be made up for before and

after. Rural industrial workers commonly took time off
to help with the harvest, and work for most of them was
intermittent, dependent on the weather, seasonal
demand, the state of the roads, which could hold up
supplies of materials in the winter, absence of wind and
water power, which could cut a vital link in the chain of
production in summer, and the casual nature of much
employment, in which many labourers were hired by the
day and rarely did a full week's work. Moreover, this
was the age of 'St Monday', and sometimes 'St Tuesday',
when domestic weavers, knitters, nailers and the like
regularly took time off for drinking, cock-fighting, hare-
coursing and other sports at the beginning of the week at
the expense of working day and night to complete their
stints at the end of it. And this pattern of life was not
unknown amongst factory and similar workers not too
dependent on powered machinery, such as potters, iron-
workers and miners, who were famous even then for
absenteeism.

There were also the ubiquitous fairs, needed in a
society where shops were few and the more durable
consumer goods, such as cloth, thread, hats, boots, pots
and pans, and even grain and cheese, were bought in
bulk once or twice a year. Some of these, such as Bartholomew and May Fairs in London, Sturbridge Fair
near Cambridge and Knott Mill Fair in Manchester,
were famous and drew traders and customers from far
and wide. But most towns of any size had at least one
fair a year, and often two or three. Macclesfield in
Cheshire had three fairs, on 6 May and 3 October and,
the main one of the year, Barnaby Fair on St Barnabas'
day in June.[9] The local fairs had two other functions
besides trading in goods. They were often hiring fairs,

where employers came to hire domestic servants, hinds or living-in farm hands, and other workers hired by the year or half-year, which necessitated the attendance of a great many people who did not want or could not afford to buy goods in bulk. And, of course, they attracted sports, games, amusements and entertainments not available at other times: side-shows, bands, puppets and the living theatre, swings and roundabouts propelled by manual or horsepower, girls running races for smocks, boys climbing a greasy pole for a flitch of bacon, men wrestling for a pig, bare-fisted prize-fighting, cock-fighting, bear-baiting, dogs killing rats, and all the other brutal sports beloved of the bloodthirsty pre-industrial English. Some, like the St Leger Fair at Doncaster, even turned into famous race meetings.[10]

Like Barnaby Fair at Macclesfield, the main fair was often associated with the saint's day of the patron saint of the parish church or of the main occupation of the town. The patron saint's day tended to be the special holiday of the year, when the fun and games were at their peak and often spilled over on to the days on either side. Hence the 'wakes' of the northern towns, from the wake, vigil or eve of a Church fast or festival, and especially that of the patron saint's day. In Lancashire and elsewhere in the north and north midlands each town had its wakes, which tended in time to become a whole week of holiday and merry-making. Manchester and the towns round about always took most of Whit week off, and still do. The 'Five Towns' (really six or seven) of the North Staffordshire Potteries supported each other's wakes, so that it was difficult to get work done in the summer when the roads were fit for getting pottery away. Josiah Wedgwood explained to his partner Thomas Bentley at the London warehouse in 1771, 'I should have sent you some good black ones this week, *if it had not been for Stoke Wake*' – Stoke was five miles away from his Burslem works. Next year he was complaining, 'the men have gone madding after these Wakes's so that we could get little done', and, later in the same year:

We are laying by for Xmass at our works. The men murmer [*sic*] at the thoughts of play these hard times, but they can keep wake after wake in summer when it is their own good will & pleasure, & they must now take a few holidays for our convenience.

And he was still complaining in 1776:

Our Men have been at play 4 days this week, it being Burslem Wakes. I have rough'd, & smoothed them over, & promised a long Xmass, but I know it is all in vain, for Wakes must be observ'd though the World was to end with them.[11]

With forty-odd saints' days spread around the year, together with fairs, harvest homes and other voluntary or involuntary holidays, there was not perhaps much call for an annual holiday of the modern kind. The decisive factor, however, was the high cost of travel and subsistence away from home. As we have seen, the stage coach and the stage waggon were beyond the means of the average wage-earner: the fare from the north of England to London would cost two or three months' wages for a labourer. Even walking cost money, in meals and lodging on the way, not to mention the time lost for work and wages. Unless they were transport workers, domestic servants, soldiers or sailors, or convicted felons, the great majority of workers never went beyond their own parish, or at most the local market town.

So that was the position up to and including most of the Industrial Revolution: holidays at home, and plenty of them, for the great majority; nothing but holidays, at home and elsewhere, for the fortunate few. Industrialism and the railways were to change all that. Industrialism was to undermine the old kind of holiday, reducing the saint's days, fairs and other casual days off almost to vanishing-point, and bringing the need for a new kind of holiday, away not only from work but from the whole environment of the industrial town. It was also, at least in the long run, to provide the wherewithal to pay for it, in higher wages and other incomes. The railways were to provide the means of getting away, first for the middle class and eventually for a large part of the working class as well. Together, industrialism and the railways were to begin that redistribution of leisure which has become much more far-reaching in its equalitarianism than the redistribution of wealth or income.

The Industrial Revolution began an attack on holidays and leisure, on pleasures and pastimes generally, more ruthless and successful than that of Praise-God Bare-bones and the Puritans of the English Revolution. The connection between industrialism and the new puritanism has never been satisfactorily explained. It is obvious that the new factory owners had an interest in keeping their establishments open and their expensive equipment in use as many full working days as possible, and they imposed stern rules of punctuality, attendance and discipline at work, with fines and other punishments for lateness, absence, or such lack of diligence as looking out of the window.[12] Long hours were nothing new, but long hours of harsh discipline behind locked doors at the rhythm of the steam engine and the behest of the overlooker were, and naturally led to protest and a demand for shorter hours, a Saturday half-day for shopping and relaxation, and eventually for annual holidays. But factory owners and workers were always a minority of the occupied population, and the successful campaign against saints' days, fairs, and brutal sports and pastimes – and against many innocent ones, too – cannot be put down to the factory system alone. It was part of the more general 'moral revolution' mentioned in Chapter Six, which affected the whole of society and transformed the whole national character.

This was the largely middle-class movement which 'bowdlerized' Shakespeare and the rest of the 'smutty' English classics, turned trousers into 'unmentionables' and everything between the ankles and the neck into 'the stomach' and then 'the liver', pregnancy into 'an interesting condition' and the privy house into the w.c. and then the lavatory (which means a place where you wash). It also put down cruel sports and pastimes, including bull-baiting, bear-baiting, cock-fighting, duelling and bare-fisted prize-fighting, all of which had officially disappeared by 1840.[13] Above all, it abolished many fairs and reduced the number of saints' days taken as holidays. The Bank of England's closing days were reduced from forty in 1825 to eighteen in 1830 and finally to four in 1834.[14] The potters had their wakes weeks gradually reduced to one, the first week in August, and lost their November hiring fair. In London the Bartholomew, May and Southwark Fairs ceased to be fairs in the commercial sense, and the journeymen's custom of taking off the eight Tyburn hanging days died out even before the public hangings ended. There was sporadic resistance to this change, by means of

absenteeism and 'going slow': a master potter complained to the Children's Employment Commission in 1843
that his workers 'often come about the premises, but will
not buckle to. If I give them a day or two at Easter, they
take a week, if at Christmas they take another week;
indeed they are not to be depended on.'[15] But in the end
the middle-class employers and moralists had their way
and imposed their own morality on the rest of the population, and the English became if not the hardest at
least the longest and most continuous workers in the
whole of Europe.

Yet the English in that same age invented the modern
holiday, simply because they needed to. As most people
came to live in the smoky industrial towns – which grew
fastest, it will be remembered from Chapter Five, in the
second quarter of the nineteenth century, just when the
railways were coming – so the need for a holiday away
from home began to be more keenly felt, first of all by the
middle class, who were also the first to benefit from the
rising incomes and standard of living of the Industrial
Revolution. The trend was set, indeed, before the railways came. James Mill, chief examiner of correspondence
at the India Office, used to take his young family in the
Regency period to Bentham's country house, Barrow
Green House in Surrey, and later Ford Abbey in Devon,
where they used to enjoy a sort of summer school with
other Benthamites.[16] Dickens took his to Broadstairs,
where he watched children building 'impossible fortifi-
cations' and elderly gentlemen 'looking at nothing
through powerful telescopes for hours'.[17] Charlotte
Brontë saw the sea for the first time at Bridlington in
1839, and was 'quite overpowered, she could not speak
till she had shed some tears . . . for the remainder of

the day she was very quiet, subdued and exhausted'.[18]

The steam-boat anticipated the railway in offering cheap and rapid transport, and was introduced to carry Londoners to Gravesend in 1815 and Southend in 1819 for as little as 3s. return, and was soon carrying them to Margate and Ramsgate in eight hours for 5s. to 7s. return. Liverpool steamers carried trippers to the Wirral for a few pence, and to Rhyl for 2s. 6d. to 4s. return. On some of these, no doubt, better-paid workers sometimes took day trips, but the longer voyages were chiefly for middle-class holiday-makers staying for at least a few days. The passengers landed at Margate and Ramsgate by the Margate Pier and Harbour Company rose from 17,000 in 1812–13 to 44,000 in 1820–1, 98,000 in 1830–1 and a record 105,625 in 1835–6.[19] The demand for seaside holidays was clearly expanding where the means of transport could meet it.

The railways therefore met a growing need. When the branch line reached Brighton, already the most popular of resorts, in 1840, it was immediately assailed by 'those swarms . . . daily and weekly disgorged upon its Steyne from the cancer-like arms of the railroad'.[20] The old coaches at their peak, thirty-six of them, carried 117,000 passengers from London to Brighton during 1835, at an average fare of 21s. inside and 12s. outside and in an average time of six hours, though it could occasionally be done in four and a half. From 1841 six trains a day each way took two and a half hours at (single) fares of 14s. 6d. first class and 9s. 6d. second; third-class passengers were carried only by the 9 p.m. goods train, but from 1843 by three trains a day, and under the 1844 Act at 1d. a mile (4s. 2d. single). In the second half of 1844 the trains carried 360,000 passengers. One excursion train of forty-four carriages drawn by four locomotives in 1846 carried 4,000 passengers.[21] In one week alone in 1859, 73,000 were conveyed. Brighton's population, already one of the fastest-growing in the country, rose from 65,569 in 1841 to 123,478 in 1901.

In spite of the railway, Brighton long remained an upper-middle-class resort. Though Queen Victoria found its inhabitants 'very indiscreet and troublesome' and never went again after 1843, Thackeray in 1845 found it full of railway directors, barristers, dandies, City men, M.P.s, well-known actors and actresses, and army officers, the West End of London by the sea.[22] Other resorts within easy reach of London were subtly graduated in the social hierarchy of middle-class values: Margate, reached by a roundabout route in 1844 and the direct line in 1863, 'merely for tradespeople', its neighbour for the somewhat higher class depicted in broad cloth and silk in W. P. Frith's painting of *Ramsgate Sands*, Dickens's Broadstairs in between, the first self-described 'select' resort for a still superior class, while Gravesend and Southend were 'low', a target for day-tripping clerks, shop assistants and artisans. Eastbourne and St Leonards, on the other hand, were for the social élite, and were developed respectively by the Duke of Devonshire and Sir James Burton, the architect, on spacious lines for a superior clientele, for whom even Brighton was too noisy and vulgar.[23] One of the functions of the railway was to separate out the classes according to taste and ability to pay, in holiday habits and resorts as in their urban and suburban homes, as we shall see in the next chapter.

This process of segregation affected in time most of the coasts of England and Wales. At least one pamphlet

opposing a projected railway to Scarborough in 1840
expressed 'no wish for a greater influx of vagrants, and
those having no money to spend',[24] but the home of sea-
bathing was reached by Hudson's York and Scarborough
line in 1845 and remained a 'fashionable watering-place'
for the millowners and industrialists of the West Riding.
In 1851 it was, with 13,000 population, the only important
resort away from the south coast, and was described by
the 1871 Census Report as 'the fair Mistress' of the
north-east coast. Tynemouth developed for the less
wealthy classes from Newcastle; Bridlington and Clee-
thorpes for those from the West Riding and Hull.
Skegness, laid out and developed by the Earl of Scarborough, only rose to fame after the railway arrived in
1875, when its population grew from 1,358 in 1881 to
3,775 in 1911.[25]

On the other side of the industrial north, Blackpool
surprisingly, with only 2,500 inhabitants in 1851, was a
more select and less populous resort than Southport,
with 5,000. A contemporary historian of Southport
expressed the great expectations from railway connection
of every seaside resort:

Upon the completion of the lines of railway which have been
sanctioned by the legislature, persons may leave the more
remote places in the kingdom without that serious consideration which under the old system of travelling was necessary.
The packet, which actually performs the passage between
Manchester and Scarisbrick Bridge (within six miles of
Southport) *in one entire day*, will, it is presumed, be converted
to some baser use; and the stage coaches, easy, safe, luxurious
vehicles, as they have been of late years, are to be superseded
by first-, second-, and third-class trains, combining the speed
of lightning with the comfort of a chair at your own homes.

The coachmen, too . . . will find their occupation gone. . . .
The road-side inns will share the fate that all similar establishments have met since the introduction of steam; and the
very turnpike roads are threatened to be usurped by green
grass and noxious weeds. Cooke, Howarth, and Fidler [coach
proprietors], farewell! the scream of the railway whistle is to
be substituted for the sonorous 'all right' of your careful
charioteers, and the progress of Southport is onward![26]

Lines from Manchester and Liverpool reached Southport in 1848, and the population bounded to 18,000 in
1871 and 48,000 in 1901, still slightly larger than Blackpool's.

Blackpool was already a well-known, if small, watering-
place in 1788 when William Hutton visited it and wrote
its history. He found 'much company, much pride, much
vulgarity accompanied with much good nature', but the
company in the four hotels and few cottages could not
have been more than about 300 and consisted, in his
daughter's words, of 'Lancashire gentry, Liverpool
merchants and Manchester manufacturers'.[27] The population of the township of Layton with Warbreck, in
which Blackpool lay, was only 473 in 1801 and still only
943 in 1831. It doubled to 1,968 in 1841, including 590
visitors, since the Census of that year was taken in June.
But it was the branch line from the Preston and Wyre
Railway, opened in 1846, which began Blackpool's rise
to fame. Cheap weekly return tickets were available from
Preston for 2s. 6d. second class and 1s. 6d. third class,
and excursions from Oldham (in 1848) for as little as '1s.
for ladies and 1s. 6d. for gentlemen'.[28] The population
rose from 2,500 in 1857 to 8,000 in 1871 and to 47,000 in
1907.

Lytham was already a well-known resort in 1821, when

it contained 1,292 people, and was described as 'a very salubrious place':

The walks are many and various for those who love exercise; the lazy will soon tire here, but the active will never be at a loss. The sands are fine – the sea breeze pleasant – the air is impregnated with health. Sailing may be had at tide time; boats are occasionally going to Preston and over the water to Southport. There are baths, showers, cold and warm for invalids. . . . The people here bathe not at all, whilst those from a distance find it a blessing. Holmes, the barber, said he had never bathed in his life, nor could I persuade him to do so. He said that he was sound in body, and if so, why dip in the briny sea at all.[29]

It was developed by the local landowners, the Clifton family, as a high-class residential resort, who also had a hand in bringing the branch line from Kirkham in 1846, after which the population grew from 2,695 in 1851 to 7,902 in 1871. St Annes-on-Sea, next door, was developed as a garden suburb for wealthy residents around the railway station by a company which took a 1,100-year lease from J. T. Talbot in 1875.[30]

Fleetwood, as we saw in Chapter Five, was a completely new town developed in the 1840s by the Talbots' neighbour, Sir Peter Hesketh-Fleetwood, as a watering-place as well as a port and fish dock. The town and esplanade were laid out by Decimus Burton, son of Sir James Burton, who designed St Leonards, who was later to plan Bournemouth. It was Sir Peter's Preston and Wyre Railway and its branches which helped to create modern Blackpool, Lytham and St Annes, and so to undermine its own competitive position as a resort. In spite of importing Zenon Vantini, proprietor of the London Euston and Victoria Hotels, to manage the leading hotel, the North Euston, and attract the 'gentry and nobility' with his famous cuisine, Fleetwood never succeeded in emulating Bournemouth and St Leonards as a resort for the élite, and became rather a poor second or third to its neighbours for holiday-makers and day-trippers from the Lancashire cotton towns.[31]

New Brighton was a similar new creation, by a speculator who bought a stretch of the Wirral coast in about 1835 for reletting in building plots for superior villas for Liverpool merchants. It soon developed into the fashionable resort which its ambitious name aimed at, before it in turn, like Blackpool, found its final role as a popular resort for working-class Lancashire.[32] It perhaps owed less than most resorts to the railway, since much of its traffic came by ferry across the Mersey, but it was equally dependent on steam transport. The North Wales coast, on the other hand, owed everything to the railway, which still dominates the front at most of the resorts, and at Colwyn Bay actually separates the town from the sea by a grass-grown embankment, much prettier than the usual row of garish hotels and amusement arcades. As a modern critic has put it, 'In 1850 the Chester and Holyhead Railway opened up an absolutely virgin coastline. . . . It was like a gold rush.' English, Scottish and later Welsh speculative builders

ran up apartment houses at competitive speeds and sooner or later a scratch town council fitted out an esplanade in front of them. . . . Thus was established the Welsh local contractor, and the Welsh town councillor, whose combined essays in the creation of 'accommodation' for visitors have done more to ruin the beauty and romance of Wales than the destructive forces of all the belligerents engaged in a world war could have done.[33]

In fact, the Welsh resorts are somewhat better looking and less commercialized than those of Lancashire or the Thames estuary, for the simple reason that they were that much further from the centres of population and had to struggle to attract 'a better class of visitor'. It is significant, too, that the further you go along the line from Prestatyn and Rhyl to Llandudno and beyond, the less 'popular' and more 'select' the resorts become, a classic case of class segregation by price. Mere villages when the railway came, Llandudno, Colwyn Bay and Rhyl grew to 9,279, 8,689 and 8,473 in 1901. Aberystwyth, the only sizeable resort in mid-Wales, had an early reputation as a watering-place for the gentry and more prosperous manufacturers of the west midlands, and had upwards of 1,500 visitors a year in the 1830s; but since it was at the end of a long and tortuous line, and was soon outpaced by the North Wales resorts, the railway did not arrive until the 1860s. In South Wales the resorts Tenby, Penarth, Saundersfoot, Barry and the Mumbles end of Swansea benefited from the broad-gauge South Wales Railway, opened in the early 1850s, but they remained small and dependent on the local industrial population of the Welsh valleys, which expanded only in the second half of the nineteenth century. Day-trippers on the seven miles of the Swansea and Mumbles Light Railway, claimed to be the first public passenger railway in the world from its horse-drawn beginnings in 1807, were characteristic of the area.

In the south-west, still more remote from the industrial areas and their growing and wealthy middle class, the resorts were small and grew comparatively slowly. Somerset's chief resort, Weston-super-Mare, got a connection to Bristol in 1841, when the population was

2,103, but, apart from horse-drawn carriages, there was only one steam train a day until 1851. Thereafter the population grew from 4,031 to 19,047 in 1901, including commuters and other well-to-do residents, but Weston's main business after 1866, when the line was doubled and a new station built with a separate excursion platform and an 'excursion hall' for cheap teas for trippers, came to be excursionists from Bristol, at 1s. 6d. return.[34] Further west, in north Devon, the railway came much later, in the 1860s, and the only sizeable resort was Ilfracombe, with 8,557 population in 1901. Still further west, Cornwall, in spite of the Great Western traffic to the Atlantic liners at Plymouth, was a foreign land to most Victorian holiday-makers, and in 1901 the only notable resort was Newquay, with no more than 3,115 inhabitants. South Devon was much better served by Brunel's magnificent if misguided atmospheric railway (soon replaced by steam loco-motives), opened between 1846 and 1848, with some of the finest coastal views of any line in the world. In con-sequence resorts which were off the line, such as Exmouth and Lyme Regis, in Dorset, lost traffic to those which were on it, such as Dawlish, Teignmouth, and above all (although on a branch line), Torquay, developed by the lord of the manor, Sir Lawrence Palk, in the 1820s, which grew from 5,982 inhabitants in 1841 to 21,657 in 1871 and 33,625 in 1907. Exmouth, an old resort which had developed during the Napoleonic Wars when the Continent was closed, tried to regain its place with a branch line in 1861, but it never quite caught up again. Lyme Regis, Jane Austen's favourite resort, did not get its branch line, in spite of numerous efforts, until 1903, and was completely left behind, until the motorist re-discovered it in the twentieth century.[35]

Further along the Dorset coast Weymouth similarly lost traffic through not getting its branch line until 1857. Bournemouth in adjacent Hampshire, on the other hand, was still a coastguard hamlet with about thirty houses, including an inn at which invalids sometimes stayed, when 'Castleman's Corkscrew', the tortuous, roundabout Southampton and Dorchester Railway promoted by a local solicitor, came to nearby Poole in 1845. Visitors had to drive the intervening five miles by horse bus. But Bournemouth had fine sands, attractive pine-clad 'chines' or gulleys in its handsome cliffs, and an enterprising landowner, Sir George Tapps-Gervis, who commissioned an architect to plan an extensive watering-place consisting entirely of detached houses standing in their own grounds. By 1850 'a number of detached villas, each marked by distinct and peculiar architectural features, have sprung into existence, affording accommodation of varying extent, so as to be suited to the convenience of either large or small families', plus hotels, a church and Westover Gardens. The work was continued after his death in 1842 by Decimus Burton, architect to the trustees, who intelligently used the existing landscape and trees to lay out walks, drives, gardens and pleasure-grounds interspersed with informally sited buildings. The result was one of the best-looking, least commercialized of seaside resorts, which attracted 'a very superior class of visitor'. It had grown to 5,896 inhabitants by 1870 when the railway was extended from Christchurch (and from Poole in 1874), whereupon the population leapt to 16,859 in the next ten years, and to 47,003 by 1901.[36]

Southampton, by contrast, which was raised by the railway into the largest oceanic passenger port, was

almost destroyed by it as a watering-place. The London
and Southampton was opened in 1838 and the following
year it was reported that 'the all devouring railway
company, and its still more grasping twin sister the dock
company, swept clean away the bath-buildings and the
bathing shores'.[37] But Southampton had a more important function to perform for holiday-makers, in the
traffic to the Isle of Wight and to the Continent. For its
size the Isle of Wight had an extraordinary number of
railways, no less than six companies sharing forty-five
and a half route miles, built mainly in the 1860s. Dependent on the ferries, and even on a horse tramway between
Portsmouth Town station and the Ryde steamers, it
attracted the lovers of solitude and scenery, like Tenny-
son, who went to live at Farringford in 1853, the Rev.
Francis Kilvert of the charming diary, who bathed naked
at Shanklin in 1874 and deplored 'the detestable custom
of bathing in drawers', and only the most determined
Victorian middle-class paterfamilias, like J. M. Richards's
father, who took the family there in 1872:

the journey [from London to Ventnor] was rarely accomplished
under five to six hours. The scramble at Portsmouth and
Ryde for tram accommodation was not an agreeable experience, and with a party of children, nurses with luggage,
perambulators and bath tubs, a man had to be something of
an organizer to get through without losing his temper and
some of his belongings as well.[38]

Shanklin and Sandown were virtually created by the
railway, and had grown from small villages to resorts of
4,533 and 5,006 inhabitants by 1907.

There were many other resorts around the coast of
England and Wales which were affected for better or worse
by the railways. Their general effect was, as with other

towns, to enlarge the bigger, better situated, more attractive and more enterprising resorts still faster than the smaller and less advantaged ones. The larger seaside resorts, notably Brighton, Hastings, Southport, Blackpool, Bournemouth, Eastbourne, Scarborough and Southend, outpaced not only their coastal rivals but also the inland spas which, like Bath, Cheltenham, Buxton and Harrogate, changed their character and became residential towns for rentiers and retired businessmen and empire-builders, with relatively few short-term holiday-makers coming to drink the waters and amuse themselves. The spas had always been by their nature aristocratic. The life of the bath, the pump room and the assembly rooms, the formal visiting and the strict etiquette imposed by the master of ceremonies, were necessarily limited to the few, who were appalled when they were invaded by middle-class interlopers and, still worse, by rail-borne day-trippers from the industrial towns. They deserted the English spas for the watering-places of the Continent.

The seaside resort, on the other hand, was potentially as democratic as cheap transport and rising living standards could make it, the attractions of sea and sands, promenades and gardens, and man-made amusements of many varied kinds strung out along the front, sometimes for several miles. At first the seaside resorts emulated the spas, with their formal etiquette and compulsory sociability. In 1856 one of the earliest self-styled social histories noted:

Watering places may be divided into two classes, (1) those in which is a circle of visiting, to which presentable people find access; (2) those without any circle of visiting or society whatever. This is an important distinction, and great effects

result from the operation of either condition. . . . Some desire
to be private, some are inadmissible. Both these classes
choose a town without a circle: to others, visiting and morning
calls, added to a sojourn by the seaside, render the place very
desirable.[39]

But visiting within a formal circle was already doomed
by the mere expansion of most resorts. It was perhaps
still possible at Blackpool in the 1830s when there were
800 to 1,000 visitors, and less than half that number at
any one time. By the later years of the century when
there were hundreds of thousands, and perhaps 50,000 at
any one time (leaving aside day-trippers), it was out of
the question.

The seaside resorts as a whole had grown up to meet a
need of industrial society as urgent as the need for Lancashire cottons or Birmingham hardware. They were,
indeed, industrial towns with a specialized product,
recreation and recuperation, made necessary by the
growth of other specialized towns and the concentration
of most of the population in an urban environment from
which periodical escape was important for mental and
physical health. As such they grew as fast as other
industrial towns, and faster than most. The 1851 Census
Report noted that the sixteen watering-places in a
classified list of 212 towns had increased in population
since 1801 by 254 per cent compared with an average of
176 per cent, and faster than any other class, including
the manufacturing, mining and hardware towns. The
four inland spas apart, the dozen coastal resorts had
grown by 314 per cent, or over fourfold, while Brighton
alone had grown nearly tenfold, faster than Bradford, the
fastest growing industrial city of the half-century. And
this was before the railways had had time to have much

effect. In the second half of the century both the number of seaside resorts and their total population increased still further. Forty-eight resorts listed by the 1871 Census increased from 430,000 in 1861 to 900,000 in 1901, by which time over 200 places were included in a current handbook of *Seaside Watering Places* (1896–7 edition).[40]

As we have seen, most of them grew up to cater for middle-class holiday-makers staying from a week to a month or more, but from an early stage a few of the most fortunate, better-paid workers emulated them. Even before the railways came, some of the Lancashire resorts were inundated with cotton workers during wakes weeks, some of whom stayed overnight, sleeping up to sixteen in a bed by means of shifts of five or six. As early as 1815 a visitor to Blackpool noticed that

Among the company are crowds of poor people from the manufacturing towns. . . . Most of them come hither in carts, but some will walk in a single day from Manchester, distant more than forty miles. . . . They rest here only three or four days . . . generally sufficient to empty their pockets. They bring tea and sugar with them, and pay ninepence a day each for lodging.[41]

In August 1824 the *Lancaster Gazette* reported of Blackpool and Lytham:

We may venture to say that these two watering places never witnessed such crowds of visitors of various social classes, as continued to flock to them in search of health, pleasure and relaxation. Cottages for six accommodated twenty or thirty, and no less than a hundred carts containing on an average eight persons each passed through Clifton Turnpike on Saturday and Sunday week.[42]

The railway made it much easier to go and return in a day, and its first effect on working-class holidays was to increase the number of day trips. A day by the sea was the Victorian worker's dream of heaven. Cheap steamer trips from London to Gravesend, Liverpool to the Wirral and Newcastle to Tynemouth were, as we have seen, within their reach from the 1820s, but it was the railway which opened the floodgates to most of the big resorts. Cheap-day tickets are as old as the railways themselves, and were offered on the Liverpool and Manchester the day after it opened in 1830 to enable people to view the line. The ordinary trains were over-crowded at traditional holiday times, and had to be doubled or trebled, as on the London to Greenwich service at Easter and Whit, 1839. The obvious solution was the cheap excursion, like Thomas Cook's celebrated trip for 1,000 temperance reformers from Leicester to Loughborough on 5 July 1841 – eleven miles and return, plus ham sandwiches, tea, dancing, cricket and games, all for 1s. – which was by no means the first. In August 1839 the organizers of a church bazaar at Grosmont in Yorkshire persuaded the local railway to offer cheap tickets on their horse-drawn trains from Whitby and Pickering. In 1840 the Manchester Sunday schools organized an excursion into the country on the Leeds and Manchester Railway for upwards of 40,000 Sunday-school children, circumventing the passenger tax by paying only for every fourth child. In the same year the Leicestershire Mechanics' Institutes organized two excursions on the Midland Railway to an Exhibition in Nottingham for about 2,000 passengers at a time, at 6s. first class, 4s. 6d. second, and 2s. third – which may have given Cook the idea. Cook continued to organize temperance excursions, but did not begin to offer pleasure trips commercially for all comers until 1845, when he organized an excursion from Leicester, Nottingham and Derby to Liverpool for 10s. to 14s., with a supplementary charge for the steamer trip to Caernarvon and the ascent of Snowdon. Most of his tours were in any case too ambitious for the working class – to Scotland from 1846 to 1863, to the Dublin Exhibition in 1853, the Paris Exhibition in 1855 – and were increasingly for the middle class.[43]

Meanwhile, Sir Rowland Hill, inventor of the penny post and now chairman of the London, Brighton and South Coast Railway, began cheap excursions in 1843. By 1844 the Board of Trade reported that 'pleasure trips prevailed extensively', and the *Railway Chronicle* commented on 'the degree in which railways are everywhere contributing to the recreation and health of all classes, by removing them in the intervals of labour from the confinement of streets and lanes to the fresh air and verdure of the country'. Works outings began to be arranged by benevolent employers, such as Horrocks, Jackson & Co. of Preston and Richard Cobden, M.P., of Crosse Hill for their cotton workers to Fleetwood in 1845 and 1846, and Heathcoats of Tiverton for their lace-workers to Teignmouth in 1854, and were encouraged by the factory inspectors, who pointed out in 1845 that 'railway carriages may be as easily hired as steamboats may be chartered for summer excursions', and praised the benevolence, practical good sense and enlightened self-interest of employers who did so.[44] Thousands of workers rushed to take advantage of both private and public excursions. In Whit week 1845 the *Manchester Guardian* estimated that 150,000 people had left Man-

chester by rail, more than had attended the traditional
festivities at the Kersal Moor races:

This is, socially speaking, one of the greatest advantages of
this annual week's holiday to a population like that of Manchester. The birth of this new and cheap means of transit is as
if the wings of the wind had been given for a weeek to the
closely confined operative, the hard-working mechanic, and
the counter-riveted shopkeeper. . . . The advantages of these
railway excursions are many; but amongst their principal
social benefits, on such occasions as the present week, we may
notice that they are greatly conducive to health, by combining
pure air with the active exercise of field sports; and that they
are eminently social and domestic in character – and in all
these respects are infinitely preferable to the tumultuous, dis-
orderly and intemperate scenes of the racecourse – scenes in
which wives and children cannot and ought not to partici-
pate.[45]

In this way the railway excursion offered the working
class some compensation for the decline of the traditional
fairs and saints' days.

The Great Exhibition of 1851, with its 5s. day trips
from the north of England for hundreds of thousands of
working men and women – the L.N.W.R. alone carried
775,000 excursionists – gave a great stimulus to excursions, which were in their heyday in the 1850s, when the
day trip from London to Brighton, Margate, Hastings or
Dover and back cost 3s. 6d. There was a set-back in the
1860s when fares rose and excursion trains were limited
to Sundays, fixed holidays and special occasions,
numbers on Brighton excursions falling to about 2,000 on
a typical summer Sunday from having totalled 6,000 or
7,000 in the 1850s, and the Royal Commission on
Railways in 1867 blamed the companies for neglecting

the mass of the people. This helped to lead to great
improvements in third-class travel and accommodation
in the 1870s, pioneered by the Midland Railway and
spreading to the other companies.

By then the tide which had been running against
holidays ever since the Industrial Revolution was
beginning to turn. The Factory Acts, which had given
children in cotton mills eight half-holidays a year in 1833
and women and teenagers (and by extension all) textile
workers the Saturday half-day in 1847, were extended to
factories and workshops in all industries in 1867. In
1871 Sir John Lubbock's Act made Boxing Day and
Easter and Whit Mondays statutory bank holidays, and
added a fourth, 'St Lubbock's Day', the first Monday in
August.[46] *The Times* grumbled that there had been

an increasing tendency of late years among all classes to find
an excuse for Holydays. Among those who are well-to-do the
annual trip to the seaside has become a necessity of which
their fathers, or at least their grandfathers, never dreamt.[47]

In 1875 the Civil Service Inquiry Commission found
that annual holidays for office workers in banks, insurance offices, stores, railway companies and other
businesses were commonly a fortnight, with three weeks
in the higher grades or for long service, and usually with
pay in the larger firms. Paid holidays for manual workers
were very unusual before the 1880s, when the practice
began to spread among a few enlightened employers,
including local government and some of the railway
companies like the L.N.W.R. Annual holidays without
pay were fairly common, especially in the north and
midlands where wakes weeks had survived. Among a few
of the more fortunate, better-paid workers, such as

cotton-mule spinners, they had long been used for holidays away from home. Henry Ashworth of Bolton told the Select Committee on the Factories Bill in 1840 that some of his workers went 'to Ireland or London or Scotland, wherever the coach or steamboat will carry them', and when Beatrice Webb visited her working-class relatives in Bacup in 1886 she found that 'parties of young men and women go off together for a week at Blackpool, sometimes on cheap trips to London'.[48]

The decisive factor, however, was not time, but money to pay for holidays away from home, and this was provided by rising real wages. These had been rising almost continuously, though at varying speeds, during and since the Industrial Revolution, at least in the progressive factory and other skilled occupations. The decisive advance, however, came only in the last quarter of the nineteenth century, when the great price fall of about 40 per cent from 1874 to 1896, coupled with slightly rising money wages, raised real wages by as much as two thirds. The better-paid working class came to have a little more to spare, to spend on Lever's soap, Harmsworth's newspapers, Woolworth's threepenny and sixpenny stores, and all the new department and chain stores of the age – and also on holidays away from home. Charles Booth in 1902 found that among all classes in London, holiday-making was 'one of the most remarkable changes in habits in the last ten years'.[49] Workers who took holidays away from home were a minority, but they were a growing minority which would turn into a majority after the First World War.

As the inland spas and seaside resorts were invaded, first by the middle class and then by working-class trippers and even resident holiday-makers, the leisured rich began to desert them, first for the smaller, more remote resorts, the Lake District and Scotland, and increasingly for the Continental spas of Germany, Austria and Switzerland and seaside resorts from Ostend, Boulogne and Deauville on the Channel to the French and Italian Rivieras. Nice had its Promenade des Anglais before the railways came, and according to Dr Arnold in 1840, 'Switzerland is to England, what Cumberland and Westmorland are to Lancashire and Yorkshire; the general summer touring place', that is, for those who could afford the time and expense for the long and tedious journey. The railways were to break even this aristocratic monopoly, and here Thomas Cook played a more important part than he did at home. He began his Continental holidays in 1855 with a grand circular tour of Antwerp, Brussels, Waterloo, Cologne, Frankfort, Heidelberg, Baden-Baden, Strasbourg and the Paris Exhibition. To the second Paris Exhibition in 1863 he conveyed 20,000 excursionists, and to the third, in 1878, 75,000 in 324 special trains. Meanwhile, he organized tours to Switzerland (1863), Italy (1864), America (1866), the Nile and Palestine (1869), Greece (1870), and round the world (1872). He was emulated by other agents, bringing holidays abroad to still wider classes. Dean and Dawson began by arranging a private excursion to Paris in 1871 from a Stockport factory. The Polytechnic Touring Association began with a holiday home at Brighton for poor members of the Polytechnic College in 1872, and was not separated from the college until 1911. Sir Henry Lunn began with a tour to Rome in 1892 for ministers of religion and their families.[50]

The English middle class, the first large group from any country with a large surplus for foreign touring, pioneered many new kinds of holiday: mountaineering and winter sports in the Alps in the 1860s, introducing skiing from Norway to Switzerland around the turn of the century, cycling tours in Holland and Belgium, walking tours in France, even motoring tours, organized by Cook's from 1902, in the last few years before the First World War. They were the Americans of the Railway Age, benefiting from the enormous sterling balances and favourable exchange rates built up by British industrial and commercial success, and turning Switzerland and the French and Italian Rivieras into English playgrounds complete with English churches, English-speaking hotel staffs and statues of Queen Victoria. In 1913 over three quarters of a million Britons left the country for Europe, most of them middle-class tourists going on holiday.[51]

Industrialism, rising living standards and the railways had brought the English full circle, from pioneering hard work and few or no holidays to pioneering shorter hours, the English week-end (*la semaine anglaise*) and holidays of every kind, at home and abroad. If at the end of the Victorian age, in Booth's London and Rowntree's York, nearly a third of the population were still living in poverty and much too poor to dream of holidays, the majority regularly left work and home at least once a year, for a month, a fortnight, a week or at least a day, according to their means and taste. As Charles Booth put it in 1902,

Amongst the upper classes holiday making has been raised to a fine art and invested with the character of a religious observance. . . . The amount of holiday taken and the way in which it is spent, from a fortnight at the seaside to a winter in Algeria or Egypt, serves very fairly to distinguish the various social grades.[52]

If we add the week or the day at Blackpool, Skegness, Weston-super-Mare or Southend, that goes for the other classes too. By the twentieth century the English, or a large part of them, were fast becoming, for a small part of each year, a nation of holiday-makers.

Some of them began to want to live at the seaside all the time. Even before the railways came, William Cobbett and Charles Lamb remarked that London stock-jobbers and brokers were living in Brighton and commuting on Monday mornings and Saturday nights by the new fast coaches of the 1820s. The railways made it possible for them to commute daily, and they could buy first-class season tickets for £12 monthly, £25 quarterly or £50 annually. Other Londoners with sufficient time and income went to live at Southend, Gravesend and other Thames estuary resorts, Liverpool merchants to New Brighton and Southport, Leeds industrialists to Harrogate, and so on. But this was only a part of the much larger migration of the wealthy middle class to the railway suburbs, as will appear in the next chapter.

Further Reading

J. A. R. Pimlott, *The Englishman's Holiday* (Faber, 1947).

J. A. R. Pimlott, *Recreations* (*A Visual History of Modern Britain* series, Studio Vista, 1968).

Anthony Hern, *The Seaside Holiday: the History of English Seaside Resorts* (Cresset Press, 1967).

G. R. Scott, *The Story of Baths and Bathing* (1939).

A. B. Granville, *The Spas of England and Principal Sea-Bathing Places* (1841).

R. S. Lambert (ed.), *The Grand Tour* (Faber, 1935).

Sir Frederick Ogilvie, *The Tourist Movement* (P. S. King, 1933).

Notes

1. Cf. J. A. R. Pimlott, *The Englishman's Holiday* (Faber, 1947), much the best book on this subject, on which this chapter heavily draws.
2. Robert Witty, *Scarborough Spaw; or, a description of the nature and vertues of the Spaw at Scarborough in Yorkshire* (1660).
3. Pimlott, *op. cit.*, chap. ii; O. Goldsmith, *Life of Richard Nash of Bath* (1762).
4. Sir John Floyer and Edward Baynard, *The History of Cold Bathing* (1702).
5. Richard Russell, *A Dissertation on the Use of Sea-Water in the Diseases of the Glands* (1755).
6. Pimlott, *op. cit.*, chap. iii.
7. *Ibid.*, chap. iv.
8. *Report of the Departmental Committee on Holidays with Pay* (1938), p. 11.
9. C. Stella Davies, ed., *A History of Macclesfield* (Manchester University Press, 1961), pp. 63–8.
10. Cf. J. A. R. Pimlott, *Recreations* (*A Visual History of Modern Britain* series, Studio Vista 1968), chap. iii.
11. N. McKendrick, 'Josiah Wedgwood and Factory Discipline', *Historical Journal*, 1961, IV. 46.
12. Cf. S. Pollard, 'Factory Discipline in the Industrial Revolution', *Economic History Review*, 1963, 2nd series, XVI. 254f., and *The Genesis of Modern Management* (Penguin, 1965), chap. v.
13. Cf. M. J. Quinlan, *Victorian Prelude: a History of English Manners, 1700–1830* (New York, 1941), Muriel

Jaeger, *Before Victoria* (1956) and F. K. Brown, *Fathers of the Victorians: the Age of Wilberforce* (Cambridge, 1961), all of which, however, put down the moral changes to the personal influence of the Evangelicals and do not see the connection with industrialism. For the latter, see Pollard, *Management*, chap. 5, iv, 'The assault on working-class morals'.

14. *Report . . . on Holidays with Pay*, *loc. cit.*

15. Report of Children's Employment Commissioners, Parliamentary Papers, 1843, XIII–XV, p. 81.

16. J. S. Mill, *Autobiography* (1873, World's Classics edition, 1958), pp. 46–7.

17. Walter Dexter, *The England of Dickens* (Palmer, 1925), p. 124.

18. Mrs Gaskell, *Life of Charlotte Brontë* (Milford, 1919), pp. 108–9.

19. Pimlott, *Holiday*, p. 77.

20. Elizabeth Stone, *Chronicles of Fashion from the time of Elizabeth to the early part of the nineteenth century* (2 vols., 1845), II. 294.

21. H. P. White, *A Regional History of the Railways of Great Britain*, II, *Southern England* (Phoenix House, 1961), pp. 78–82.

22. *Punch*, 1845.

23. W. Ashworth, *The Genesis of Modern British Town Planning* (Routledge & Kegan Paul, 1954), p. 39; Pimlott, *Holiday*, p. 114.

24. George Knowles, quoted by K. Hoole, *A Regional History of the Railways of Great Britain*, Vol. IV, *The North East* (1965), p. 79.

25. G. H. J. Dutton, *Skegness and District* (1922), pp. 52–3.

26. Frank Robinson, *A Descriptive History of the Popular Watering Place of Southport* (1848), p. 49.

27. Ll. Jewitt, ed., *Life of William Hutton* (1872), p. 207; W. Hutton, *A Description of Blackpool in Lancashire; fre-*

quented for Sea Bathing (1789); C. H. Beale, *Reminiscences of a Gentlewoman of the Last Century* [Catherine Hutton] (1891); W. J. Smith, 'Blackpool: A Sketch of Its Growth, 1740–1851', *Transactions of Lancashire and Cheshire Antiquarian Society*, 1959, LXIX. 70f.

28. Smith, *loc. cit.*

29. Quoted by John Porter, *The History of the Fylde of Lancashire* (Fleetwood and Blackpool, 1876, reprinted Wakefield, 1968), p. 440.

30. *Ibid.*, pp. 429–53.

31. J. H. Sutton, 'Early Fleetwood, 1835–47' (unpublished M.Litt. dissertation, University of Lancaster, 1968), esp. pp. 126–7, 222.

32. Ashworth, *op. cit.*, p. 39.

33. Howard Marshall in Clough Williams-Ellis, ed., *Britain and the Beast* (Dent, 1937), p. 166; Pimlott, *Holiday*, p. 123.

34. D. St. J. Thomas, *A Regional History of the Railways of Great Britain*, I, *The West Country* (1963), pp. 9–10.

35. *Ibid.*, pp. 40–1, 53; Ashworth, *op. cit.*, p. 44.

36. Thomas, *op. cit.*, p. 138; Ashworth, *op. cit.*, pp. 42–3.

37. Pimlott, *Holiday*, p. 110.

38. White, *op. cit.*, pp. 122–3, 145–50; William Plomer, ed., *Kilvert's Diary, 1870–79* (Cape, 1956), pp. 249–50.

39. George Roberts, *Social History of the Southern Counties of England* (1856), p. 559.

40. Listed in Pimlott, *Holiday*, Appendix I.

41. Richard Ayton, *A Voyage Round Britain undertaken in the summer of 1813* (8 vols., 1814–25), II. 102–5; Smith, *loc. cit.*, p. 84.

42. *Lancaster Gazette*, 21 August 1824; Smith, *loc. cit.*, p. 91.

43. Information kindly supplied by Thomas Cook and Son Ltd.

44. Sutton, *op. cit.*, pp. 226–7; Thomas, *op. cit.*, plate 28; Pimlott, *Holiday*, pp. 90–4.

45. Quoted by Pimlott, *Holiday*, pp. 94–5.

46. *Twentieth-Century Dictionary of National Biography*, *sub*. Sir John Lubbock.
47. Quoted by Pimlott, *Holiday*, p. 142.
48. Select Committee on the Regulation of Mills and Factories, Minutes of Evidence, Parliamentary Papers, 1840, X; B. Webb, *My Apprenticeship* (1926), p. 145.
49. C. Booth, *Life and Labour of the People of London*, XVIII (1903), p. 50.
50. Pimlott, *op. cit.*, p. 158.
51. *Ibid.*, p. 261.
52. *Ibid.*, p. 158.

Chapter Nine

The Commuter Age

WE live today in the commuter age. Over half of us live in towns of over 50,000, and more than one in three in great conurbations of from nearly a million to over eight million people. And many of us who live in smaller places, even of the quarter of the population who live in rural areas, work or go to school in large towns and cities. Most of us live a bus-, car- or train-ride from our place of work or education, and have to commute daily. Strictly speaking, commuting means travelling daily by *train*. *Commuter* is an American word, invented in the last century, for a season-ticket holder. The railways in Britain orginated the practice, though they did not use the word 'commutation ticket', and both commuting and the growth of far-flung suburbs were a product of the Railway Age.

Before the suburban railways came, even London (the City and Metropolitan Police area), with $3\frac{1}{4}$ million people in 1867, was physically quite small, stretching

scarcely more than four miles in each direction from
Charing Cross, from Camden Town and Hackney in the
north to Clapham in the South, and from Paddington and
Kensington in the west to Stepney and Greenwich in the
east. By 1901 Greater London, with 6½ million, just twice
the population, had spread over an area ten times as
large, stretching from Barnet, Enfield and Loughton in
the north to Croydon and Sutton in the south and from
Harrow, Hounslow and Kingston in the west to Barking,
Woolwich and Bromley in the east – though of course
there were large empty spaces in between. And even this
huge area did not include all those who worked in
London: some commuters were travelling from as far
afield as Watford and Epping, Southend and Brighton, as
far indeed as any do today.

In other regions commuting was on a smaller but still
significant scale. Manchester cotton merchants and millowners went to live out at Altrincham, Wilmslow or
Alderley Edge, Liverpool merchants and shipowners at
New Brighton, West Kirby or Southport, Newcastle coal
factors at Hexham or Tynemouth, Birmingham ironmasters and factory-owners at Solihull or Stratford,
Bristol merchants at Bath, Clevedon or Weston-super-
Mare, and so on. Everywhere the suburban railways were
making it possible for the well-to-do middle class to live
miles from their work in the fresh air of the country or at
the seaside, and for an increasing number of lower
middle-class clerks and even well-paid artisans to live on
the fringes of the built-up areas. At the same time horse-
buses, numerous from about the middle of the century,
and horse-trams from the 1870s, sorted out the classes
within the built-up areas into distinct sections, according
to social status and the rent they could afford to pay. The

horse-buses were comfortable but expensive and served a wider area, thus enabling the middle class to live further out, though, since they averaged only about four miles an hour, not so far out as the railway commuters. The trams were cheaper but generally restricted to a few roads and areas, and increasingly served the lower middle and upper working class in a more restricted area. Generally speaking, the semi-skilled factory workers and the unskilled and casual labourers, such as dockers and market porters, never used any form of transport, since they were too poor to pay the fares and they had to live close to their work to be sure of getting there early enough to get any work at all. Thus the suburban railways, the buses and the trams all helped to segregate the classes into separate residential areas, where they came to live their own distinct kind of life, with important consequences for the whole of society.

Suburbs, of course, were not new, and migration to the edge of town and into the countryside in search of health and fresh air began long before the railways came. John Aston's *Manchester Guide* in 1804 noted that 'many persons whose business is carried on in the town reside some little way from it that the pure breath of heaven may blow freely upon them' – in suburbs of handsome dwellings and commanding views like Ardwick Green and the Crescent above Salford. Everywhere the increased wealth produced by the Industrial Revolution enabled many merchants and manufacturers, lawyers, engineers and accountants to afford saddle-horses or carriages and to live on the more salubrious edge of town. Some even went to live in the countryside on new estates, without giving up business: Josiah Wedgwood bought a country seat at Barlaston ten miles from his potteries, and Matthew Boulton one at Great Tew in Oxfordshire, over fifty miles from his Soho works. The long-distance travellers before the railways came, however, were few, and most of them were probably anticipating retirement from business either for themselves or for their families. The most common pattern for the successful business or professional man was to build a detached house on the edge of what was still in every case except that of London a comparatively small town. In Manchester, the biggest town outside London, as late as 1850 the best middle-class residential areas, Buile Hill, Higher Broughton, Cheetham Hill, Oxford Road and Fallowfield, were all within two or three miles of the centre, and even the detached suburban villages of Withington and Didsbury, served by horse omnibuses, within four or five miles. The flight of the wealthier classes to the suburbs, or into inner suburban enclaves behind walls and toll-gates like Victoria Park set up under a trust in 1837, had begun, but it had still not taken them out of touch with the town which they still dominated by their physical presence.

It was the railways which were to break up the compact, if immensely swollen, towns of the Industrial Revolution and scatter many of their inhabitants, beginning with the wealthiest, over the surrounding countryside, like seeds from an exploding seed-pod. The early railways were too concerned with the basic task of connecting up the towns themselves with each other and with the ports and markets to think about suburban services. Only a few far-sighted railwaymen could envisage the possibility of large numbers of people living a railway journey from their work, like the editor of the *Railway Times* who asked in 1850 why 100,000

Londoners could not live further out and be brought
in by train:

> If house rent, twenty miles from the City, and travelling by
> rail, could be made to be not more than equivalent to house
> rent in crowded streets, is it not clear that the same motives
> which prompted the citizen to fix his habitation within an
> hour's walk of his place of business, would at once induce him
> to exchange the dirty suburb for the pure and invigorating
> atmosphere of the country? Who, for instance, would prefer
> living at Paddington, Islington, Kingsland or Walworth, if he
> could for the same cost reside at Kingstead, Banstead Downs,
> Stanmore Common, Bushey Heath, Northfleet, Slough,
> Epsom, Hainault Forest, Barnet or Reigate? These pleasant
> salubrious sites are all accessible by railway and are within
> half an hour's ride of the metropolis.[1]

Yet the upper-middle-class towndwellers were quick to
seize the opportunity for themselves. The first lines from
Manchester to the south – main lines to Birmingham and
Chester – were opened in 1839 and 1849. Within a
decade of the latter a high-class suburb had developed at
Alderley, fifteen miles out, where 'the greater part of the
edge is covered by gardens and villas', while at Altrincham and Bowden, ten miles down the Chester line, broad
sweeping avenues of detached houses had grown up. And
around the stations in between – Sale and Stretford on the
Altrincham line, Heaton Moor, Cheadle Hulme,
Bramhall and Wilmslow on that to Alderley – suburbs of
substantial though not quite so imposing houses grew up.
Other main lines as they developed came to share this
commuter traffic and suburban growth, though later and
on a smaller and less precisely graduated scale. The
Warrington line from 1873 initiated the growth of
Urmston and Flixton, the Bury line from 1879 that of

Heaton Park, Crumpsall and Prestwich, while the belated
Midland connection to London, extended across south
Manchester to the new Central Station in 1880, began
suburban development of Heaton Mersey and Cheadle
Heath and gave a new and powerful boost to the 'horse-
bus villages' of Chorlton, Withington and Didsbury,
which increased in population by 50 per cent during the
next decade.[2]

By the end of the century Manchester and Salford had
been classically 'suburbanized', over an area as wide as
today, though without the 'infilling' of the areas in
between the railway stations since brought about by the
motor-bus and car. The inner core was given up to shops,
offices and the huge warehouses of the cotton trade.
Around this was a tight ring of mills, factories, railway
yards and sidings, interspersed with the worst slums.
Immediately surrounding this was a wider ring of more
substantial but bleak and monotonous terraces of
working-class housing, graded from the two-up-and-
two-down cottages of the labourers to the bay-windowed
houses of the artisans. Further out still but still contiguous was a broken ring of lower middle and middle-
class estates, graded from pleasant terraces for clerks and
small professional people to substantial if now slightly
ageing villas for businessmen of moderate wealth.
Finally, there were the railway suburbs, strung like beads
along the railway lines, each a compact self-contained
village within walking distance of the station. The nearer
ones were characterized by substantial semi-detached
houses, much larger, more elegant and imposing than
their twentieth-century namesakes but still instantly
recognizable from their lack of ground space for garages
and the like, the further ones by their handsome if

ponderous villas, often with stables and coach-houses, now turned into garages. Some of the inmost railway suburbs were connected by ribbon development along the horse-bus or tram route to town, but for the most part they, like the outer ones, were still surrounded by green fields, woods and heaths. The city and its suburbs were like a complex planetary system, the 'sun' dense and massive at the core and shading to a more open texture at the expanding margin, and surrounded by satellites of a size and density which varied with the distance from the parent body.

The same process affected all the great cities. Already in 1859, according to the historian of Liverpool, Thomas Baines, 'Comparatively few large and beautiful dwelling houses are now built in town, while thousands are scattered over the sea-shore from Southport to Hoylake', and the wealthy were deserting Abercromby Square for the 'pleasant villages from Bootle to Aigburth'. This migration, however, was mainly due to the steamboat and the horse-bus and -carriage traffic, and most of it was concentrated within four miles of the centre, especially by way of the Bold Street–Church Street–Lord Street shopping avenue to the wealthy southern suburbs. The railway suburbs developed only from the 1870s onwards, when the lines and stations were completed and the companies began to provide suburban train services and special fares.[3]

In Birmingham, too, the early inner suburbs of New Hall, Edgbaston and Islington were a product of the private carriage and omnibus, as were the slightly later and less exclusive ones at Small Heath, Sparkbrook, Aston and Ashstead. The railway suburbs came in the last quarter of the century – Selly Oak, Bournville and King's

Norton along the Birmingham West Suburban line authorized in 1871, Handsworth, Perry Bar and Harborne along lines opened in 1874, Hay Mills, Acock's Green and Yardley a little later. Many of these were deliberately restricted in growth by railway policy and local feeling: the *Birmingham Daily Mail* remarked of Acock's Green and Olton in 1903 that for a long time 'a railway service suited to the few rather than the many, kept them select, and the absence of any other popular means of conveyance adapted to the needs of the multitude enabled both places to set at defiance the advancing tide from a great town'.[4]

In Glasgow there was a curious inversion of the normal pattern, and the railways played a much smaller part. Prosperous inner middle-class suburbs did develop at Langside, Pollokshields and Kelvinside within three miles of the centre, but the suburban railways came late, mainly in the 1890s, and Glasgow never developed the suburban 'explosion' of other cities in the Railway Age. Instead, as great steel, engineering and chemical works were built on the outskirts, the city itself became a dormitory for workers travelling daily, on foot and by tram, to the outskirts, and when workmen's trains were at length provided towards the end of the century, the flow was mainly outward in the morning and inward in the evening.[5]

London was of course the prime example of commuting, then as now. The City in a sense had always had suburbs, at least since the early Middle Ages: Southwark, the East End, the Strand, all the 'Bills of Mortality' without the walls, began as suburbs from which people generally walked into the Cities of London and Westminster. In 1836, when the first London railway, to Greenwich, was opened, about 100,000 people walked daily over London Bridge in both directions, and probably as many more into the City from other sides. The Thames steamboats, which expanded in the 1820s and 1830s, were much used for commuting, and season tickets could be had from places as far away as Gravesend for 6 guineas a year. The short-stage coaches, some 600 of them in the 1820s making about 1,800 daily journeys with four to six inside and as many again on top, brought wealthy citizens at 1s. 6d. or 2s. a head from as far afield as Paddington, Edmonton, Clapham and Hammersmith. These were supplemented from 1828 and later overtaken by the 'sixpenny omnibus', as it became in the 1830s and 1840s, about 620 of them in 1838 (as against about 200 remaining short-stage coaches), which carried fourteen to twenty passengers, mainly of the lower middle class, City clerks and the like, from the inner suburbs. By the mid-1850s when most of the buses, nearly 600 out of about 700, were monopolized by the French-owned London General Omnibus Company, the basic fare had come down to 3d. or 4d., and the route mileage had spread over a wider area, but they were still out of reach of the bulk of the population. Out of about a quarter of a million daily travellers into the City in 1854, about 200,000 still went on foot and only about 26,000 by bus, while 15,000 went by steamboat, from points as far up and down river as Greenwich and Richmond. Only between 6,000 and 10,000 went by rail, since the railway companies still thought chiefly in terms of main-line haulage of passengers and goods, and only a few provided enough early-morning trains, still less the cheap fares, to attract large numbers of commuters. In a city of three million people the horse-bus for the middle class and walking for the great majority were still the chief means of getting to work.[6]

The main-line railway companies around mid-century became more concerned to reach the heart of London. The main-line termini, especially on the north side, where property values were higher, had been deliberately sited on the edge of the built-up area. Paddington (1838), Euston (1837) and King's Cross (1852) had all been built within sight of green fields, woods and waving corn. As the streets of London became congested with horse traffic they joined forces with a movement for *urban* rather than suburban railways, for the movement of people and goods *within* the built-up area. The London and North Western's solution was to foster a separate company, later called the North London Railway, to build a line from Camden Town north of Euston right along the northern edge of the built-up area, finally swinging down via Bow to reach the West India Docks and Fenchurch Street. Opened in 1850, it was connected next year to the L.N.W.R. at Hampstead Road (Chalk Farm), and so joined the main line to the north-west. Though originally intended for goods, it soon developed a heavy inner suburban traffic, supplementing the horse-buses from Hampstead, Camden Town, Islington and Hackney; but though the L.N.W.R. offered a free pass for eleven years to anyone taking a house at not less than £50 rental at Harrow, and for twenty-one years at Tring and Leighton, very few were taken up and suburban traffic from the main-line stations was very light. Nor was it much increased by its ally, the North London's branch to a City terminus at Broad Street in 1865.[7]

The more successful and spectacular solution, adopted by the Great Western, Great Northern and later the

Midland Railways, was the building of the first underground railway in the world. They set up the separate Metropolitan company, opened from Paddington and King's Cross to Farringdon Street in the City in 1863, and extended to Moorgate in 1865. This was a remarkable piece of engineering by the 'cut-and-cover' method, which involved digging a vast trench along the main street, building a brick-arch tunnel up to a hundred feet wide, and re-laying the road on top of it. The trains, after an unsuccessful experiment with a fireless locomotive powered by pre-heated firebrick called 'Fowler's ghost' after the engineer, were hauled by ordinary steam engines, and additional broad-gauge lines were provided to take the G.W.R. trains on from Paddington. The Metropolitan, however, was an independent company, under the chairmanship successively of two of the most powerful personalities in the railway industry, John Parson and Edward Watkin, which concentrated on its own 'street traffic' and the suburban traffic from its feeder lines to Hammersmith (1864), Kensington (1868) and Swiss Cottage (1868). This naturally led to quarrels with the main-line companies, especially the Great Western, only partially settled by the building of the 'widened lines' alongside the original track, opened in 1868, which also served trains from the new London, Chatham and Dover Railway. The Midland Railway, which reached St Pancras in 1868, also fed trains on to the Metropolitan, and was soon providing suburban services from Camden Town, Kentish Town, Hendon, Hampstead and Tottenham.[8]

Within the built-up area and its growing extensions to the north-west and the south-east, 'the Drain', as the Underground was called, was in spite of its smoke and

stench a tremendous success, and was promptly emulated
by others. A Select Committee of the House of Lords in
1863 recommended the connecting-up of all the main-
line termini by means of an underground 'inner-circuit'
formed by the Metropolitan from Paddington to Moorgate 'and connecting the extremities of those lines by a
line on the north side of the Thames'.[9] To construct this
a separate company, the Metropolitan District, was set
up, with overlapping directors and the clear intention of
amalgamating with the Metropolitan. It was beset by
financial difficulties, however, and the 'inner circuit' –
the modern Inner Circle – was not completed until 1884,
by which time the two companies, the Metropolitan
under Watkin and the District (as it was now called)
under J. S. Forbes, had become involved in the larger
rivalry between their chairmen's main-line companies,
the South Eastern and the London, Chatham and Dover.
The rivalry bordered on the ridiculous and even on the
violent: in 1884 the District chained a train to a disputed
siding and the Metropolitan sent three locomotives to
try, unsuccessfully, to pull it away.[10] The Metropolitan,
with its main-line connections, was twice as successful in
terms of passengers, receipts and dividends as the
District, which suffered from the fact that the main-line
companies on the south side all had termini within
walking distance of the centre and so it could attract little
suburban traffic except from its own West London
Extension to Kensington (1869), where it connected
with the L.N.W.R. and the G. W. R. The completion of
the Inner Circle as such was a failure, both financially and
in practice. As one of its joint engineers said, it was
'rather the joining of two parallel lines than the completion of a circle'.[11] The two parallel lines in 1875

carried about 72 million passengers a year (two thirds of them on the Metropolitan), about half the urban and surburban railway passengers of the London area.[12]

The other half was divided between the southern and the north-eastern main-line companies, which had the advantage of reasonably central termini. On the south side of the river the London to Greenwich had achieved a coup right at the start with its elevated track on a brick-arched viaduct to London Bridge (1836), always the busiest commuter station for the City, which came to serve also the South Eastern and the Brighton lines. Between 1850 and 1858 the number of passengers using it rose from $5\frac{1}{2}$ million to $13\frac{1}{2}$ million a year, and 266 out of 320 daily trains carried suburban traffic. Waterloo, opened in 1848, brought in commuters on the London and South Western from Putney, Barnes, Richmond and Twickenham, and on the London and Southampton from Clapham and Wimbledon. Victoria Station was projected in the 1850s to serve the excursion traffic from the West End of London to the Crystal Palace when the latter was moved out to Sydenham, but by the time it was opened in 1860 the excursion traffic had fallen off and, connected to the Brighton and Chatham lines, it began its modern role as a commuting and continental station. The other southern companies saw the advantage of cross-river termini, and the South Eastern got powers to build Charing Cross (opened in 1864) and Cannon Street (1866), and the London, Chatham and Dover to build Ludgate Hill (1866). Together with connecting lines to the west linking up with the Kensington and Richmond line and the L.N.W.R. lines to Willesden and beyond, these southern termini were capable of serving commuters from a huge semicircle of suburbs running round from north-west Kent to west Middlesex.[13]

The most vigorous suburban railway expansion came on the north-eastern edge of London. From 1862 the newly amalgamated Great Eastern Railway pursued a deliberate policy of developing the suburban lines out through Stratford, Walthamstow and Hackney to Ilford, Loughton, Chingford, Edmonton and Enfield, all converging on their new terminus at Liverpool Street (1874). With cheap workmen's trams and half-fare trains for clerks, this quarter of the compass was to have the most densely packed working and lower-middle-class suburbs and to provide more railway commuters than any other. The London County Council report on Workmen's Trains in 1892 was to describe the Great Eastern as 'especially the workman's London railway – the one above all which appears to welcome him as a desirable customer'.[14] In the solidly working-class area of Edmonton and Walthamstow the population increased tenfold between 1861 and 1901, when the north-eastern suburbs housed 50 per cent more than any other quadrant and the housing densities and rate of immigration were twice as great.[15]

This was the most spectacular example of that outward movement of the metropolitan population which has gone on ever since. Edmonton in the 1860s, according to the general manager of the Great Eastern, who lived there himself, had been 'a very nice district indeed, occupied by good families, with houses of £100 to £250 a year, with coach-houses and stables, and gardens, and a few acres of land'.[16] As the workmen and clerks moved in, the well-to-do sold their few acres, at a considerable profit, for building-sites for terraced or semi-detached houses, and moved further out. Meanwhile, the central

areas began to lose population, by night at least, to the
suburbs: the residential population of the City itself fell
from 128,000 in 1851 to 75,000 in 1871, and that of
Westminster and the West End began to decline in the
1860s and fell more rapidly from the 1870s. Not only did
the lost residents move out to the suburbs, but most of
the newcomers to the metropolis, still more numerous,
moved directly there, to swell the outer fringe, rather than
going first to live in the centre. As a result the growth of
London, like that of other large cities but on a larger
scale, took the form of a wave travelling outwards from
the centre, like the ring from a stone thrown into a pond
and producing a spectacular if short-lived burst of
population increase in each circle of suburban census
districts as it passed by. Between 1861 and 1871 nine of
the twenty-two towns in England and Wales which grew
by more than 30 per cent (some of them much more)
were the London suburbs of Battersea, Croydon,
Hackney, Hammersmith, Hampstead, Islington, Kensington, Lewisham and Poplar. Between 1871 and 1881
six of the twenty were Camberwell, Deptford, Leyton,
Stoke Newington, Tottenham and West Ham. Between
1881 and 1891, ten of the fourteen were East Ham,
Enfield, Hornsey, Fulham, Walthamstow, Wandsworth,
Willesden, Wimbledon, Wood Green and Woolwich.
Between 1891 and 1901 four out of the eight were
Edmonton, Gillingham, Ilford and Wimbledon again
(and three of the others were suburbs of Birmingham or
Liverpool). And between 1901 and 1911 two out of the
three were Ealing and Hendon, and the third was
Southend, London's East End by the sea.[17] Altogether,
while the population of inner London (the L.C.C. area)
between 1871 and 1901 increased by less than half, from

3.2 million to 4.6 million, that of Outer London, almost
entirely made up of railway suburbs, increased more than
threefold, from 623,000 to over 2.0 million.[18]

Yet all this outer suburban development must be seen
in perspective. In the first place the majority of Londoners continued to live within the, admittedly growing,
built-up area and either to walk or to go by horse-bus to
their work. From 1870 onwards the horse-buses were
joined by the horse-trams which, though banned from the
central streets themselves, served all the inner suburbs
from Wood Green and Edmonton in the north to Brixton
and Dulwich in the south. In the last quarter of the
century, with the great fall in the price of grain and horse
fodder, the trams and buses held their own and, with
their much smaller capital outlay and declining costs,
were able to pay higher dividends than the railways.
They had, of course, the important advantage of being
able to pick up and set down their passengers anywhere
on their route, their fares were cheap and kept down by
competition – and still cheaper on the trams with their
wooden benches and larger numbers of passengers than
on the buses with their upholstered seats and higher-class
clientele – and they served the more densely packed inner
suburbs. In 1875 the buses carried about 70 million
passengers, the trams about 50 million, as against the
local railways' 400 million. By 1896 the buses carried 300
million, and the trams 280 million, compared with 600
million railway passengers.[19]

In the second place, not all this growth of traffic by
road and rail was for commuting purposes between
centre and suburbs. A great deal of it, particularly on the
buses and the underground, was purely urban, carrying
business and professional men and – until the telephone

developed in the last few years of the century – messengers and porters around the central streets. Another large
part consisted, especially as the department stores and
early chain stores developed in the 1870s and 1880s, of
well-to-do shoppers and sightseers from the suburbs in
the middle of the day, and another of week-end and
holiday trippers to London parks, commons, museums,
exhibitions and beauty spots. Still more was within and
between the suburbs themselves, which developed a life
of their own, with work journeys and shopping trips for
the majority of the population who did not commute to
the centre. In 1906 about 410,000 passengers arrived in
central London daily by rail, perhaps 250,000 early
enough to be considered commuters – a vast tide of
people, but still no more than one in four of the working
population of the inner and outer suburbs.[20]

In the third place, most of the railway and especially
the long-distance commuters were rich upper middle-
class and substantial middle-class people, who could
afford the fares, and still more the time, for commuting.
That is why most of the outer suburbs, although growing
impressively after the railways reached them, remained
fairly small, loosely settled communities compared with
the inner ones until the present century. Those who
travelled furthest, the City merchants, bankers, insurance
underwriters and stockbrokers with perhaps £1,000 to
£5,000 a year and first-class season tickets from Epping or
Epsom, Kingston or Chislehurst, wanted and could
afford a villa with twenty or thirty acres, up to a dozen
servants, and a carriage and riding horses. Every commuter of this kind implied, with his family, household
domestics and the shopkeepers, craftsmen and other
service personnel to meet their daily needs, at least a

score of other, non-commuting residents in the neighbourhood. Even a few dozen such commuters, departing
from one station, could represent a considerable village
or small town, quite apart from any rural market or
industry which it might already possess. Further in, in
suburbs like Willesden, Highgate, Richmond, or Dulwich, would live the lesser City and larger professional
men, with perhaps £500 to £1,000 a year, a villa with one
or two acres, three to six servants, and a riding horse or a
gig. Still further in, in suburbs like Swiss Cottage, Earls
Court, Clapham or New Cross, on the edge of the built-
up area would live the small business and lesser professional men on £250 to £500 a year, with substantial
detached or terraced houses overlooking the green or
common, two or three servants, and the choice between
commuting by rail or by horse-bus. Further in still,
within the built-up area, Camden Town, Somers Town,
Islington, Pimlico and Newington,were the inner and increasingly dense circles of clerks, artisans, and other skilled
workers, on salaries or wages of 30s. to £4 a week,
who could just barely afford to take the bus into, or
more commonly the tram to the edge of, the City, but
often preferred to walk. Finally, there were the densely-
packed neighbourhoods on the margins of the City and
the West End themselves, Shoreditch, Bow, Stepney,
Lambeth and the Borough, crowded with unskilled labourers, porters, dockers and other casual labourers, on
earnings of 15s. to 20s. a week, who could not afford
either the money or the time to ride to work. As the chairman of an L.C.C. committee dealing with the housing
problem put it in 1899, the railway network had become
'an imperfect system of transit devised almost entirely for
middle -and upper-class requirements'.[21]

The only substantial exception to this pattern was in the north-eastern quadrant. There the Great Eastern, partly in pursuit of suburban traffic of any kind and partly by the accident that, in order to gain parliamentary assent to its Liverpool Street terminus, which entailed clearing a large area of working-class housing, it had been forced to provide workmen's trains at the unheard-of rate of a 2d. return for journeys of up to ten miles. This had encouraged the development of very large working-class suburbs at such places as Ilford, Leytonstone, Walthamstow and Tottenham, and of lower middle, mainly clerical, class suburbs at Chingford, Enfield and Wood Green beyond. In that quarter the circles of better-class suburbs were pushed further out, to Epping and Barking, and there were fewer of them. Only Woodford within the quadrant formed an island of superior middle-class property. In 1901 the Great Eastern brought in 20,000 out of the 27,600 workmen commuting on twopenny tickets, 41,000 out of the 114,000 on workmen's tickets of any price (up to 11d.), and over 14,000 out of the 18,000 clerks and others commuting on half-price tickets. Altogether nearly half, 55,000 out of 117,600 daily arrivals, were on cheap tickets intended for workmen and clerks, as against a fifth to a third on other lines.[22]

It might be thought from this that the rigorous segregation of Greater London's population into single-class suburbs was not only caused by the railways but was the result of deliberate policy. It is true that all the railway companies preferred the wealthier first- and second-class commuters and sometimes took special steps to encourage them, such as offering them cheap or even free season tickets for a period after moving out, and that some, like the Great Western or the L.N.W.R., actively discouraged lower-middle-class and working-class commuters by offering few or no cheap trains at an early enough hour for them. Yet even the Great Eastern had not set out to encourage such segregated working-class suburbs: the policy was thrust upon it by Parliament. Indeed, the company complained that it made a loss on the two-penny workmen's trains, and that the half-fare trains scarcely covered their cost. It would obviously have preferred a larger first- and second-class commuter traffic and, as successive general managers complained, the cheap workmen's fares to Edmonton and Walthamstow 'utterly destroyed the neighbourhood for ordinary passenger traffic', while the extruded middle-class residents 'do not move further down the Great Eastern line, they move over to the Brighton and other companies' lines, where the workman does not exist to such an extent'.[23]

The truth was that the railway companies themselves were not the principal agency in determining which classes should live where. Except in the sense that railway lines with frequent early-morning services were a necessary factor in the growth of suburbs beyond the reach of the horse-bus and -tram, they were not even the principal cause of suburban growth. No suburban railway was deliberately built ahead of need. Suburbs grew up around existing towns and villages or in a few cases such as Anerley around country stopping places, on main lines, or else lines were built out to already existing suburbs previously dependent, albeit for a smaller traffic, on the short-stage coach or the bus. Under the existing state of the law almost no railway stood to gain from suburban growth except in the traffic itself: only the Metropolitan

Railway, for reasons connected with the rehousing of evicted tenants in central London, was allowed to hold on to and redevelop or sell at a profit land purchased under its Act, and in other cases all the increased land values created by the railway went to the adjacent landowners (who admittedly might include railway directors and officials in their private capacity). Thus the railway companies as such had a smaller interest in suburban development than might be thought, especially as suburban traffic operation was expensive, locking up capital in rolling stock only used at peak hours, and inconvenient, interfering with the more profitable main-line passenger and goods traffic. If at the same time the suburban traffic was at cut-rate fares for workmen and clerks, it was not even adequate compensation for what the Great Eastern came to call its 'suburban incubus'.[24]

What really determined the segregation of the classes in distinct suburbs was the cost (in time as well as money) of transport, by other means as well as railways, and the cost of suburban housing, due to the policy not of the railway companies but of the suburban landowners. And behind both these lay the extraordinary powerful deter-mination of the classes themselves to buy the best accommodation at the best place, and therefore the highest social status, which they could afford. From the 1840s to the early 1900s philanthropists, social reformers and politicians concerned with London's overcrowded and unhealthy houses and streets advocated the move-ment of large numbers of lower middle-class and working-class families to the railway suburbs. *The Economist* in 1844 began its perennial call for the railways to serve 'the great masses of the working population' as well as 'the higher and wealthy middle classes'.[25] In 1846 Charles

Pearson, Solicitor to the City of London, suggested to the Royal Commission on Railway Termini that if a central station was to be built at Farringdon Street an estate of 10,000 cottages should be built seven miles down the line to house the displaced artisans and clerks, who could be offered rents lower than their old ones by more than the 2d. a day it would cost to carry them by train.[26] Watkin of the South Eastern made a similar suggestion in 1868, after introducing workmen's trains:

Let us find the wealth of London ready to grapple with this great evil of crowding out the working man. Let us see the capital raised at 5 per cent to build working men's houses for 100,000 in any healthy place down our line and we shall be ready . . . to carry the people at times to suit [them] and at prices not greater than the difference in rent and taxes between unhealthy London and the healthy open fields beyond.[27]

But the houses had still not been built when he appeared before the Royal Commission on the Housing of the Working Classes in 1884, apart from those around the railway works of his other London company, the Metropolitan, at Neasden, seven miles out of London. He argued that the companies themselves should be empowered to 'build little colonies in places contiguous to their railways', but the Metropolitan, uniquely, already had that power and, apart from Neasden, which was strictly a railway town like Crewe or Wolverton, had not used it. He did not deny the Commissioners' suggestion that the effect of cheap housing was 'to drive out the richer class, who are more profitable customers'.[28] Charles Booth, whose great *Survey of London* had convinced him that squalor and overcrowding were among the major causes, through disease, drink and despair, of poverty, argued in 1901 that cheap railway services were the first step towards draining of people the 'stagnant, water-logged land' of the slums.[29] The Royal Commission on London Traffic of 1905–6 advocated the same policy, and supported the proposal that the railway companies should be allowed to recoup by engaging in land-speculation and development, but it was ignored by the government.[30]

That so little came of this, except in the north-eastern suburbs, was not the fault of the railway companies, who gained so little from the enormous increase in land values produced by their lines, and who could not be expected to subsidize house rents or wages more than they already did with fares at 2d. to 11d. return for journeys of up to a dozen miles. Nor was it due to the reluctance of the working classes who, when real wages rose by as much as two thirds in the great price fall between 1874 and 1896 at the same time as average working hours shrank from ten and a half to about nine a day, at last began to able to afford both the time and the money for commuting. The great success of the trams, which became an almost exclusively working-class mode of conveyance, with 1d. fares by the 1890s from the crowded inner suburbs, shows that they were only too willing to move, as the chairmen of London Tramways claimed in 1884: 'We have relieved London of an immense number of poor people by carrying them out to the suburbs.'[31] The chief reason for their failure to move out still further, and for the segregation of the classes, was the fact that in all but a few of the railway suburbs, chiefly on the north-eastern side, the cost of housing was still too high, i.e. the rent plus workman's fare was much greater than the rents in central London and so beyond the reach of most working men. And the chief reason for this was the soaring cost of suburban land and the policy of the suburban landowners.

It was the local landowners who determined the social character of the suburbs. No one could compel a land-owner to sell or develop at all. Baroness Windsor at King's Norton near Birmingham would not sell any land for building purposes, and the suburb developed only after she died. The landowners at Solihull would not, except for the existing villagers, allow any houses under £500 to be built. At Radlett, near St Albans, the land-owners held up development until 1894 and then, except for a small working-class estate for domestic servants, tradesmen's assistants and other service occupations, mostly allowed only detached houses at no more than four to the acre. In parts of Wimbledon the building of houses worth less than £1,000 or £1,500 was ruled out by the landowners' conditions of sale. On some estates in Croydon the minimum house value specified by covenant was £600.[32] Everywhere the landowner, or his agent or his successor the developer, determined the class of people for whom the houses were intended. This no doubt was in response to the demand, and not every land-owner could aim at the highest level of the market. But the market, and the preference of landowners and developers for as select a clientele as they could get, effectively decided which class should live where. And once the good-class property came, the local landowners and residents joined together to prevent any 'contamina-tion' by the less affluent. At Tunbridge Wells, for example, the residents petitioned the South Eastern in 1874 against reduced fares, which might lead to a lower-ing of the district's social tone.[33] If, in spite of all, cheaper property was built, the wealthy residents would sell up, at a profit, as at Edmonton, and move further out.

The railways, like other modes of transport, were thus only the means used by the classes to segregate themselves. This process went furthest in London, where the range of wealth and of fares and housing costs was greatest and most finely graded, but it affected all the great cities. Manchester, Liverpool, Birmingham, Leeds, Bristol, Glasgow and Edinburgh, whether or not they were rail-orientated, had their superior, middling and inferior suburbs, as well as their central working-class areas and slums. The smaller towns were less affected, but every town of over 20,000 had its worse and better neighbourhoods: the difference was that they were still close enough together for the well-to-do, and especially the local employers and professional men, to belong to the town and take an interest in its affairs. In small towns like Glossop or Lancaster, for example, millionaire employers continued to belong to the borough council and to engage in competitive philanthropy – giving hospitals, libraries, public parks and so on to the town – down to the First World War and sometimes beyond. But in the larger towns and cities the employing class increasingly came to live outside the boundary, with profound social consequences to the communities which they, and still more their families, left behind.

In their brand new outer suburbs the middle-class commuters and their families began to live a life of their own – a new kind of life which came to be called 'suburban'. It was in effect a single-class life, cut off from the inferior classes left behind in the cities, and cut off too from the old society of the surrounding countryside, from the landed gentry of county society, who would have nothing to do with the *nouveaux riches* unless they were rich enough to buy a whole estate and become gentry

themselves. The outer suburbanites were like white
settlers in a colonial land: they could not mix with the
native princes, and their only dealings with the rest of the
native population were as employers of servants and
customers in the local shops. They lived unto themselves,
in a round of leisure-time pursuits divorced from work:
dinner parties, garden parties, whist and bridge parties,
croquet or tennis on the lawn (lawn tennis, significantly,
was patented by Major Wingfield in 1874), and golf,
which became popular in the 1870s and 1880s. Team
games, rugby, football and cricket, flourished in the
suburbs, where the single-class club with its exclusive
subscription provided the ideal environment for suburban
gentlemen who had neither the time nor the entrée to
aristocratic field sports such as hunting and shooting.
Suburban ladies and their daughters, with nothing to do
in their large, many-servanted villas after the head of the
household had left by the morning train, went through
elaborate rituals of calling on each other and leaving
their visiting cards. Only families of the same social
standing were visited: for a newcomer to leave her cards
without first being visited and accepted was to invite a
polite but firm rebuff, and every new family was scruti-
nized and its antecedents checked before the ladies of the
suburb pronounced it respectable. On the other hand,
the suburban ladies avoided like the plague calling on the
ladies of county society, out of fear of the same rebuff
and of being accused of social climbing by their peers.

All this is delightfully and sympathetically described by
the sharp-eyed Katharine Chorley in *Manchester made
Them*, a description of the upper-middle-class suburb of
Alderley Edge in her late Victorian and Edwardian
childhood.[34] Lady Chorley, who later married a

university don who became a Labour M.P. and peer, was the daughter of an engineer and business manager from a well-known Manchester family who moved from one of the inner suburbs to 'the residence of the merchant princes of Manchester', as *Baddeley's Guide* described the Edge. 'Every morning in my childhood,' she writes, 'the businessmen caught the 8.25 or the 8.50 or the 9.18 trains into Manchester.' They travelled in first-class compartments with their cronies, and any wife or daughter who had to travel at that time went third, since

to share a compartment with the 'gentlemen' (we were taught never to call them just plainly 'men') would have been unthinkable. Indeed, the ladies always avoided the business trains if they possibly could. It was highly embarrassing, a sort of indelicacy, to stand on the platform surrounded by a crowd of males who had to be polite but were obviously not in the mood for female company.

On weekdays the village was given over to the ladies:

After the 9.18 train pulled out of the station the Edge became exclusively female. You never saw a man on the hill roads unless it were the doctor or the plumber, and you never saw a man in anyone's home except the gardener or the coachman. And yet it was a man-made and a man-lorded society . . . the men were the money-lords, and since for every family the community values were fundamentally economic, it followed that their women were dependants. They existed for their husbands' and fathers' sakes and their lives were shaped to please masculine vanity.

A woman's place was firmly in the home, ministering to the needs of husband and children, but since most of the ministration was done by servants there was almost nothing to occupy their time, and no husband would admit 'the right of his wife to produce a set of activities of her own which in any way threatened the vested interest in her time and personality which he had secured for himself'. A small amount of charitable work was in order, sewing for the poor, sitting on committees or, for the very determined and daring, slum visiting in Ancoats, but paid work was out of the question: 'A paid job for one of his womenfolk would have cast an unbearable reflection of incompetence upon the money-getting male.'

So most of the women were idle in the sense that there was very little work which they had to set their hands or minds to do whether they liked it or not. Like a large house and garden, a wife or daughter with nothing to do was an emblem of success. There were plenty of servants and nurses about so domestic chores were mostly limited to ordering the meals and doing the shopping, and domestic responsibility to captaining the staff. Of course, on the nurse's half-day, mothers with small children inexpertly looked after their young and usually longed for the nurse's return. For the rest, they all 'filled in time'.

One method of filling in time was paying calls, which meant setting aside two afternoons a week for visiting ladies of equal standing, and two more for receiving them and serving them tea and cakes. But this was complicated by agonizing decisions about who could and could not be visited and received.

Snobbery was also geographical; it was almost an axiom for instance that, socially speaking, no good thing would be likely to come out of Wilmslow, the neighbouring village nearer Manchester. On the other hand, Peover, a village deeper in Cheshire than Alderley Edge, where the manager of the Manchester branch of the Bank of England lived in semi-county state, was regarded by most of our ladies with equal though different scorn as the preserve of people who liked to be 'in with' the county. The people who lived round about Peover reciprocated, of course, and suspected a good many of us as we suspected the Wilmslow families. The complications were endless. Mother and Mrs Schill, for instance, both got on admirably with 'the lower classes' because these they could meet without any fear of being drawn in or needing to draw them in to their own entourage. It was the people immediately below and immediately above that caused the trouble. The 'aboves' were as troublesome as the 'belows' for mother and Mrs Schill had twisted their sturdy self-respect into a ridiculous pattern of inverted snobbery. . . . Wives with the views of mother and Mrs Schill had to walk on a social tightrope.

Bridge and embroidery for the older ladies, tennis and golf for the younger, were the main pastimes – and even these had to be confined to weekday mornings and afternoons, since the evenings and week-ends were devoted to the pleasures of the 'gentlemen', who monopolized the courts and links except for the occasional gracious invitation to doubles. Even the football and cricket teams, unlike in the real country villages, were confined to one class, for 'with us there was no squire's son and the shopkeeper's sons and the grooms had to get their cricket at second-hand by watching between the slats of the tall fence which shielded the club from the road'. The tradespeople were neither servile nor sycophantic, but 'accepted the situation with a sort of agreeable cynicism', charging even higher prices to the rich suburbanites than to the rest of the inhabitants.

The poor people were almost exclusively the personal retainers of the Alderley Edge houses, the gardeners, the coachmen and later the chauffeurs. . . . As a social institution the village was bad, for it had no life-blood of its own. It was a parasitic growth. It was not even the vestigal remains of a feudal village grouped around one big house. It was grouped around several dozen houses whose masters' roots and economic interests lay elsewhere.

Nor was the city where their roots and interests lay enhanced by their nightly desertion: '. . . the exodus of the well-to-do into Cheshire produced a vacuum in the city life which had not existed before and which began steadily to spoil the looks and to a large extent the character of Manchester'. It spoilt the looks by emptying the square-built, red-brick houses along Manchester's Upper Brook Street and Ardwick Green, where the merchants and industrialists used to live close to the city centre, and turning them over to cheap offices, tawdry shops and shoddy tenements. It spoilt its character by leaving it without its natural leaders. They no longer sat on the city council or the committee of the Chamber of Commerce, supported the Literary and Philosophical or the Statistical Society, or endowed libraries, art galleries and hospitals as their fathers had done. At best they attended the Hallé concerts at the Free Trade Hall and the occasional straight play at the Opera House or Miss Horniman's Gaiety, and they or their wives sat on the Infirmary Committee or the Gentlewomen's Employment Association.

The city became the place they worked in by day and abandoned in the evening as quickly as might be. Their leisure interests were elsewhere and the time they gave to civic duties dwindled. The city was no longer the centre of their cultural lives. . . .

Many of them even gave up the Nonconformist faith of their ancestors, preferring the more genteel and less strenuous ritual of the Anglican Church, and still more abandoned the sturdy, radical Liberalism of their Manchester youth and, alienated by 'Socialism', direct taxation and Home Rule, drifted, like Katharine Chorley's father, into the Tory party. This drift, which was not peculiar to the Manchester area, coincided with the break-up of the old county parliamentary constituencies dominated by the county families (1885) and of the old county government of mainly landed J.P.s and its replacement by the new elected county councils (1888). Thus, instead of the suburbanites capturing the new constituencies and councils for the Liberals and giving them a built-in majority in both central and local government, they gave the built-in majority to the Conservatives. In Cheshire, certainly, the old county families and the new middle-class suburbanites came together, in spite of their social differences, on the same political platforms in an alliance which has never since been shaken, abandoning the nearby cities of Liverpool and Manchester to their social inferiors and political enemies.[35]

For the growth of commuting was still more important for what it left behind in the neglected cities. In the squalid central slums and packed inner suburbs increasingly abandoned by the middle classes, the working classes now felt an increased sense of isolation and deprivation. Not that their material conditions of life were worse than before. On the contrary, the towns were getting cleaner and healthier, as the Public Health Acts, the pure water supplies, the new sewerage, street paving and lighting did their work. And with the great fall in prices from 1874 to 1896 – 40 per cent in twenty-two years, while average money wages held up, or even rose by 10 per cent – real wages rose by as much as two thirds, and the bulk of the working class had pennies to spare

for more and somewhat better food – more meat and
butter and less bread and potatoes – for clothes, furniture, soap and newspapers, and other luxuries, such as
trips to the seaside and, for a few, even holidays away
from home. Yet that very improvement in living standards made the working classes more aware of their condition, more aware of what money could buy, more aware
of the insecurity of their lives, and of what the cessation
of work could mean in terms of the rapid descent into
poverty. The modest prosperity of those with small
families and in full work only exposed the degraded
condition of those with large families or without work:
the casual labourers, dockers and others whose usual
wages were too small to keep a family of two or more
children adequately fed, clothed and sheltered, the
unemployed with families of any size, the sick, the aged,
the submerged layers of paupers, beggars and street folk
who swarmed in the slums of the great cities. In the
1890s Charles Booth in London and Seebohm Rowntree
in York conducted the first modern social surveys, and
found nearly a third of the population – over a third of
the working class – living below the poverty-line: that is,
receiving too little income from all sources to keep themselves and their families alive in full health and fit for
work.[36]

This situation, with the working classes left behind in
the cities, and growing at once stronger in material terms
and more aware of the problems that remained, was the
ideal soil for a renewed outburst of class resentment, and
the 1880s and 1890s saw the rebirth of two powerful
working-class movements. On the political side there
were the new Socialist societies, Hyndman and William
Morris's Social Democratic Federation, the Fabian

Society, and Keir Hardie's Independent Labour party. On the industrial side there was the New Unionism, beginning with the famous dock strike of 1889; the new mass trade unions of unskilled and semi-skilled workers which, along with the surge of expansion they evoked by their example among the skilled unions, carried union membership from under a million in the 1880s to nearly two million in 1900 and to four million by 1914. The working class now had the vote – householders and lodgers in the towns since 1867 and in the counties since 1884 – and the Liberal and Tory parties under Gladstone and Disraeli, and still more under radical, reforming politicians like Joseph Chamberlain and Lord Randolph Churchill, began to compete for their support with measures of social reform, such as public education and improved factory and trade-union law. But in the new atmosphere of class segregation and mutual hostility they could not prevent the polarization of politics along class lines. The new suburbanites, as we have seen, were incensed by the expensive social reforms and the taxation policy of the advanced Liberals, and drifted into the Tory Party. The two wings of the working-class movement, the political and the industrial, were frustrated by their failure to make headway in the 1890s, and came together in the Labour Representation Committee, the progenitor of the Labour party, in 1900. The ground was thus laid in the Victorian commuter age, and to a large extent by the social consequences of commuting itself, for the class politics of the twentieth century, with a predominantly working-class Labour party on one side and a middle-class-led Conservative party on the other.

By way of postscript it is worth mentioning two movements by middle-class philanthropists which tried to stem the tide of working-class resentment and to provide antidotes to the class segregation of the commuter age. One was an attempt to revive in the modern city the paternalism of the old village community by bringing the rich back to live in the urban slums. The other was the town-planning movement, which set out to build model towns and suburbs in which the classes could once more live in harmony with each other. Though they failed in their immediate objectives, they both had important consequences for the twentieth century, the first for the Welfare State, the second for the New Towns and community planning generally.

The first is known as the settlement movement, which began in the 1860s with Edward Denison's return to live in the East End of London and with Octavia Hill's Marylebone rent-collecting scheme. The son of the Bishop of Salisbury, Denison's plan was to revive the philanthropy in education and other charitable work of the country parson; the granddaughter of the public health reformer Southwood Smith, Octavia Hill's was to buy, with the art critic John Ruskin's money, some London slums and to revive the benevolent rule of the country squire so as 'to bring order into the lives of her tenants'.[37] In 1869 they came together with Canon Barnett, Rector of Whitechapel, to found the Charity Organization Society (now the Family Welfare Association), to do what the good squire and parson had always done : divide the deserving or 'hopeful' cases of poverty – those which could be helped to stand on their own feet – from the undeserving or 'hopeless', those which should be left to the Poor Law authorities. From this unpromising beginning, rapidly imitated in other cities in Britain and the United States, there developed modern social

casework and the family services of the Welfare State.[38]
Through Canon Barnett it pioneered the University
Settlement, the little colony of young graduates living for
a time in the slums and helping with educational,
charitable and local government work. Among the first of
these was Arnold Toynbee from Balliol College, Oxford,
who gave lectures to East End working men on the
Industrial Revolution. When Toynbee unexpectedly died
at the age of thirty, in 1883, Canon Barnett founded
Toynbee Hall, the first University Settlement. It was
emulated by others in other cities, such as the Manchester one in the Round House in Every Street, Ancoats,
where the Chartist Convention had met in 1842. At
Toynbee Hall many famous Oxford men got their first
knowledge of working-class life and their passion for
social reform: W. H. Beveridge, R. H. Tawney, Hugh
Dalton, Clement Attlee.[39] One might almost say that the
Welfare State was born there. But the settlement movement failed to bring back the middle class to the city
centres in more than isolated handfuls.

The other movement, the town-planning movement,
goes back also to the country village, but to the model
industrial villages which early factory masters like Arkwright, Samuel Greg, David Dale and Robert Owen
built around their water mills. Through Owen and his
followers, including influential community planners like
James Minter Morgan and John Silk Buckingham, the
ideal of building model co-operative communities, in
which life should be higher and purer than in the competitive world outside, descended to become an important
strand in the garden-city movement of the 1890s. Meanwhile, later industrialists attempted a more practical
application of the ideal, in model villages and towns for

their workers. The railway towns at Crewe, Wolverton and elsewhere were models by the standards of the age, but more self-conscious models include Titus Salt the alpaca manufacturer's Saltaire, built near Bradford in the 1850s, W. H. Lever the soap king's Port Sunlight and George Cadbury's Bourneville, opened in the 1890s. The two strands, ideal and practical, came together in the garden-city movement of the 1890s, best represented by Ebenezer Howard's book *Tomorrow* (1898) and by the first garden city, Letchworth, founded in 1903. The garden-city movement had a tremendous influence on the Town Planning Acts of 1909, 1932 and 1947 and on the New Towns of the mid twentieth century.[40] But, like the settlement movement, it was too little and too late to cure the urgent social problems and divisions of the early commuter age. Increasingly these social problems and divisions were to become the political problems of the later Railway Age, as we shall see in the final chapter.

Further Reading

J. R. Kellett, *The Impact of Railways on Victorian Cities* (Routledge & Kegan Paul, 1969).

T. C. Barker and Michael Robbins, *A History of London Transport*, II, *The Nineteenth Century* (Allen & Unwin, 1963).

H. P. White, *A Regional History of the Railways of Great Britain*, III, *Greater London* (Phoenix House 1963).

Asa Briggs, *Victorian Cities* (Odhams, 1963).

W. Ashworth, *The Genesis of Modern British Town Planning* (Routledge & Kegan Paul, 1954).

Katharine Chorley, *Manchester made Them* (Faber, 1950).

J. M. Lee, *Social Leaders and Public Persons: a Study of County Government in Cheshire since 1888* (Oxford University Press, 1963).

Notes

1. *Railway Times*, 29 June 1850.
2. Cf. H. B. Rodgers, 'Suburban Growth of Victorian Manchester', *Journal of Manchester Geographical Society*, LVIII, 1961–62.
3. Cf. J. R. Kellett, *The Impact of Railways on Victorian Cities* (Routledge & Kegan Paul, 1969), pp. 355–7.
4. *Ibid.*, pp. 360–4.
5. *Ibid.*, pp. 354–5; J. R. Kellett, *Glasgow: a Concise History* (Blond Educational, 1967), pp. 43–52.
6. T. C. Barker and Michael Robbins, *A History of London Transport*, I, *The Nineteenth Century* (Allen and Unwin, 1963), chap. ii; H. P. White, *A Regional History of the Railways of Great Britain*, III, *Greater London* (Phoenix House, 1963), pp. 1–2, 19–22; Kellett, *Impact of Railways*, pp. 365–7.
7. Barker and Robbins, *op. cit.*, pp. 44–56; Kellett, *Impact of Railways*, pp. 268–78; White, *op. cit.*, chap. vi.
8. Barker and Robbins, *op. cit.*, chap. iv; White, *op. cit.*, chap. iv.
9. S.C. of H. of L. on Metropolitan Communications, 1863, VIII. iv–v.
10. *North London Advertizer*, 30 August 1884.
11. J. W. Barry, 'The City Lines and Extensions (Inner Circle Completion) of the Metropolitan and District Railways', *Proceedings of Institution of Civil Engineers*, 1884–85, LXXI. 41.
12. Barker and Robbins, *op. cit.*, pp. 164–5.
13. *Ibid.*, chap. V; White, *op. cit.*, chaps. ii, ix.

14. L.C.C., 'Report on Workmen's Trains', *London Statistics* (1891–92), II. 325.

15. Kellett, *Impact of Railways*, p. 376.

16. William Birt, quoted in *ibid.*, p. 371.

17. W. Ashworth, *The Genesis of Modern British Town Planning* (Routledge & Kegan Paul, 1954), p. 12.

18. Barker and Robbins, *op. cit.*, pp. 220–2.

19. *Ibid.*, chap. viii.

20. Kellett, *Impact of Railways*, pp. 377–9.

21. B. F. C. Costelloe, *The Housing Problem* (1899), p. 56.

22. Kellett, *Impact of Railways*, table, p. 378.

23. William Birt, quoted in *ibid.*, p. 377.

24 For this whole argument, cf. Kellett, *Impact of Railways*, chap. xii.

25. *The Economist*, 20 July 1844.

26. *Royal Commission on Metropolitan Termini*, Parliamentary Papers, 1846; XVII, qq. 2811ff.

27. *Herapath's Railway Journal*, 29 August 1868.

28. Royal Commission on Housing of Working Classes, Parliamentary Papers, 1884–85, XXX, qq. 10479, 10483.

29. Charles Booth, *Improved Means of Locomotion as a First Step towards the Cure of the Housing Difficulties of London* (1901), p. 17.

30. *Royal Commission on London Traffic*, Parliamentary Papers, 1905 (Cd. 2597), XXX, pp. 16, 30, 71.

31. *Herapath's Railway Journal*, 19 January 1884.

32. Examples from Kellett, *Impact of Railways*, pp. 411–16.

33. *Ibid.*, p. 411.

34. Katharine Chorley, *Manchester made Them* (Faber, 1950), on which the following six paragraphs are based.

35. Cf. J. M. Lee, *Social Leaders and Public Persons: a Study of County Government in Cheshire since 1888* (Oxford University Press, 1963).

36. C. Booth, *Life and Labour of the People: London* (1891) II. 21; B. S. Rowntree, *Poverty: a Study of Town Life* (1901, popular edition, n.d.), pp. 150–1 (the percentages

are: London, 31% of population, 40% of working class; York, 28% of population, 43% of working class).

37. Sir Baldwyn Leighton, ed., *Work among the London Poor: Letters and Other Writings of the late Edward Denison* (1872); E. Moberly Bell, *Octavia Hill* (1942); Octavia Hill, 'Blank Court, or Landlords and Tenants', *Macmillan's Magazine*, 1871, XXIV. 456ff.

38. C. L. Mowat, *The Charity Organisation Society, 1869–1913* (1961); Kathleen Woodroofe, *From Charity to Social Work: in England and the United States* (Routledge & Kegan Paul, 1962), chap. ii.

39. S. A. Barnett, *Practicable Socialism* (Longmans, 1915); Henrietta Barnett, *Canon Barnett, his Life, Work and Friends* (2 vols., John Murray, 1918); J. A. R. Pimlott, *Toynbee Hall: Fifty Years of Social Progress, 1884–1934* (Dent, 1935); Mary Stocks, *Fifty Years in Every Street: the Story of the Manchester University Settlement* (Manchester University Press, 1945).

40. Cf. Ashworth, *op. cit.*, esp. chap. v.

Chapter Ten

The End of an Age

THE last thirty years before the First World War were the great age of the railways. Nothing could touch them for long-distance travel or heavy suburban traffic. Speed, comfort, elegance, reliability were all approaching present-day standards, while the rival motor-car and motor-bus were still in their ponderous and excruciatingly uncomfortable infancy. Great express trains roared and snorted across the English shires and the Scottish moors, at average start-to-stop speeds of over 50 m.p.h. Races on the West and East Coast routes to Scotland in 1888 and 1895 reduced the scheduled time from London to Edinburgh from over twelve to eight and a half hours, with average speeds on some stretches approaching 70 m.p.h. Similar feats were regularly performed on all the great trunk lines, especially where there was competition, as between the London and North Western and the Great Western for the 'city-to-city' traffic to Birmingham, between the L.N.W.R. and the Midland to Manchester, or the G.W.R. and the London and South Western in the race to the Atlantic liners at Plymouth. And the cross-country trains in the Edwardian age were somewhat faster and, of course, much more plentiful than on today's much reduced lines.

At the same time the railway companies were meeting the public demand for greater comfort and more elegant surroundings. From the 1870s the larger companies, the Midland, the Great Western and the Great Northern, began to introduce much bigger and more comfortable passenger coaches than the old standard six-wheeler, with eight or twelve wheels, often on bogies which improved the springing and the 'ride', and sprung buffers instead of the old, jarring 'dumb' ones. Lighting, by oil, gas or sometimes electricity from batteries or dynamos on the axles, was improved, and heating, by steam or by oil-fired hot-water circuit, added. The clerestory, an elevated portion of the roof with window panels to help light and ventilation, was a fashion of the period. Lavatories, and side-corridors to give access to them, were added, and so for longer journeys were dining-cars and sleeping-cars. The last were mainly on the American model, developed by George Pullman, whose sumptuous day carriages and efficient, obsequious staff were first introduced to Britain by the Midland in 1874. In the early stages these bigger and more comfortable carriages were only for the first-class passengers on the most important routes, but they gradually spread to other classes and lines. The Great Western introduced a through-corridor train in 1891, and the Great Eastern for its York to Harwich Continental express a standard set with a dining saloon between a third-class carriage and a first- and second-class composite. Meanwhile, the Midland pioneered comfort for third-class passengers, including heating and padded seats instead of wooden benches, and forced its competitors to follow suit. One of the side-results of this was the decline of the old second class, which, being neither 'uppish' enough for the rich and the snobbish nor cheap enough for the poor and economizing, tended to disappear altogether.

All these improvements added to the cost and weight of trains without any corresponding increase in passengers carried. Indeed, they often reduced the number, the side-corridor for example taking the room of one passenger in every five, and the dining-car taking the place of a whole carriage of fare-paying passengers. The standard six-wheeler weighed about fifteen tons, the larger side-corridor or Pullman day-car over twice as much, while a sleeper or dining-car could weigh over forty tons. The enormous increase in the weight of trains, from under 100 tons to over 250 tons for a typical express, and the increasing length of goods trains, meant that locomotives had to be much bigger and more efficient. Their very names suggest their size: Francis Webb's 'Jumbos' and 'Dreadnoughts' on the L.N.W.R., William Adams' 'Moguls' on the Great Eastern, David Jones' 'Big Goods' on the Highland Railway, Harry Ivatt's 'Atlantics' on the Great Northern, Churchward's 'Stars' and Gresley's 'Pacifics' on the Great Western, and Russell's mighty ten-coupled (driving wheels) 'Decapod' on the Great Eastern, which could out-accelerate a suburban electric train from a standing start. Compound engines (using the steam twice over at high and at low pressure), superheating (reheating and drying the steam to temperatures in excess of 100° Centigrade), heated feed-water, and many other sophisticated devices were all used in the pursuit of additional power and speed. Locomotive

weights rose in proportion, from the thirty or forty tons
of mid-century to the more than 100 tons of the Atlantics
of the 1890s; and they were correspondingly voracious of
coal and water.

The companies invested, too, in improving and
strengthening the permanent way to take these monsters
and their heavier trains. The leading routes had sixty-foot
rails weighing ninety-five pounds and upwards to the
yard, and sleepered and ballasted to match. The track
was quadrupled, allowing faster through-running for
expresses, on many main lines. The Great Western
converted to standard gauge, and got rid of its last
broadgauge sections in 1892. Automatic signalling with
continuous track-circuiting and the automatic application
of the brakes when a train passed a signal at stop began
to come in in the early years of the century, and the modern coloured light signals on the Underground. Although,
apart from the London Tube and a few light railways in
out-of-the-way places, there was little new railway
building, there were some important and expensive
route-shortenings achieved by great engineering works
like the Tay Bridge (rebuilt after the first one, of 1878,
blew down in 1879), the Severn Tunnel (opened in 1886
after being twice drowned by hidden springs and unexpectedly high tides), and, greatest of all, the Forth
Bridge (opened in 1890); and, less spectacularly, by
humble though still costly short-cuts like the Castle Cary
cut-off of 1906 which by-passed Bristol and won the race
to Plymouth for the Great Western.

All these developments cost money, however, and the
mainline companies – though still by far the largest
economic organizations in the country, with capitals
ranging from £30 million to over £200 million – were not

making the high profits of their early days. For one thing, as we saw in the last chapter, powerful rivals survived and even increased their competition for suburban traffic, in the shape of the horse-bus and the horse-tram, given a new lease of life by the cheapening of horse fodder in the last quarter of the nineteenth century. And new rivals began to appear, in the shape of the steam-tram, introduced in Glasgow in 1877 and North London in 1883, and, far more menacing, the electric tram, which was tried out in London between 1889 and 1893, and was finally adopted on a large scale in the Edwardian age both there and in many other cities. In 1900 there were 1,000 miles of street tramways in Britain; by 1914 there were 2,500 miles, and they were practically all electric.

The competition of the trams for urban and inner suburban traffic, which preferred their cleanliness and convenience to the smoke and stench of 'the Drain', was the most important factor in the electrification of the old, shallow Underground. The deep Tube had already proved the success of electric traction, and the Metropolitan and District companies were experimenting with a joint electric train in 1900 when an energetic, swash-buckling American, Charles Tyson Yerkes, came on to the scene. In rapid succession he bought up the projected but uncompleted tubes, the Charing Cross, Euston and Hampstead (nucleus of the present Northern Line), the Baker Street and Waterloo (Bakerloo Line), and the Brompton and Piccadilly Circus and the Great Northern and Strand (united in the Piccadilly Line), and captured the District Company. Although he died in 1905 long before his schemes were complete, he left his mark on London's transport system, with a unified Underground system, electrified on his third-rail system, which also spread via the South Western Railway to the Southern Railway of later times. To beat the trams the London, Brighton and South Coast Railway electrified its Victoria and London Bridge line in 1909, and from 1914 the L.N.W.R. electrified the lines to Watford and from Broad Street to Kew and Richmond. For the same reason the Mersey Railway and the Lancashire and Yorkshire had already electrified their Liverpool lines (1903–4), and the North Eastern its lines on the north side of Newcastle-upon-Tyne – the first steam railways to be wholly converted to the new form of traction. With such urban and suburban exceptions, however, the railways were still committed to steam, which was still supreme for heavy and long-distance transport.

There were other rivals, it is true, ultimately more deadly than the tram. Daimler and Maybach in Germany patented their petrol-driven horseless carriage in 1886, and Lanchester the first British four-wheel car in 1895. Next year the first British car built for sale, Lawson's Coventry Daimler, appeared, and in 1899 the first petrol-driven London bus, a German-built Daimler. From 1903 the motor-bus came into general use in London. Its main victim was the horse-bus: the last one ran in London in 1907. The trams did not disappear until after the Second World War. As for the railways, they saw nothing to fear in the motor-car, which was still a rich man's toy, very uncomfortable and unreliable, and mainly used for short local trips in place of the private carriage, while they welcomed the motor-bus, for which some of them quickly found a use. The Great Western, for example, bought two Milnes-Daimlers in 1903 to save them extending the Helston branch line to the Lizard, and found such a brisk demand for feeder services and organized tours in Devon and Cornwall that they built up a fleet of eighty vehicles. The North Eastern started a bus service between Beverley and Beeford, the Great North of Scotland one between Ballater and Braemar via Balmoral, the Great Eastern built its own buses at Stratford, and the L.N.W.R. operated two bus fleets, around Watford and in North Wales. Wherever there was a scattered population to be linked to the rail network the motor-bus was a useful ancillary, but as yet it was no threat to the railways as such. As for the aeroplane, invented in America by the Wright brothers in 1903 and flown across the Channel by Blériot in 1909, it was still an interesting experiment rather than a means of transport.

Yet in spite of their unchallenged supremacy in every major field of transport, the railways were not happy in the enjoyment of their monopoly but were powerfully threatened from other directions. Not only were their costs rising to meet the demand for more comfortable travel, but their profits were subjected to a double squeeze, from their customers on the one side, acting through the government, and from their workers on the other, acting through the trade unions. This double squeeze and the railway companies' reaction to it brought them into the forefront of national politics and the battle-field of industrial relations. From the 1880s to the brink of the First World War, the railways were the constant butt of public criticism, rising at times to a state of national crisis demanding the intervention of Parliament, the government and ultimately of the prime minister himself.

For this unwanted glare of publicity the railway companies were themselves largely to blame. They had become enormous and arrogant monopolies, riding roughshod over their customers and workers alike. They charged what freight rates they liked to their customers, discriminating on the principle of 'what the traffic would bear' not only between hundreds of different commodities but between different places – charging much more, for example, for carriage to and from inland towns than between ports with the alternative of coastal shipping – and even between customers for the same goods on the same routes, where bigger or shrewder ones could drive harder bargains than the smaller and less persuasive. In the 1880s there was a great public outcry against these high and discriminating freight rates. It was occasioned by the so-called 'Great Depression', the great fall in prices of 1874–96, which, whatever its ultimate cause, was undoubtedly aggravated by the international competition of new, rising industrial powers. Britain was ceasing to be the only workshop of the world, and was being rivalled in industrial production and even overtaken in certain fields such as iron and steel by other countries, notably Germany and America. British industrialists complained that they were handicapped, not only by high railway rates, but by unfair discrimination against British goods and in favour of foreign imports. It actually cost less to send a ton of American goods from New York to London via Glasgow or Liverpool than to send a ton of British goods from Glasgow or Liverpool to London. It was to beat the stranglehold of the railways, particularly on the import of grain and raw cotton and the export of engineering products and cotton piece goods, that Daniel Adamson and other Manchester businessmen built the Manchester Ship Canal, projected in 1884 and opened ten years later – a notable riposte to the first modern railway, which had only been built so as to break the stranglehold of the waterways on the traffic between Liverpool and Manchester.

Manchester's solution was not open to every inland city, however. The various chambers of commerce continued to agitate for revision of the freight rates, and their association commissioned Sir Bernhard Samuelson to investigate the question. He reported in favour of a 'prompt and thorough revision of British railway rates' under the control of the Railways Commission. The result, after some parliamentary skirmishing, was the Railway Regulation Bill which A. J. Mundella, President of the Board of Trade, introduced for Gladstone's government in 1886. It was opposed tooth and nail by the eighty-six railway M.P.s and the forty-six railway peers, who found an unexpected salvation in the Irish Home Rule crisis, which split the Liberal party and forced Gladstone out of office.[1] The Liberal attempt to control the railways – the first real attempt since Gladstone's 'parliamentary trains' Act of 1844 – contributed, along with Home Rule, to that drift which we noticed in the last chapter, of businessmen, led by some of the greatest railway directors, into the Tory party.

The fall of Gladstone did not save the railways from parliamentary interference, however. It was one thing to split the Liberal party when there was a Tory party to migrate to. It was quite another to oppose a Tory government which was also under pressure from united chambers of commerce to do something about railway rates. When Lord Salisbury's government in 1888 introduced a Railway and Canal Traffic Act requiring the companies to submit a revised classification of merchandise and a revised schedule of maximum freight charges, they meekly submitted. It was a complicated operation. Two

special commissioners examined the companies' revised
lists and the 4,000 objections to them during 1889 and
1890, the Board of Trade submitted thirty-five Provisional Orders with maximum rates to Parliament, and
the new rates eventually came into force on 1 January
1893. Whether out of cunning or imprudence, the railway
companies immediately raised all rates to the maximum,
though they later claimed that this was merely pre-
liminary to negotiating 'reasonable' rates. The result was
a furore of protest from the united traders, who believed
that they had been cheated, either by the Board of Trade
or the railway companies or both. There followed a
further parliamentary committee and, in 1894, when
Mundella was again at the Board of Trade, a short,
brusque Act, passed in a fit of parliamentary exaspera-
tion with the railways. This allowed any member of the
public to challenge as 'unreasonable' any increase in
railway freight charges made since 1892, and in effect
pegged the rates at the 1892 level.

This Act was the source of immense difficulty for the
railways until 1913, when it was finally repealed. Passed
at the very trough of the great price fall, it allowed
practically no increase in charges during all the years of
rising prices which followed. The effect of this was to peg
the railway companies' profits at the very time when they
were under pressure to improve the service they provided
and when wages, in money terms, were on the move again
for workers in other industries.

The railways were thus in an impasse. Working
expenses as a proportion of gross receipts from fares and
freight charges rose steadily from 55 per cent or less in
the 1870s and 1880s to 62 per cent or more between 1900
and 1913. Dividends equally steadily declined. Three to

6 per cent came to be usual, and many companies could not even pay that: those of the Great Central, Watkin's old Manchester, Sheffield and Lincolnshire, declined from $2\frac{7}{8}$ per cent in 1877 to nothing at all in the early 1900s. Why a gross profit of more than a third of total receipts could support only so small a net profit is explained chiefly by the railways' over-capitalization: they had cost too much to build – too much for land, too much for lawyers' and surveyors' and parliamentary expenses, too much for company promoters' rake-offs and other unproductive items, and, it must be admitted, too much for the pioneers' inevitable experiments and mistakes.

The railways were in fact symbolic of the British economy at this stage of its development: remarkably efficient and still progressive, though notably in the less productive areas of development, but handicapped over against competitors by a backlog of old and costly capital investment which still had to be paid for out of current profits. This was the price which Britain still had to pay for pioneering the first industrial revolution, and the railways for pioneering the revolution in transport. But it was too late to do much about that now, and the only way out of the impasse was to economize in running costs. The only large item of running costs which could be economized was labour, and this meant overworking and underpaying the men. This in turn inevitably meant trouble with the trade unions, and a history of industrial conflict which in the last twenty years before the First World War went from crisis to crisis and became an issue in national politics.

Not that there was much room for economizing in labour costs. Except in the very early days, when skilled railwaymen were scarce, railway wages were never high compared with other occupations. In the 1840s they were good: engine drivers earned from 5s. 6d. to 7s. 6d. and firemen 3s. 6d. to 5s. 6d. a day according to grade and length of service, i.e. from 33s. to 45s. and 18s. to 33s. a week, compared with 26s. to 33s. for skilled engineers in the Manchester area. Porters averaged 18s. 7d. a week, but this was better than most town labourers, and much better than farm labourers, who averaged 11s. 6d. a week in the north and only 8s. 5d. in the south of England. But over the years railway wages lagged behind those of other workers. At the end of the century the maximum for drivers was generally still only 8s. a day, and very few earned this. In 1907 railway wages for all grades averaged only 25s. 10d., and 100,000 men, two fifths of the labour force, earned less than 20s.[2] And this was at a time when Rowntree in York estimated that the poverty-line for a man, wife and three children was 21s. 8d. The railways only kept their men because of the attractions of the work – the pride and pleasure of controlling their magnificent charges for the drivers and firemen, the escape from the boredom and heavy labour of the factory or the mine for the guards and porters and, above all, the regularity and certainty of work and wages for all grades of railwaymen who, short of dismissal for incompetence or 'insubordination' – a word of very elastic meaning, covering most kinds of trade-union activity – could feel they had a job for life.

For these wages, the companies exacted more than their pound of flesh. Practically all grades of railway workers, except for signalmen at exceptionally busy boxes, worked a basic twelve-hour day, but the minimum was in many cases notional. Porters were expected to

arrive at 6 a.m. and continue until the last passenger of
the day required their services. Signalmen could not leave
their boxes until their relief arrived, and if he failed to
turn up might be required to do a double shift. Double-
shift working was automatic for one set of signalmen at
the weekly or fortnightly changeover of shifts, and
occasionally these could stretch out to a marathon
thirty-six hours. Drivers and firemen, under the almost
universal custom that only one team worked a particular
locomotive, did double journeys of such length that they
could almost never be confined within a twelve-hour
period, and in foggy or bad weather could stretch out to
eighteen hours or more. Guards on the same trains
necessarily did similar stretches. To modern eyes the
most extraordinary feature of this overwork, apart from
its inhuman length, is the fact that in most cases it was not
paid for. Nor merely were overtime rates not paid: in
most cases no extra wages were paid, even at ordinary
rates of pay. Railwaymen of all grades were treated as
'staff', permanent employees whose loyalty to the company and security of tenure justified an expectation that
they should always continue on duty as long as they were
needed, in return for no additional reward.

Whether paid for or not, excessive hours of this length,
especially for signalmen, drivers and guards, were a
danger to the travelling public. This became obvious
from the reports on railway accidents made by the inspectors of the Board of Trade. In the 1860s a number of
disasters were blamed on the excessive hours of signalmen, and one inspector reported that 'many accidents
occur from men being overworked'.[3] The question was
taken up by the medical journal, the *Lancet*, which in
1861 appointed a special commission into the effect of

railway travel on health. It reported that the greatest danger came from nodding drivers, signalmen dazed from want of sleep and guards with faculties blunted from long unrest, and as a remedy recommended 'the simple one of fixing a maximum time of work'.[4] The Royal Commission on Trade Unions of 1867 remarked that

There is abundant evidence to show that on exceptional occasions men on whom the safety of trains mainly depends are either required or permitted to continue on duty for an excessive length of time, and we find also that in certain cases the duties ordinarily exacted from men of these classes are too protracted.[5]

The travelling public were naturally alarmed, and even *The Times* declared in 1871:

We are not among those who would desire to stimulate or befriend trade combinations or strikes, but we confess that a great part of the excessive labour exacted from railway servants might have been avoided or mitigated if railway servants, like other skilled workmen, had known how to combine for the purpose of striking a bargain with their employers.[6]

In fact, the different grades of railwaymen, especially in London, had been trying to do just that, and for that very purpose. In 1865 a Railway Clerks Association was formed to present a list of demands to the companies, but it failed to recruit members outside London and was ignored by the directors. In 1866 the Railway Guards, Signalmen and Switchmen's Society of the United Kingdom was founded at a meeting in Paddington, and demanded from the mainline companies an eight-hour day and 30s. a week for signalmen in junction boxes and

26s. a week for men in ordinary boxes. Although the companies refused to recognize it, three of them did in fact raise the wages of signalmen and guards by 1s. to 3s. a week. In the same year the locomotive men, starting at New Cross, formed the Engine Drivers and Firemen's United Society, which at one point claimed to have 15,000 members in sixty-four branches. They demanded a ten-hour day, payment for overtime, time-and-a-half for Sunday work, a 150-mile daily maximum for main-line drivers and 120 miles for local ones. Five of the largest companies gave way, but the Brighton and North Eastern Railways resisted, and strikes followed, which broke the union and led to the imprisonment of the Brighton line leaders for breach of contract and the permanent dismissal and replacement of over 1,000 North Eastern drivers and firemen.[7] These early failures served to underline the futility of 'sectionalism', separate unions for different grades, and turned railwaymen's thoughts towards appealing to the public and to Parliament.

The companies' attitude was that trade unionism was incompatible with the discipline required for running a public service like a railway. As one leading railway director put it in 1893, 'You might as well have trade unionism in Her Majesty's Army as have it in the railway service. The thing is totally incompatible.'[8] Strike action was mutiny, union activity of almost any kind was in-subordination, even individual complaints of overwork smacked of ingratitude and invited dismissal or at least marked a man as unfit for promotion. For the railway companies regarded themselves as good employers, models of paternalism, who looked after the welfare of their 'servants' – the very name they gave to their em-ployees is significant of their attitude – without any need for 'outside interference' either by the unions or the state.

If the companies had lived up to this ideal they might have escaped the attention of the public and of Parliament, but they did not. By 1871 public concern at railway accidents caused by overwork was at its height, and at the instance of some of his railwaymen constituents – who since the 1867 Reform Act now had the vote – the brewer Michael Bass, M.P. for Derby and an important shareholder and customer of the Midland Railway, raised the matter in Parliament: thirty or forty drivers on the Midland had during the previous two months worked 'nearly double the time usually assigned to them', an average of nineteen and a half hours instead of the standard ten, and in one case as long as twenty-nine and a half hours. When W. P. Price, M.P., chairman of the Midland, rose to deny that there was 'a shadow of foundation in the charge', he was laughed at, and he failed to respond to Bass's challenge to disprove 'a single point in which he was inaccurate'. The argument continued in the press, and Bass was supported by *The Times*, the *Lancet*, the *Daily News* and the *Daily Telegraph*. His campaign brought him into contact with other middle-class sympathizers like the Rev. W. Griffith, the radical minister of Eccleston, and Canon J. D. Jenkins, and active railwaymen like John Graham, a Derby pointsman, and Charles Vincent, a London railway clerk, all of whom were to play a leading part in railway unionism. Bass employed Vincent and his friend James Greenwood, a feature writer on the *Daily Telegraph*, to tour the railways and inquire into working conditions, organize meetings, and write letters and articles in support of the agitation.[9]

Meanwhile, railwaymen everywhere were stimulated by

the upsurgence of trade unionism in other industries, particularly by the engineers' campaign for a nine-hour day, which was conceded for their workshop men by the Midland at Derby, the L.N.W.R. at Crewe and the Great Northern at Doncaster. A series of meetings of railwaymen addressed by Vincent at Liverpool, Mansfield, Bolton, Wolverhampton, Taunton, Stafford, Manchester and Leeds – at the last of which the rules for a union were adopted – culminated in a meeting in London in December 1871 at which the Amalgamated Society of Railway Servants (A.S.R.S.), parent of the modern National Union of Railwaymen (N.U.R.), was founded. It was chaired by the Rev. G. M. Murphy, a well-known temperance leader, and received apologies for absence from Michael Bass and the Archbishop of Canterbury. The society thus began under the most exalted auspices. Bass refused the presidency on the ground that he could best help from a position of independence, but financed the journal, the *Railway Service Gazette*, edited by Vincent. Samuel Morley the philanthropic hosier and Thomas Brassey the great railway contractor, along with two other M.P.s, became vice-presidents, and Dr J. Baxter Langley, a radical publicist, and Canon Jenkins were among the early presidents. True to its middle-class patronage, the A.S.R.S. emphasized its friendly society benefits for sickness, unemployment, superannuation and death, passed rules against drunkenness on or off duty, and declared itself as 'decidedly opposed to strikes'. But its programme of a ten-hour day and increased wages was bound to lead it into conflict with the companies which could only end in strike action.[10]

The A.S.R.S. did not remain the only union in the industry. Some of the footplatemen formed unions of

their own, notably the (tautologically named) Associated
Society of Locomotive Enginemen and Firemen of 1879,
which still survives, though the A.S.R.S. at various times
claimed to have a larger fraction of the drivers and firemen. A General Railway Workers Union (G.R.W.U.),
chiefly of workshop men, porters, vanmen and other
ancillary workers, was formed in the wave of militant,
unskilled New Unionism in 1889, as 'a fighting union' not
'encumbered by any sick or accident fund', though it
remained much smaller down to the time of its amalgamation with the A.S.R.S. in the N.U.R. in 1913.[11] And
there was until 1892 a separate A.S.R.S. for Scotland,
which from Christmas 1890 conducted one of the bitter-
est, most costly and unsuccessful strikes in railway
history, lasting six weeks and costing the companies
£300,000 in lost traffic.[12] The main A.S.R.S., however,
which in the years of the New Unionism of the late 1880s
became less of a friendly society and more of a militant
trade union, bore most of the burden of the struggle for
shorter hours, better working conditions, higher pay and,
above all, recognition by the companies of the right to
negotiate for their members. This last object was the crux
of the matter. The railway companies were, with a very
few exceptions like the North Eastern after the strike and
arbitration of 1890, adamant in their refusal to deal with
any representative but their own employees, whom they
could of course intimidate and victimize. Quite apart
from their dislike of unionism in principle, the companies
were well aware, particularly from 1888 when the state
began to control freight rates, that recognition could only
lead to concessions which would cost money and eat
further into their declining profits. This explains why the
railways were so much more stubborn in their resistance

to confrontation than other employers, and why it took all the pressure and persuasiveness of the government to bring them to the negotiating table.

Meanwhile, the public and parliamentary campaign to limit the hours of railwaymen in the interests of safety continued. The Duke of St Albans in 1877 unsuccessfully introduced a Bill to limit the hours to twelve in any twenty-four, and Lord de la Warr in 1887 and 1888 carried proposals for returns of the hours worked. Such returns, with their evidence that gross overworking was 'not an abnormal incident but a part of a system', led to a debate in 1891 in the House of Commons which passed a motion that 'the employment of railway servants for excessive hours is a source of danger both to the men themselves and to the travelling public' and appointed a Select Committee to inquire whether the hours should be restricted by legislation.[13] The committee not only found plenty of evidence of excessive hours 'habitually worked without adequate reason' and of lack of effort by the companies generally 'to deal earnestly and thoroughly with the matter', but inadvertently revealed that railway employees were intimidated and victimized for giving evidence against their superiors. The most scandalous case was that of John Hood, the locally respected stationmaster at Ellesmere, who was dismissed after twenty-two years' exemplary service by the Cambrian Railway after he had given evidence contradicting that of the general manager. In this case the general manager and two other directors of the railway were called to the Bar of the House of Commons, and a fourth, who was an M.P., ordered to appear in his place, to purge their contempt of Parliament. They apologized and were admonished by the Speaker – but Stationmaster Hood was not reinstated.[14] One result was that Parliament passed the Witnesses (Public Inquiries) Act, 1892, providing penalties of a fine of up to £100 or three months' imprisonment for anyone who threatened, punished or otherwise injured any person giving evidence before a public inquiry.

In 1893 Mundella, President of the Board of Trade, got a Railway Regulation Act through which provided for the Board to inquire into complaints of overwork, require revised duty schedules from offending companies, and fine them up to £100 a day for non-compliance with the board's instructions. The machinery, which depended on the men risking their jobs by complaining and on the companies making honest returns to the Board of Trade, did not work very well, and the A.S.R.S. spent a good deal of money in the ensuing years in 'protection grants' to men who had been dismissed for making complaints and other union activities.

With their failure to bring the companies to negotiate and their success in getting public and parliamentary support for their case, the railwaymen naturally favoured political rather than industrial action. The A.S.R.S. came to play a larger part in the creation of the Labour party than any other union. It was the society which sponsored the famous resolution at the T.U.C. at Plymouth in 1899 for the conference of representatives of the unions and Socialist societies which set up the Labour Representation Committee in 1900. And it was also the society which, accidentally of course, became involved in two great legal decisions which, because of their hostility to the working-class industrial and political movements, served to unify and strengthen the infant Labour party against its enemies.

The first was the Taff Vale Judgement. The Taff Vale Railway was an important company, carrying nearly as much coal over its 124 miles of line, chiefly from the Welsh valleys down to Cardiff, as the Great Western did over its 3,000. The A.S.R.S. had already had a brush with it in its first official, and highly successful, local strike, for a sixty-hour week in 1890, and relations between the union and the company were reasonably harmonious until a 'strong man' who disliked trade unions, Ammon Beasley, became general manager. His efforts to maintain the Taff Vale's record as one of the highest paying railways in the country at the expense of overworking led to a series of strikes, culminating in a complete stoppage from 20 to 31 August 1900. The issues were complex, but the fundamental question was recognition of the union, which Beasley refused to concede. He was in the end forced to negotiate a settlement, however, which included the setting up of a conciliation board for the South Wales railways and the dropping of legal proceedings which he had brought against some of the strikers for offences connected with picketing. In the course of the latter, however, on the last day of the strike, Mr Justice Farwell had given an injunction against Richard Bell and James Holmes, leaders of the union, which not only threw doubt on the supposed freedom, since an Act of 1875, of peaceful picketing, but also on the supposed immunity of the unions from legal proceedings for non-criminal acts arising out of industrial disputes. This decision was reversed by the Court of Appeal, but upheld by the House of Lords.

The House of Lords' judgement was a serious blow to the trade union movement as a whole. The vindictive Beasley, despite his promise to drop the proceedings, seized the opportunity to sue the union for damages for loss of trade, and was awarded £23,000 plus costs. The total cost to the A.S.R.S. was £42,000. More important to the trade union movement was the complete loss of the strike weapon. If any union engaging in a dispute could be sued for crippling damages, strikes had become impossible. The cock-a-hoop Beasley was awarded gratuities of £2,000 by the Taff Vale company 'in recognition of his services'.[15]

The ultimate result, of course, was the reverse of what Beasley and the railway companies expected. The Taff Vale Judgement rallied the trade unions to the Labour Representation Committee, their main hope of getting the law changed by Parliament. At the general election of 1906, with their help and money, it returned twenty-nine M.P.s (apart from twenty-four other trade union members, chiefly miners and cotton workers, who received the Liberal whip). This was the real birth of the Labour party. According to the defeated Conservative premier, Arthur Balfour,

We have here to do with something much more important than the swing of the pendulum or all the squabbles about Free Trade and Fiscal Reform. . . . Unless I am greatly mistaken, the Election of 1906 inaugurates a new era.[16]

Under the pressure from the new Labour M.P.s with the trade union vote behind them, the Liberal government reversed the Taff Vale Judgement by the Trade Disputes Act of 1906, which gave British trade unions a unique privilege, enjoyed in no other country: complete immunity from legal proceedings in respect of civil wrongs committed in the furtherance of a strike. This was the only certain way in which Parliament could prevent the courts from tampering with the right to strike.

The other legal decision involving the A.S.R.S. and the Labour movement was the Osborne Judgement of 1909. This concerned the right of the trade unions to spend their funds for political purposes, notably on the election and support of M.P.s, and threatened to strangle the infant Labour party in the cradle. It arose out of an action which the secretary of the Walthamstow branch, Walter Osborne, head porter at Clapton Station, and a member of the Walthamstow Liberal Association, brought against the A.S.R.S. to restrain them from using the union's funds to support Labour candidates. Osborne financed his case, which went as far as the House of Lords, by a public appeal, which found a ready response among members of the traditional political parties. The House of Lords gave judgement in his favour, and the trade unions were prevented, on the eve of the 1910 general election, from supporting Labour party or any other parliamentary candidates.[17]

Once again, the ultimate result was the reverse of that expected. The trade unions were confirmed in their commitment to the Labour party, and the latter managed to defeat the judgement, in two stages: first, in 1911, by persuading the Liberal government, now in a minority and dependent on their support, to enact payment of M.P.s, and secondly by obtaining the Trade Union Act of 1913, which allowed the unions to set up a political fund to which members contributed, as part of their subscription, a voluntary 'political levy'. Members were allowed to 'opt out' of paying the levy, but most did not bother to take the initiative to do so. ('Opting out' was replaced by 'opting in' by Baldwin's government in 1927 as a retaliation for the General Strike, and restored by Attlee's in 1945.) On this financial foundation the Labour party became, after the First World War, the official Opposition and was able to form the governments of 1924 and 1929.

On the industrial side the railway unions took a full share in the turbulent industrial unrest of the decade before the First World War, and were in the vanguard of the movement which for the first time brought the government itself into the negotiation and settlement of industrial disputes. The root cause of the unrest was an exceptional set of economic circumstances, almost unknown since the railways first came: rising prices at a time of stagnating industrial production and national income per head, which meant that money wages were exceptionally difficult to raise and real wages actually declined. No group of workers was more affected by this stagnation and decline than the railwaymen, whose employers were still caught in the grip of state-controlled fares and freight rates which restricted their profits. The demand of the unions for better pay and shorter hours and the refusal of the companies to negotiate with or recognize them were bound to lead to a head-on collision which in 1907 threatened and in 1911 actually produced a national railway strike. Since in the days when motor transport was incapable of carrying more than a tiny fraction of the traffic a national railway strike could bring industry and the whole economy to a standstill, the government was forced to step in on both occasions to avert disaster.

The first occasion resulted from the 'all grades movement' of 1906, when the A.S.R.S., released at last from the shackles of the Taff Vale Judgement, demanded an eight-hour day for locomotive and traffic men and a ten-hour day for the rest, and an immediate wage increase of

2s. a week, plus various improvements in working conditions. They were able to show that only 11 per cent of railwaymen earned more than 30s. a week and only 61 per cent more than 20s., and that only 7 per cent worked a basic eight-hour, two-thirds a ten-hour and the rest a twelve-hour day, not including long hours of overtime. The Railway Companies Association refused even to discuss the claim, and repeated their refusal to recognize the unions on the ground that 'full control by the directors was essential for the maintenance of strict discipline' and the safety of the public. Most of the national press condemned the companies' attitude, so out of line with that of other employers. The A.S.R.S. and G.R.W.U., after balloting their members, gave notice of a strike in November 1907.

At this point the President of the Board of Trade, David Lloyd George, stepped in. He persuaded the union leaders and the directors' representatives to meet him, not together but at different times, on the same day (6 November 1907). The companies still refused recognition of the unions, but accepted a conciliation scheme under which the railwaymen in each company, but not their union officials, could take their demands and grievances before a sectional board for each grade and on to a central board, both consisting of workers' and employers' representatives, and in case of disagreement could refer them to an arbitrator. The scheme was to operate for at least six years, down to November 1913.[18] It did not work very well. The companies treated it as an alternative to recognition of the unions, and not only used its lengthy procedures to delay and frustrate the settlement of claims but adopted their old tactic of intimidation of the men's representatives, who were mostly union men. G. S. Churchward, the famous engine builder and locomotive superintendent of the Great Western, wrote to the men's secretary of one sectional board: '. . . if you and those you represent are not satisfied with conditions in my department, I shall be pleased to receive your notices'.[19] They resorted to tricks to evade arbitration awards, by moving men to other grades or stations or by regrading the work. When challenged they took the line that interpretation of an award was for the companies alone, and had nothing to do with the conciliation boards or even with the arbitrator himself. Under this system railwaymen's average money wages actually fell, from 25s. 10d. in 1906 to 25s. 9d. in 1910, and because of rising prices declined still more in real terms.[20] Small wonder that the exasperated A.S.R.S. at this period adopted as its ultimate aim the nationalization of the railways.

The years 1910–13 saw an unprecedented number of strikes and days lost throughout British industry, as one group of workers after another tried to raise their wages in line with the mounting cost of living. The rank-and-file railwaymen became increasingly frustrated as the dockers, miners and other workers made gains while the railway companies took refuge behind the conciliation scheme and refused to negotiate in any other fashion. At last, in the summer of 1911, a wave of unofficial railway strikes involving 50,000 men, about a fifth of the labour force, led on to the first national railway strike. On 15 August the executives of the four manual railway unions jointly gave the companies twenty-four hours to decide 'whether they were prepared immediately to meet the representatives of the unions to negotiate the basis of a settlement'. The managers of the main railways, called to the Board of Trade next day by the president, Sidney Buxton, declared that they would rather face a strike than negotiate, and the government promised to provide troops to help them. The prime minister himself, H. H. Asquith, met the unions' representatives next day and promised them a Royal Commission to investigate the working of the conciliation scheme, but with no guarantee that it would be speedy or settle any other grievance. The union leaders refused to accept this evasion, and sent out 2,000 telegrams calling on the men to strike.

The strike was very nearly complete. Two hundred thousand railwaymen stopped work, and the jobs of millions of other workers in mills, factories and steelworks were threatened by the shortage of coal. The government mobilized 58,000 troops, which had the effect of goading the strikers and their sympathizers into demonstrations and riots. There were violent scenes in Liverpool, and in Llanelly two rioters were shot dead by the troops. Winston Churchill, the home secretary, who gave orders that the troops were to be used whether or not they were called on by the civil authorities, never lived down his reputation with the working class, reinforced in the General Strike in 1926, as a man of violence. Public opinion and most of the national press swung round to the strikers, and blamed the railway directors for refusing even to meet the union leaders to discuss a settlement. It was also the time of the Agadir crisis, when the German Kaiser Wilhelm II was engaging in gunboat diplomacy in Morocco and the government was anxious about the supply of coal for the Navy. Within two days, therefore, the government and the railway companies climbed down, and at the instance of Lloyd George arranged a round-table meeting between the union leaders and the spokesmen of the managers. This in itself amounted to recognition and a victory for the unions, who called off the strike in exchange for a Royal Commission of Inquiry, now instructed to report speedily, and a rapid convening of the Conciliation Boards to consider their claims.[21]

When the Royal Commission's report appeared in October it contained points which the unions would not accept without further discussion, but the companies refused yet again to meet their leaders. It required a further threat of strike and a resolution by the House of Commons to persuade them to change their minds. In the course of the debate one M.P. spoke for the majority when he said:

The obstinate refusal of the railway directors in the country to meet the representatives of the trade unions has gone far to convince the public that the railway management is not in the hands of level-headed businesslike men. . . . We, who are neither trade unionists nor directors of great businesses but simply members of the public, see in the coal trade, in the cotton trade, in the iron trade – the great masters of industry, welcoming trade unions, co-operating with trade unions, working with trade unions, and we do not understand why the directors of the railway companies decline to follow what seems to us this wise plan.[22]

The joint meetings finally took place in December, at which a settlement was reached on the reform of the conciliation scheme. The new system abolished the central boards for each railway and by concentrating on the sectional boards had the unfortunate effect of encouraging sectionalism and the playing off of one grade against another. But it led to modest wage increases of 1s. to 2s. a week for most railwaymen and the shortening of hours for some grades, though most continued to work a sixty-hour minimum week. And the root cause of the trouble, the statutory limitation on fares and freight rates, was lifted by Parliament in 1913.

The main effect of the strike was to teach the railway unions the vital importance of standing together and of co-operating with other unions in the transport and adjacent industries, especially the dockers and miners. By 1913 the A.S.R.S., the G.R.W.U. and the small signalmen's union, the United Pointsmen and Signalmen's Society (U.P.S.S.), amalgamated in the National Union of Railwaymen, covering 180,000 members, the first really successful industrial union covering all grades of workers in a great industry. At the same time the famous 'Triple Alliance' of railwaymen, transport (mainly dock) workers' and miners' unions came into existence, and was agreed in principle at a joint conference in March 1914. These were years in which Syndicalism, the idea that industrial action by the united unions could be used to achieve social reform and even a Socialist state, was a force in the trade union world, and the N.U.R. passed a resolution in June 1914 that the alliance would 'encourage the growth of greater solidarity and a vast improvement in the social condition of the workers and be a powerful lever in the cause of working-class emancipation'.[23] The leadership had more modest hopes of the alliance, that the threat of a strike for increased wages or improved conditions by one of the groups would be backed by all three, and a threatened stoppage by one and a half million men would be irresistible. In the summer of 1914 the N.U.R. was preparing a further round of demands which the companies would have to respond to by December or else face the prospect of what amounted to a general strike. But it never came to that. By 4 August the country was at war.

The railways, both management and men, played a heroic part in the First World War. All thoughts of strike action were cast aside, and at a meeting on 1 October the railway managers and the union leaders agreed an industrial truce which lasted, in spite of some tough bargaining over cost-of-living bonuses and a few unofficial strikes in South Wales and elsewhere, until the Armistice. The government assumed control of the railways, through a Railway Executive Committee composed of the principal company managers. The railways sent in all 184,000 men, nearly a third of their labour force, into the armed forces, together with 675 locomotives, 30,000 waggons and other rolling stock, thirty ambulance trains, and materials for 2,300 miles of standard-gauge and 1,300 miles of narrow-gauge track in and behind the front line in France. Practically the whole burden of supplying the British troops in France and the Navy, especially the Grand Fleet at Scapa Flow, fell on the railways, which provided £126 million worth of free services to the government. But it was all at a tremendous cost in the strain on men and equipment. The little Highland Railway almost broke down in its task of supplying Scapa Flow, and was rescued only by massive loans of locomotives from other companies. By 1918 all the companies' motive power, rolling stock and permanent way were run down and badly in need of repair.[24] The railways needed a new period of prosperity to restore their equipment and earning power to bring back the proud years of the Railway Age.

But the proud years were gone, and prosperity with

them – for Britain, as well as for the railways. The old
triumphant industries of the Victorian age in which
Britain had led the world – coal, iron, cotton and
railways – had lost their place in the world economy and
were giving way to new and more powerful competitors –
oil, hydroelectricity, man-made fibres, light engineering
and the motor-car. Ill-equipped for this new age, Britain
was soon to face massive unemployment, which after
1920 never fell below 10 per cent and sometimes rose to
over 20 per cent. The railways in particular had to face
new rivals which they had scorned before the war, the
motor-lorry and the motor-bus which broke their
monopoly of heavy transport and of outer suburban
traffic, and even began to challenge them as the most
popular means of long-distance, and especially holiday,
travel.

At the same time the companies were under both
industrial and political pressure from the unions, who
wanted better pay and conditions and, especially after the
example of successful state control during the war,
nationalization of the railways. In pursuit of the first and
against the withdrawal of war bonuses they called a
national railway strike in 1919 which lasted nine days
and was settled only after meetings with the Prime
Minister, Lloyd George, and other members of the
Cabinet at 10 Downing Street. The revived Triple
Alliance involved the N.U.R. in the struggles of the
miners against wage cuts in 1921–6, culminating in the
General Strike, in which the railways came to a standstill.
But with the large-scale advent of the motor-lorry – not
to mention the armoured car, which the government
called on to guard the food convoys in 1926 – the
railwaymen were no longer in a position to hold the

country to ransom. This was the final proof that the railways were no longer indispensable.

According to Winston Churchill in a pre-election speech, the government had made up its mind in 1918 to nationalize the railways, and the new Coalition government introduced a Ways and Communications Bill in 1919 containing power to purchase any railway, tramway, canal or dock undertaking.[25] The new Parliament, however, contained a majority of businessmen who would have no truck with nationalization, and the clause was deleted. Instead, the Railways Act of 1921 was passed, by which, on 1 January 1923, 121 main-line railway companies were reduced to the 'Big Four', the London, Midland and Scottish (L.M.S.), the London and North Eastern (L.N.E.R.), the Great Western (G.W.R.) and the Southern (S.R.). (The London Underground group remained separate, to be absorbed in the London Passenger Transport Board in 1934.) The Big Four still had much work to do and some remarkable improvements to make – high-speed expresses like the *Flying Scot*, the world's record speed for a steam locomotive by the *Mallard* in 1938, the electrification of the Southern Railway – before they were finally nationalized in 1947.

But the 'great grouping' of 1923 could not hold back the clock. The great age of the railways was at an end. The new age was dominated by a new prime mover, the internal combustion engine, and by new means of transport, the automobile and the aeroplane. As the dominant symbol of a distinct epoch of history, the Railway Age came to an end with the First World War.

*

This book has tried to show through the effects of transport on society the beginnings and the decline of a particular civilization, as unique and memorable as ancient Greece or Rome – the middle-class civilization of Victorian and Edwardian Britain. The Railway Age saw the rise and fall of Victorian class society. It began in the old, pre-industrial society, dominated by the man on horseback, the landed aristocrat and country gentleman. It transformed it into the new class society, dominated by the man of the iron horse, the middle-class industrial capitalist. What would the Automobile Age bring? The new professional society, dominated by the professional expert, the scientific manager and the technologist? We shall have to wait and see. But one thing is certain: whatever the future may bring in the shape of 200 m.p.h. linear-motored, hover-trains or the like, half a century before 11 August 1968, when the last steam train ran in Britain, the undisputed reign of the 'real' railway, the steam railway, was already over.

Further Reading

C. Hamilton Ellis, *British Railway History, 1877–1947* (Allen & Unwin, 1959).

Jack Simmons, *The Railways of Britain: a Historical Introduction* (Routledge & Kegan Paul, 1961).

P. S. Bagwell, *The Railwaymen: the History of the National Union of Railwaymen* (Allen & Unwin, 1963).

Lord Askwith, *Industrial Problems and Disputes* (Murray, 1920).

Sidney and Beatrice Webb, *The History of Trade Unionism* (Longmans, 1920 edition).

Henry Pelling, *A History of British Trade Unionism* (Macmillan, 1963).

H. A. Clegg, A. Fox and A. F. Thompson, *A History of British Trade Unions Since 1889*, Vol. I: *1889–1910* (Oxford University Press, 1964).

Henry Pelling, *The Origins of the Labour Party* (Macmillan, 1954).

F. Bealey and H. Pelling, *Labour and Politics* (Macmillan, 1958).

Notes

1. Cf. W. H. G. Armytage, 'The Railway Rates Question and the Fall of the Third Gladstone Ministry', *English Historical Review*, LXV, 1950, pp. 18f.
2. P. S. Bagwell, *The Railwaymen: the History of the N.U.R.* (Allen and Unwin, 1963), p. 265.
3. *Ibid.*, p. 36.
4. *The Lancet*, 4 January 1862.
5. Quoted by C. Hamilton Ellis, *British Railway History, 1877–1947* (Allen and Unwin, 1959), p. 206.
6. *The Times*, 15 September 1871.
7. Bagwell, *op. cit.*, pp. 38–43.
8. *Ibid.*, jacket.
9. *Ibid.*, chap. ii.
10. *Ibid.*, *loc. cit.*
11. *Ibid.*, p. 132.
12. *Ibid.*, pp. 62–3, 141–9, 312; Ellis, *op. cit.*, pp. 212–16.
13. *Hansard's Parliamentary Debates*, 1890–91, Vol. 349, Col. 905f., 23 January 1891.
14. Bagwell, *op. cit.*, pp. 160–7; Ellis, *op. cit.*, pp. 218–22.
15. Bagwell, *op. cit.*, pp. 208–27; Henry Pelling, *A History of British Trade Unionism* (Macmillan, 1963), pp. 121–6.
16. Arthur Balfour to Lord Knollys, the King's Private Secretary, 17 January 1906, in Sir Sidney Lee, *King Edward VII* (1925–27), II. 449.

17. Bagwell, *op. cit.*, pp. 241–57; Pelling, *op. cit.*, pp. 128–31.
18. Bagwell, *op. cit.*, pp. 263–9.
19. *Ibid.*, p. 279.
20. *Ibid.*, pp. 275–84.
21. *Ibid.*, pp. 289–99.
22. Leif Jones, M.P., Hansard, 1911, Vol. 31, Col. 1256, 22 November 1911.
23. Bagwell, *op. cit.*, p. 307.
24. Ellis, *op. cit.*, pp. 299–308.
25. Bagwell, *op. cit.*, pp. 405–6.

Important Dates Affecting Communications

GENERAL	ROADS	WATERWAYS	RAILWAYS
1485–1603: THE TUDORS			
1492–3: Columbus discovers the New World			
		1512: Trinity House (pilots, later light-houses, etc.) founded	
	1516: Sir Brian Tuke, first Master of the Posts		
			1519: Earliest print of railway, *Der Ursprung Gemeyner* ('The Origin of Mining Law')
1520–1: Circum-navigation of globe by Magellan's crew			

312

1531–2: Act confirming freedom of passage on navigable rivers

1556: Detailed drawings of railways, Agricola's *De Re Metallica*

c.1540: *Blast furnace introduced into England*
1542: Discovery of Japan by de Mota
1555: Muscovy Company

1555: Highways Act: 'Statute labour'
1556: Coaches first mentioned

1563–7: Exeter Canal (first pound-lock canal in England)
1571: River Lee Improvement Act

1577–81: Circum-navigation of globe by Drake
1583: Newfoundland annexed (first English colony)

GENERAL	ROADS	WATERWAYS	RAILWAYS
1600: East India Company			
1601: Discovery of Australia by de Eredia			
1603–49: THE EARLY STUARTS	1603: Postmasters granted priority in provision of post-horses		c.1605: Horse-drawn wagonway, Wollaston – River Trent
1618: Africa Company	1621: First of many Acts regulating weight and wheels of road vehicles		
1622: *Weekly News*, first English newspaper	1623: Hackney coaches first mentioned		c.1630: Huntingdon Beaumont introduces wagonways from Leicestershire to Tyne coalfield

314

Fens

introduced by
Sir Sanders Duncombe
1635: Stage coaches first
mentioned

1642–9: CIVIL WAR
1649–60: THE
INTERREGNUM

1654: Postmasters granted
monopoly of
provision of post-
horses (tended to
lapse c.mid 18th cent.)

1657: Act establishing
Post Office (confirmed
1660)
1660–88: THE LATER
STUARTS
1660: The Royal Society
1662: *Boyle's law of
gaseous pressures*

1662: Act: Highway
rates levied

1663: First Turnpike Act
1669: 'Flying coaches',
London–Oxford

1662–5: River Improve-
ment 'boom': Acts for
9 rivers, including
Medway and Mersey–
Weaver

GENERAL	ROADS	WATERWAYS	RAILWAYS
			1671: Earliest section of modern railway system: Tanfield tramway
1680: Dockwra's London Penny Post			
1682: *Newton's law of gravitation*			
1688: THE REVOLUTION			
1688–1702: WILLIAM III	1691: Act 'for settling the Rates of Carriage of Goods' (by J.P.s)		
	1694, 1729, 1751 Acts: Thames Navigation regulated		
1694: Bank of England			
1698: *Savery's steam-pump*			
1702–14: ANNE			
1702: *Daily Courant*, first daily newspaper	1706: First Turnpike Trustees Act		

316

1708: *Newcomen's atmospheric engine*
1709–14: *Darby's coke-smelting of iron*
1714–1837: THE HANOVERIANS
1715: Old Pretender's rising

1717–20: River Navigation 'boom': Acts for 6 rivers, including Weaver and Mersey–Irwell

1726: Oldest railway bridge, Causey Arch, Tanfield tramway

1726–33: General Wade's Highland military roads

1730–42: Newry Navigation, Northern Ireland
1736: *John Harrison's chronometer (for measuring longitude)*

1745: Young Pretender's rising
1749: *Roebuck's mass-production of vitriol and soda*

GENERAL	ROADS	WATERWAYS	RAILWAYS
1750 onwards: Great increase in Enclosure Acts	c.1750 onwards: Great increase in Turnpike Acts		
		1755–57: Sankey Brook Canal	1758: First Railway Act: Rev. Charles Brandling's Middleton Colliery line, Leeds
		1758–72: James Brindley, canal engineer (active)	
		1759–61: Bridgewater Canal (first deadwater canal)	
1760–1850: INDUSTRIAL REVOLUTION			
1764: *Watt's steam-engine*	c.1765: Cugnot's steam carriage		
	1765–92: John Metcalfe, road engineer, active	1766–77: Grand Trunk Canal (Mersey–Trent)	

318

Coalbrookdale
Ironworks

1776–7: *John Curr invents 'plateway' (for untanged wheeled vehicles)*

1773: General Highways Act and General Turnpike Act

1784: Mail coaches introduced by John Palmer

1786–1834: Thomas Telford, road engineer, active

1768–79: Cook's South Sea voyages

1769: *Arkwright's water-frame*

1770: *Hargreaves's spinning jenny*

1776: AMERICAN REVOLUTION

1779: *Crompton's mule*

1783: *Cort's puddling and rolling of wrought iron*

1783: *Bell's calico-printing machine*

1784: *Cartwright's power-loom*

319

GENERAL	ROADS	WATERWAYS	RAILWAYS
		1787: *John Wilkinson's iron boat*	1788–9: *Edge rails,* Loughborough Canal Dock railway
1789: FRENCH REVOLUTION		1789: *William Symington's steam boat* 1790: Canal 'Cross' completed (Humber–Severn and Mersey–Thames) 1791–94: Canal 'Mania': 81 Acts passed	
1792: *William Murdock's coal-gas* **1793–1815:** GREAT FRENCH WARS	1797: *Cartwright's alcohol engine* 1798–1836: J. L. Macadam, road engineer (active)	1793–1834: Thomas Telford, canal engineer, active	
1799–1800: Combination			

1801: First Census
1801: General Enclosure (model clauses) Act

1801: Richard Trevithick's steam-carriage

1801–3: Surrey Iron Railway: first public railway (horse-drawn, freight only)

1802: First Factory Act

1802: Symington's Charlotte Dundas (steam-boat)
1803–22: Caledonian Ship Canal

1804: Trevithick's tramway locomotive, Penydarran
1804–7: Oystermouth Railway (Swansea Bay): first passenger line (horse drawn)
1805: Trevithick's flange-wheeled locomotive, Newcastle Colliery

1808–9: Sir George Cayley's gunpowder engine, and theory of flight

GENERAL	ROADS	WATERWAYS	RAILWAYS
1812–17: Luddite Riots			*1812:* Matthew Murray and Blenkinsop's rack-and-cog locomotive, Middleton Colliery: first regular steam haulage
			1812–48: George Stephenson, railway engineer (active)
			1813: Blackett and Hedley's locomotives, Wylam Colliery first regular steam haulage on smooth rails
			1814: Stephenson's first locomotive, *Blücher*
		1818: Dover–Calais steampacket begins	
		1819: Savannah crosses Atlantic by steam and sail	
	1819: Cartwright's pedal quadricycle		
1819: Peterloo			
			1820: John Birkinshaw's rolled wrought-iron rails

1821: *Faraday's electro-magnetic rotation*

1821: *Aaron Manby*, first iron steamer

1821–5: Stockton and Darlington Railway: first public steam-hauled railway (freight only; passenger service horse-drawn until 1834)

1823–59: Robert Stephenson, railway engineer (active)

1825–8: Bolton and Leigh Railway (steam-hauled freight; passenger service horse-drawn until 1831)

1825–60: Joseph Locke, railway engineer, active

1826–30: Liverpool and Manchester Railway: first public steam-hauled passenger-and-freight railway

1826: Consolidation of Metropolitan Turnpikes

1826–36: *Walter Hancock's steam omnibuses*, London–Paddington

GENERAL	ROADS	WATERWAYS	RAILWAYS
	1829: *Goldsworthy Gurney's steam coaches,* London–Bath	**1829:** Mail steamers begin	
	1829: George Shillibeer's (horse-drawn) omnibus, London		
1831: *Faraday's induction and transformer*			
1832: GREAT REFORM ACT			
		1833: *Royal William* crosses Atlantic by steam alone	**1833–7:** Railway 'boom': Acts for London–Birmingham, Grand Junction, London–Southampton, Great Western, Manchester–Leeds, Great North of England, and other Railways
			1833–59: I. K. Brunel, railway engineer, active

Brassey, railway contractor active

1835–52: George Hudson, railway promoter (active)

1836: *John Ericsson's screw propeller*

1840: First excursion train (Eastern Counties Railway)

1840: Railway Department of Board of Trade

1841: Thomas Cook's first excursion

1843: Telegraph line, Paddington–Slough (G.W.R.)

1834: Owenite general strike

1835: *Morse's electric telegraph*

1835: 'Statute labour' on roads abolished

1836–48: Chartist movement

1837–1901: VICTORIA

1838–46: Anti-Corn Law League

1839: *Macmillan's treadle bicycle*

1840: Rowland Hill's Penny Post

1841–3: 'Rebecca Riots' against Welsh turnpikes

GENERAL	ROADS	WATERWAYS	RAILWAYS
1844: General Enclosure Act	**1844:** South Wales turnpikes abolished		**1844:** Railways Act: 'parliamentary trains', state's right of purchase, etc.
			1844: Midland Railway: first great amalgamation
			1844–7: Railway 'mania'
			1845–1901: Sir Edward Watkin, railway and Channel Tunnel promoter (active)
	1845: *Thompson's pneumatic tyre*	**1845:** Canal companies allowed to act as carriers	**1846:** Gauge Act: standard gauge (except G.W.R.), 4' 8½".
1847: Ten Hours (Factory) Act			
1848: First Public Health Act			**1849:** First express train (Paddington–Exeter)
1851: GREAT EXHIBITION			
1851: Channel Cable			

326

1852: *Giffard's steam airship*
1854–6: CRIMEAN WAR
1854: First 1d. daily newspapers, *War Telegraph* and *War Express* (both Manchester)
1855: First ½d. evening paper, *The Events* (Liverpool)
1857: Atlantic cable
1859: *Bessemer's mass-production of steel*

1852: Completion of main trunk lines

1854: *John Elder's compound marine engine*

1859–69: Suez Canal

1860: *Lenoir's gas engine*
1861: Horse trams, London
1862: *Lenoir's liquid-fuel engine and carriage*

1865: 'Red Flag Act': maximum speed for 'horseless carriages' 4 m.p.h.

1863: Metropolitan (underground) Railway opened
1865–66: Three Railway trade unions (clerks, guards, etc., and engine-drivers, etc.)

GENERAL	ROADS	WATERWAYS	RAILWAYS
1867: SECOND REFORM ACT		1867: Steel ships on Lloyd's Register	
	1871 onwards: Turnpike Trusts allowed to lapse		1871: Amalgamated Society of Railway Servants
1873: Clerk-Maxwell's laws of electro-magnetic radiation			
1876: Bell's telephone	1877: Steam trams, Govan (Glasgow)		
1879: Siemen's electric traction			1879: Associated Society of Locomotive Engineers and Firemen
			1881: Sir William Siemen's electric railway (Berlin)
1882: Henry Fawcett's parcel Post	1882: Electric trams, Kew–Hammersmith		1883: Siemens electrifies Portrush Railway
1884: THIRD REFORM ACT	1884: Daimler's petrol engine	1884: Sir Charles Parson's	

1886–94: Railway freight rates agitation

1889: General Railway Workers Union
1890: Electric 'Tube' (London)
1894: Railways and Canal Traffic Act (freight rates pegged)

1888: Trunk roads transferred to new County Councils
1888: *Dunlop's pneumatic tyre*

1894: Non-trunk roads transferred to new Urban and Rural District Councils
1895: Last public road toll abolished (Anglesey)
1895: *Lanchester's motor-car*: first British four-wheeler
1896: "Red Flag Act" repealed: Maximum speed 12 m.p.h.

1896: *Marconi's wireless telegraphy*
1896: *Daily Mail*, first ½d. daily

GENERAL	ROADS	WATERWAYS	RAILWAYS
	1897: *Diesel's heavy-oil engine*	1897: Parsons' *Turbinia* (turbine-driven ship)	1897: Railway Clerks Association
	1898: First British motor-bus		
1899–1902: BOER WAR			
1900: Labour Representation Committee			
1900: Taff Vale Judgement			
1900: *Zeppelin airship*	1900–7: Electric tramways 'boom'		
1901–10: EDWARD VII		1901: *King Edward* (first commercial turbine-driven ship)	
1903: *Wright brothers' aeroplane*	1903: Tillings's motor-buses, London		
	1903: Motor-Car Act: Maximum speed 20 m.p.h.		1904: Electrification of (shallow) Underground
1906: Trades Disputes Act			
	1907: Last horse-bus in London		

Judgement

motor-cars licensed
and petrol taxed

1910–36: GEORGE V

1911: Telephone
companies
nationalized

1911: General rail strike

1912: Railway Executive
Committee (for co-
ordination in War)

1913: National Union of
Railwaymen

1913: Repeal of Railway
and Canal Traffic Act,
1894

1914: 'Triple Alliance' of
Railwaymen, Miners,
and Transport
Workers

1914: Government
assumes control of
railways

1913: Panama Canal
opened

1914–18: FIRST WORLD
WAR

1918: UNIVERSAL
SUFFRAGE (for women
21–30, 1928)

1919: Ministry of
Transport

GENERAL	ROADS	WATERWAYS	RAILWAYS
1919: First regular air service, London–Paris			
			1921: Railways Act: 121 companies reduced to four from 1923
1922: Broadcasting begins			
1924: Imperial Airways			
1926: General Strike			
	1934: London Passenger Transport Board		1934: London Passenger Transport Board
1936: EDWARD VIII			
1936: Television begins			
1936–52: GEORGE VI			
1939–45: SECOND WORLD WAR			
1947: Airways nationalized	1947: Road transport nationalized	1947: Canals nationalized	1947: Railways nationalized
1952: ELIZABETH II	1952: Road transport denationalized		
1957: First earth satellite (Russian sputnik)			

1961: First manned
space flight (Gagarin,
U.S.S.R.)
1962: American manned
space flight
(John Glenn)
1962: Telstar communi-
cations Satellite

1963: Waterways Board

1963: Railways Board
1968: Last regular steam
train on British Rail
(11 August)

1969: First man on Moon
(Armstrong, U.S.A.)

Note: Where two dates are given for a canal or railway, the first normally denotes the Act authorizing it or other formal commencement, the second the official opening or substantial completion.

Index

Panther Science

The Environment Game
Nigel Calder 42½p

The author, until recently editor of *New Scientist*,
argues that the agricultural method of producing
food has become too wasteful of the world's
land areas. We must plan to produce our food
as we produce motor cars or clothing – in
factories. An abundance of food
photo-synthetically produced – and, hand in
hand, an abundance of reverted land to play
with. Present agricultural areas will return to their
pristine condition; vast tracts of a splendidly
re-invigorated Mother Earth will become our
playground. Not, as today, faraway, exclusive,
expensive playgrounds for a small minority – but
a world for all of us.

'Any solution to the problems posed by the
present expansion of the world's population and
the still accelerating productive capacity of
technology in other directions must be to some
extent Utopian. Mr. Calder's Utopia is curious,
original and logical'
Times Educational Supplement